Gestalt Therapy

A Guide to Contemporary Practice

Philip Brownell completed a doctoral program in clinical psychology from George Fox University in which he was trained as a scientist-practitioner. Following completion of his Psy D, he completed six years of post-graduate level training in Gestalt Therapy through the Portland Gestalt Therapy Training Institute and worked as a Mental Health Therapist for four years on the Intensive Care Unit of a dual-diagnosis psychiatric facility. Dr. Brownell is the Editor of the *Handbook for Theory, Research, and Practice in Gestalt Therapy*, which is being translated into several languages. He has facilitated the gestalt-focused discussion group, Gstalt-L, for thirteen years, is co-chair of the AAGT's Research Task Force, and is actively engaged in supporting research focused on gestalt therapy. He is a licensed clinical psychologist, gestalt therapist, organizational consultant, and coach. He is seminary educated, an ordained clergyman, and President of the Gestalt Training Institute of Bermuda.

Gestalt Therapy

A Guide to Contemporary Practice

PHILIP BROWNELL, MDiv, PsyD

SPRINGER PUBLISHING COMPANY
NEW YORK

Springer Publishing Company, LLC
11 West 42nd Street
New York, NY 10036
www.springerpub.com

Acquisitions Editor: Nancy S. Hale
Production Editor: Peter Rocheleau
Project Manager: Molly Morrison
Cover design: Mimi Flow
Composition: Newgen

E-book ISBN: 978–0–8261–0455–7

10 11 12 13/ 5 4 3 2 1

Library of Congress Cataloging-in-Publication Data

Brownell, Philip, Psy. D.
Gestalt therapy : a guide to contemporary practice / Philip Brownell.
p. ; cm.
Includes bibliographical references and index.
ISBN 978-0-8261-0454-0
1. Gestalt therapy. I. Title.
[DNLM: 1. Gestalt Therapy—methods. WM 420.5.G3 B884g 2010]
RC489.G4B76 2010
616.89'143—dc22 2009048998

Printed in the United States of America by the Hamilton Printing Company

I dedicate this book to all the people who trained me in gestalt therapy; most profoundly that would be Maya Brand and Carol Swanson and my discussion partners at Gstalt-L. My gestalt training group with Maya and Carol broadened my view beyond my doctoral program and Gstalt-L broadened my view beyond my gestalt training group.

I also want to thank my wife, Linda, and my children, Matt, Zac, and Stasia, and my good friend Pat Roberts. Pat is a writer and lover of books and in many ways has been like a spiritual mother.

So, here's to good friends, stacks of books, and cups of coffee around which to talk about the Kingdom of God.

—Philip Brownell

Contents

Foreword

It is raining in Bermuda as Phil Brownell writes the Preface to his comprehensive look at contemporary gestalt therapy. The rain fills cisterns all over his island and fills dry streams. It is fitting that this is how he begins his Preface since gestalt therapy is a metaphorical stream. Or rather, gestalt therapy is the convergence of many streams: streams that flowed from Europe, America, and Asia; converging streams of existentialism and pragmatism, phenomenology and hermeneutics, biology and psychology, social science and neuroscience, psychoanalysis and politics, the arts and sciences, Buddhism and Western theology. With such a broad headwater, no single view of gestalt therapy can be the final word on the subject. This is Dr. Brownell's encyclopedic overview, which is both traditional and original.

I have described gestalt therapy's development with the earthbound metaphor of water; Dr. Brownell characteristically looks to the heavens for his metaphor: "Gestalt therapy is not a supernova shining alone in the darkness. It is built from an assimilation..." (p. 35) Dr. Brownell's book describes today's gestalt therapy as a widely accepted theory and method (praxis).

This book is accessible as an introduction for the reader who has heard something about gestalt therapy and wants to know more. It is also a resource for the experienced gestalt therapist who needs a deeper understanding of gestalt therapy history, development, theory, and practice. He accomplishes this by offering a book that meets these varied needs of readers at different levels of interest, modality, and experience.

In this Foreword I will situate Dr. Brownell's contribution within the history and the current world of gestalt therapy, from my own point of view, of course.

Dr. Brownell describes the founding of gestalt therapy some 60 years ago by Fritz Perls, Laura Perls, and Paul Goodman, who brought together their diverse European and American backgrounds to synthesize a new psychotherapeutic and social theory. He takes the reader through gestalt therapy's later development and makes gestalt therapy come alive by introducing actual practitioners who, in their own words, describe how they became gestalt therapists. Dr. Brownell offers his personal insights into gestalt therapy to show heretofore unexplored possible influences on its founders and original practitioners as they developed gestalt therapy. At all times, he is ecumenical in his presentation of the various contemporary approaches within gestalt therapy, offering the reader a sense of a world of differences in the gestalt therapy universe. The world of gestalt therapy is, and has always been, a world of differences. However at relative peace these various approaches may now be with one another, gestalt therapy's history was not without conflict.

The postwar years in the United States were a time of social conformity; this was reflected in the dominant psychotherapies, which encouraged individual adjustment to social pressures. Gestalt therapy "debuted" in 1951. This new modality offered reform of traditional or authoritarian modalities of psychotherapy that stressed a model of health based on adjustment to societal norms dictated by the psychotherapist himself (the therapist was most often a man).

To some people's perceptions, the established psychotherapies offered an often-cerebral process of social adjustment, while gestalt therapy offered an opportunity to release the creative potential of the person. Gestalt therapy presented a psychotherapy with creative novelty at its core and proposed an egalitarian psychotherapy relationship of more or less mutual partners. Most importantly, and famously, gestalt therapy accented a person's creative potential and supported individual difference, not conformity. It is no wonder that in its early days it attracted so many artists, social nonconformists, and miscellaneous "refugees" from then authoritarian mainstream psychotherapies. The social complacency of conformity and the psychotherapies that supported it were begging to be challenged, to come under siege. Gestalt therapy would be the modality most identified with supporting this siege.

The 1960s was a time of social tumult; it was the time of this siege. "The human potential movement" and the social revolutions of the decade formed a synergy with the social and clinical values of gestalt therapy. Gestalt therapy became the unofficial "anti-Establishment" psychotherapy. Its popularity got ahead of itself. In the hands of popularizers and amateurs, "gestalt therapy" sometimes seemed to morph into often-unidentifiable variations and sometimes careless or reckless parodies of the original, serious psychotherapy. The reputation caused by this popularization, that is, the mistaken impressions that gestalt therapy is nothing but theatrical techniques that could be done to people, that mere emotional catharsis such as pillow banging and screaming was psychotherapy, that gestalt therapy is nothing but its techniques, and so on, is something gestalt therapy continues to have to correct. Dr. Brownell's book is an important contribution to gestalt therapy's ongoing work of addressing what remains of these false beliefs.

Claims of dilution as a consequence of gestalt therapy being outstripped by its popularity were further complicated by gestalt therapy's initial success among serious psychotherapists in the 1950s, too. Clinicians were eager to learn gestalt therapy as one of the modalities in the humanistic reformation of psychotherapy. There was an increasing demand to learn gestalt therapy quickly. Trainers from the original institute, The New York Institute for Gestalt Therapy, were invited to teach gestalt therapy around the country and soon across the world. These skilled trainers were under pressure to teach gestalt therapy as quickly as possible. There was a need to streamline the training of gestalt therapists, and indeed, to streamline the gestalt therapy.

Fritz Perls rejected the original model of gestalt therapy that he helped develop in New York. He developed a new, simple, more easily understandable and learnable version of gestalt therapy. His version of gestalt therapy became widespread and identified as gestalt therapy itself. Those in New York who continued to practice and teach the model he rejected felt Perls's new version of gestalt therapy strayed too far from its source in the service of simplification. They insisted that gestalt therapy could not be taught quickly since it was a nuanced, phenomenological approach. Unfortunately, the tensions between what was known as the "East Coast Model," identified with Laura Perls in New York, and the "West Coast Model," identified with Fritz Perls in California, colored gestalt therapy's history.

As gestalt therapy spread, gestalt therapy institutes sprang up and flourished as people who were trained by the original trainers trained their own students. Newer conflicts emerged as institutes inevitably offered their own understandings of gestalt therapy to which other institutes objected, sometimes aggressively. The differences among various models, approaches, or perspectives within gestalt therapy proliferated over the decades. There was no peace among the adherents of the different models. Intramodality conflicts are not unique to the history of gestalt therapy. A glance at the history of psychoanalysis, for example, shows similar scuffles.

Over time, gestalt therapy itself continued to develop as a modality that embraces change. The fractionalization of gestalt therapy eased from the rigid defense of particular perspectives on gestalt therapy to inclusive notions that we each may have different points of view within a common heritage.

The streams of gestalt therapy that once flowed apart have come together. Naturally, different approaches to gestalt therapy remain and there are hearty disagreements. These energize gestalt therapy and assure its development.

Gestalt therapists meet in conferences with attendees from all over the world. There are transnational organizations such as the Association for the Advancement of Gestalt Therapy, an international community, to transcontinental organizations such as the European Association for Gestalt Therapy, Gestalt Australia and New Zealand, and the International Gestalt Therapy Association, which is primarily oriented toward the Spanish communities. There are many national and regional organizations as well. Gestalt therapy has its own journals such as *Gestalt Review*, *Studies in Gestalt Therapy: Dialogical Bridges*, *The British Gestalt Journal*, and *Gestalt!* to name only the English language journals, and its own publishers (The Gestalt Press, The Gestalt Journal Press).

This brings me back to this book. Dr. Brownell's description of gestalt therapy is an example of the contemporary perspective in that he offers us a broad view of gestalt therapy itself. But this is not to say that he offers us a generic, one-size-fits-or-pleases-all model of gestalt therapy. To be sure, he offers an excellent survey of the basic, important concepts and offers illustrative clinical examples. The latter are crucial for any reader to be able to see how gestalt therapy is applicable across so many different dimensions of practice. Dr. Brownell excels in reaching out to the broadest audience of readers. At the same time, he offers the more informed reader an opportunity to see gestalt therapy from his own perspective.

Make no mistake about this. Just as in this Foreword I offer my own perspective on the history of gestalt therapy, Dr. Brownell does the same in this book. Readers may differ with my point of view here; and readers may sometimes differ with Dr. Brownell's. Gestalt therapy's liveliness often comes from its support of differences and its commitment to meeting one another on the basis of our differences. It is this liveliness that now characterizes gestalt therapy as its different perspectives continue to develop around the world. Each perspective is a special point of view from a different vantage point, yet each looks upon a world of shared experiences. Gestalt therapy continues to develop, like the stream with which I began this Foreword. Dr. Brownell's contribution adds to this development.

Dan Bloom

Preface

As I put the finishing touches on this book it is raining in Somerset; it's raining all over Bermuda. That is good, because in Bermuda people catch their water as it rolls off limestone painted roofs and lands in cisterns beneath the houses. It's been dry here for weeks and we were just about ready to order a truckload of water.

When one's line of work goes dry, it's hard to imagine getting excited because everything seems stale, washed out, and bleached from overexposure. The same may be true of gestalt therapy. Many books have been written exploring one aspect or another, such as those of Perls, Hefferline, and Goodman (1951), Erving and Miriam Polster (1973), Joel Latner (1989), Gary Yontef (1993), Sylvia Crocker (1999), Jennifer MacKewn (1997), Gaie Houston (2003), Edwin Nevis (2000), and Ansel Woldt and Sarah Toman (2005) to name just a few in the English language. So why another one?

The most honest answer is because I wanted to write one. I wanted to include things in this book that I've been discussing with my friends and colleagues at Gstalt-L, an online community of gestalt theorists, trainers, trainees, and practitioners. For more than thirteen years it's been like a think tank where people have fought for their opinions and argued passionately and cogently for their ideas. Recently, Seán Gaffney (2009) indicated that his article in *Gestalt Review* came about in part due to such discussion at Gstalt-L. Because of the drama that can be seen there, some people report that they maintain a subscription to see what the characters are going to do next. It's like watching a soap opera. At any rate, some of the ideas expressed there over the years have not made it to print yet, and I want to give them voice in a different format.

I also wanted to give myself the gift of writing. For me, writing is a learning experience. I frequently propose projects to publishers because I want to pursue a particular idea and learn from it. Then I go into research mode as I prepare to write. Even in the process of writing, as I thrash about with something, I discover resources I never knew existed and expand my world. I run sections of the manuscript past friends and colleagues to see how they play with them. Their responses help me calibrate what I'm doing.

Finally, I wanted to write a book that would inform people who are unfamiliar with gestalt therapy–perhaps to bring them a little water if what they already knew had gone dry. That is why, for this book, I have selected the mainframe of gestalt praxis—phenomenology, dialogical relationship, the field, and experiment. I don't want to blur that focus. There are many other things that could have been put into this book, but if a mental health professional wants to understand gestalt therapy, especially with a view to eventually becoming fully trained and to practice it, then the starting place is to grasp these four tenets. In addition, I knew from years of experience, both in private practice and in community mental health, that there are pragmatic concerns, if not sound professional protocols, that needed to be included. So, I chose the issues of assessment, treatment planning, and training.

My hope is to bring a little water to people who have become thirsty in their work, including established gestalt therapists. I've tried to keep the jargon to a minimum, but I realize it is necessary to use the terms that have meaning within the field in order to help those unfamiliar learn the necessary concepts. I've also included some subjects gestalt therapists have thus far neglected in the literature, as well as new slants on subjects that have already been covered.

I guess the last thing is that I speak from where I'm at. Where I'm at is partly due to where I've been. I'm the oldest of five children. I grew up in an alcoholic, dysfunctional family, and I went through years of therapy to deal with it. I've been a road manager for a rock band. I've been a neuropsychiatric technician in the United States Navy during a time of war. I've been a longhaired counter-culture freak, and I've been a Jesus freak. I'm still a Jesus freak. I've been a seminary student. I've worn three-piece suits trying to fit in while working as a minister of children at a large, multistaff church in central California, and I've been a laid-back pastor of a rural congregation along the north Tillamook coast in Oregon. I've ridden a motorcycle to work. I've been a liberal and I've been a conservative. Right now I'm what I like to call a *conliberative*. I'm the father of three great children, and I've been married three times. I've been a single parent. I've been homeless, and I've lived in beautiful, even luxurious, homes including the place from which I write at the moment, which is located atop a hill looking south and west across the expanse of the Atlantic Ocean.

Each therapist brings to his or her work as a professional his or her whole self. That means that if I am to be of help to others I must attend to myself, making sure that I'm grounded, balanced, available, and courageous enough to meet the courage that brought my clients to me in the first place. When I do that, I bring my *whole self* to that meeting. People get a whole person—an integrated person at peace. That is what I also hope the reader picks up on in this book, even though what they get is a huge dose of my mind grappling with various issues.

Philip Brownell
June 2009

REFERENCES

Crocker, S. (1999). *A well-lived life: Essays in gestalt therapy*. Cambridge, MA: Gestalt Institute of Cleveland Press.

Gaffney, S. (2009). The cycle of experience re-cycled: Then, now . . . next? *Gestalt Review*, *13*(1), 7–23.

Houston, G. (2003). *Brief gestalt therapy*. Thousand Oaks, CA: Sage Publications.

Latner, J. (1989). *The gestalt therapy book*. Highland, NY: The Gestalt Journal Press.

Mackewn, J. (1997). *Developing gestalt counselling* (Developing Counselling Series). Thousand Oaks, CA: Sage Publications.

Nevis, E. (Ed.). (2000). *Gestalt therapy: Perspectives and applications*. Cambridge, MA: Gestalt Press.

Polster, E., and Polster, M. (1973). *Gestalt therapy integrated: Countours of theory and practice.* New York: Vintage Books.

Woldt, A., and Toman, S. (Eds.) (2005). *Gestalt therapy history, theory and practice.* Thousand Oaks, CA: Sage Publications.

Yontef, G. (1993). *Awareness dialogue and process: Essays on gestalt therapy*. Highland, NY: The Gestalt Journal Press.

Acknowledgments

There are many people to thank. First, I want to thank Phil Laughlin at Springer for his encouragement and his work as editor. Phil left before the project was done in order to follow a great opportunity in publishing elsewhere, and so I also want to thank Jennifer Perillo, who took over for him.

Second I want to thank Dan Bloom and Peter Philippson who at various times read and commented on portions of the book. As always, we did not agree on everything, but that is the beauty of having people like this in one's life. No matter how much we may struggle over various things, no matter how different we are from one another, we find a common ground in our interest in gestalt therapy theory and practice. I have gone to war with Peter while conducting organizational business, but then I can turn the page and find in him a thoughtful and considerate thinker who will take what I write seriously and give his best shot at critical response. I respect that very much. Dan is much the same way, except in him I have found a man who thinks like me on crucial subjects and sometimes speaks directly and forcefully as I also tend to do. Neither of these men share my faith in Jesus, and what I find truly amazing and priceless is that we can talk with one another the way we do and can respect, if not love one another, in spite of what has separated other people.

Last, I want to acknowledge the sacrifice that my wife has made as I have worked on this book. I have been unavailable to her, and that has been difficult. While I worked hard writing, she worked hard waiting—waiting to get her husband back. And now the book is done; and now I am back.

Introduction

This is a book about gestalt therapy, but it is not a book that tells everything there is to know about gestalt therapy. Some things are left out and other things are only treated in passing. Why? It is because I want to keep a focus on the core of gestalt therapy. To practice gestalt therapy, one must know these core concepts.

So the claim is that this book tells the reader what gestalt therapy is and that it can serve as a template or treatment manual.[1] However, this would only be a beginning for a true student of gestalt therapy. Vast sections on gestalt therapy's theory of self, especially as it relates to contact in the person-world/organism-environment field, are either left out or only mentioned in passing. Why is that? Because to utilize the core of gestalt therapy praxis will inexorably lead one into person-world/organism-environment self-formation. Self emerges from the action of the person in his or her world. Utilize the core, and all else will follow.

The primary audience for this book is practicing clinicians; counselors and psychotherapists who are working with people in a variety of settings (or those in training to do so). This would also extend to anyone interfacing with people in a helping profession such as nursing, the clergy, corrections, or social work.

During my internship at a large hospital on the southeast side of Portland, Oregon, I was an adjunct instructor at the Walla Walla School of Nursing. My purpose was to teach the nurses about the field of psychology during their rotation through the psychiatric units in the hospital. What I emphasized was making good contact with the patients they served instead of simply coming into a room, attending to the medical necessities, and charting. Contact is healing. Often, one of the greatest factors leading to positive outcomes can be the support that meaningful human contact can have for a patient during a stay in the hospital. Nurses can benefit from learning how to do gestalt therapy.

I was a line staff member at several residential treatment centers for children and adolescents. The line staff are the ones who spend most time with the residents. I realize now that I could have done a much better job if I had been trained in gestalt therapy back then, and that goes for my time as a pastor or minister to children as well. So, with a bit of hindsight, I contend that anyone in a position that requires working in groups and interfacing with other people could benefit from learning gestalt therapy.

There are people who train in gestalt therapy, however, with no intention of using it professionally. They just want to live by its philosophy. They like how it contributes to an existentially satisfying way of life and they want to know more about it and to use it as a discipline for living. This book is for those people as well.

Gestalt therapy is an experiential approach and must be learned in experiential training groups (an explanation of this will be included in chapter 11). But the reader can gain a foothold in obtaining the expertise needed to practice gestalt therapy by reading this concise and practical guidebook written about complex clinical and interpersonal processes in mostly ordinary language even though the subjects in question do require reference to technical terms used in the field.

The practicing and experienced clinician, on the other hand, will recognize many of the elements covered in the book, but might know them under different titles and terms and might disagree with my conceptualizations. That's okay. I don't expect everyone to agree with all of my claims. However, I do believe this book will contribute to the establishment of a baseline in the core of gestalt praxis and extend into new ground on several facets of that core. This book, then, could provide self-study enrichment for those currently in practice. It would be appropriate for professional organizations of counselors and psychotherapists, formal academic programs and gestalt postgraduate-level training organizations. It could also be used as an ancillary text in any people-helping training program, including pastoral counseling programs in seminaries, school counselor training programs in college, and graduate programs for clinical social work.

Following an orientation to psychotherapy in chapter 1, chapters 2 and 3 address the question, "What is gestalt therapy?" These chapters grew from a conceptual statement of the theory of gestalt therapy to its practice and then into the actual community of gestalt practitioners. I realized the reader needed to sense *who* gestalt therapy was and not just *what* it was (the "who," and how they did what they did, helps define the "what"). So I contacted many of the people mentioned there and asked what attracted them to gestalt therapy in the first place, with whom they trained, and how they began training others. Chapter 3 gives a feel for how gestalt therapy spread throughout the world since its birth at the first gestalt training institute in New York in the early 1950s.

Part II of the book, How to Do Gestalt Therapy, presents the core of gestalt therapy praxis.

Chapter 4, "Deal with Personal Experience," covers the role of phenomenology in gestalt therapy and presents a modified phenomenological method that adapts a philosophical practice to a psychotherapeutic purpose. This is a mild corrective to many previous writings in gestalt therapy that called for the phenomenological method and pointed rightfully to Edmund Husserl, but did not distinguish between his projects and the domain of psychology.

Chapter 5, "Work the Therapeutic Relationship," first deals with the issue of *alterity*, an important concept for anyone working with people. It then goes into the nature of dialogical relationships and the concept of contact.

Chapter 6, "Use the Context of Life," addresses field theory in gestalt therapy, showing that gestalt therapy is not unique as a field-oriented approach. It orients the reader as to the place of phenomenal experience and relationship within a unified field that has both phenomenal and ontic dimensions.

Chapter 7, "Move to Action," deals with the experiential aspects of gestalt therapy, which are for some people what gestalt therapy is all about. It defines what a gestalt therapy experiment *is* and shows how experiment is integral to every other theoretical tenet.

Chapter 8, "Practice a Unified Approach," describes how every part of gestalt therapy is related to and organized by the whole of gestalt therapy. Gestalt therapy is not multimodal; it is holistic and a unified praxis. It is not possible, while working with a client, to be phenomenal without being relational and field theoretic within a process that is experienced by both therapist and client. It's all of the same tapestry.

The last two parts of the book deal briefly with some clinical and professional matters: assessment, treatment planning and case management on the one hand and training, continuing education and professional associating on the other.

If I had to choose the top five books on gestalt therapy to recommend to an English-language reader, aside from this book, I would choose:

1. *Gestalt Therapy: Excitement and Growth in the Human Personality* (Perls et al., 1951)
2. *Gestalt Therapy Integrated: Contours of Theory and Practice* (Polster and Polster, 1973)
3. *Gestalt Therapy History, Theory and Practice* (Woldt and Toman, 2005)
4. *Handbook for Theory, Research, and Practice in Gestalt Therapy* (Brownell, 2008)
5. *Brief Gestalt Therapy* (Houston, 2003)

I chose the first book because it's the seminal book on the gestalt approach. In number 2 the Polsters moved the focus from individual experiencing to contact between one person and the environment or one person and another person, and that moved the emphasis to dialogue. Woldt and Toman (number 3) is a thorough and contemporary treatment of gestalt therapy that also does well by the classic theory behind it and it presents field theory as an encompassing tenet in the core of gestalt therapy. I chose number 4 (the book I edited with an international team of contributors) because it establishes the core of gestalt therapy as represented in this book, and it addresses the issue of research in the gestalt community, something absolutely necessary for gestalt therapists to undertake. Gaie

Houston's description of gestalt therapy (number 5) used in a brief approach is particularly relevant to today's concern for cost reduction that does not reduce effectiveness as a by-product.

This book fits somewhere around numbers 3, 4, and 5 for relevance. My hope is that it will be clear and understandable to the novice and provocative enough for the seasoned gestalt therapist so as to help in the evolution of gestalt therapy praxis.

NOTES

1. Most gestalt therapists loathe the term "treatment manual," because it brings to mind a positivist approach to science and research they feel is out of place in gestalt therapy's worldview. I do not share that opinion. I think every treatment manual is a map and every gestalt therapist learns that the map is not the territory. A treatment manual is also a tool; it's just one kind of tool for a special job. Only an idiot would try to use one tool to do every job. Just so, a treatment manual is created for the purpose of guiding practice and to accomplish the job of random, controlled research studies. And I'm okay with that. A treatment manual, and certainly this book, is not a cookbook with recipes or a paint-by-numbers project that makes robots out of therapists, and it doesn't tell everything there is to know and do about any given clinical approach.

REFERENCES

Houston, G. (2003). *Brief gestalt therapy*. Thousand Oaks, CA: Sage Publications.

Brownell, P. (Ed.). (2008). *Handbook for theory, research, and practice in gestalt therapy.* Newcastle, UK: Cambridge Scholars Publishing.

Perls, F., Hefferline, R., and Goodman, P. (1951). *Gestalt therapy: Excitement and growth in the human personality.* New York: Julian.

Polster, E., and Polster, M. (1973). *Gestalt therapy integrated: Contours of theory and practice.* New York: Vintage Book/Random House.

Woldt, A., and Toman, S. (Eds.). (2005). *Gestalt therapy history, theory and practice.* Thousand Oaks, CA: Sage Publications.

PART I

Orientation

1 What Is Psychotherapy?

This chapter provides a working definition of psychotherapy, describes common factors present in all established approaches to psychotherapy, and explores the issue of whether or not psychotherapy is effective. In dealing with the evidence-based movement, it advocates for practice-based evidence that is more relevant to the clinical work mental health professionals do.

If you regard yourself as a mental health professional, then chances are you already think you know what psychotherapy is. You are either doing it now, have seen someone do it, have been a patient/client/customer in the process, or help manage it in some way. If you are just starting out, however, you might approach psychotherapy with wonder and excitement. You might also feel uneasiness about your future as a psychotherapist.

This chapter provides a description of psychotherapy as a general ground for the subsequent exploration of gestalt therapy in particular. Various types of psychotherapy are mentioned (i.e., individual, dyad, or group). Psychotherapy research is discussed, including those common factors identified as being effective to positive outcomes across all major clinical perspectives. Regarding evidence-based practice, forms of warrant are briefly discussed so as to identify the means by which justification is established and to orient toward "evidence" as warrant for the practice of any particular approach to psychotherapy.

THE TALKING CURE

If you were a bug on the wall in a therapy session, what might you see? You would see two people sitting in a room talking. You might see one of the people crying, fidgeting, speaking rapidly, or you might see two people sitting in relative quiet, but the tension in the room would throttle your senses. You might see three people in the room, or you might see a whole group. You might see a family in the room with the therapist acting like a policeman directing traffic.

Many people believe the concept of psychotherapy originated with Sigmund Freud in 1900 (Bankart, 1996), in his work titled *The Interpretation of Dreams* (since republished in numerous editions and translations). Others trace the origins of psychotherapy to the collaboration five years earlier between Josef Breuer and Freud, and the publication of their book *Studies in Hysteria*; Breuer's patient, Anna O., is said to have called the hypnosis she experienced "the talking cure" (Winick, 1997). Because of these associations, psychotherapy, "the talking cure," has been attributed largely to Sigmund Freud. With the advent of such a talking cure, the psychotherapist became the doctor of the *interior* (Cushman, 1992), and psychotherapy's focus became what takes place when two people sit down to speak with one another about one person's subjective experience. It is any form of treatment using verbal or nonverbal communication between a therapist and a patient/client/consumer that is understood to be a professional relationship (Winick, 1997).

The word *psychotherapy* is a compound word coming from two Greek words: *psychē* and *therapeuō*. Psychē means "soul" and therapeuō means "heal" or "cure"; the compound, therefore, refers to a process that heals the soul. Perhaps more difficult to put into a compound was another Greek word, *iaomai*. Therapeuō originally meant to serve a superior, and eventually it came to include curing a person of various ills. Iaomai was the more direct word for healing; it resulted in a person becoming *hugiēs*, or healthy. Iaomai included healings and cures from physical and psychological ills. Thus, the implication in the compound "psychotherapy" is that the therapist serves the client for the purpose of healing the client's soul and making him or her healthy, sensible, and of sound mind (Brown, 1976).

Psychotherapy is not a legal matter, even though it often has legal implications or focuses on someone's legal process. Psychotherapy is not just a conversation; it is a dialogue. Psychotherapy is not a medical procedure (even though clinical psychology bought into the medical model years ago), so no linear process of cause and effect is involved in the cure. Psychotherapy is not social work, so the emphasis is not on procuring community services, even though it may result in the client becoming more proactive and researching these same resources on his or her own. Psychotherapy is also not a game in which two people waste each other's time and energy; it is not a farce or a futile process.

When I was a neuropsychiatric technician for the U.S. Navy during the Vietnam War, I worked on a ward with a psychiatrist who was rumored to have been associated with Harvard before joining the ranks of the officers involved in the war effort. I knew nothing of analysis, but many of the other corpsmen were saying that making an appointment with this psychiatrist was "the thing to do," so I did. At the first appointment, he sat in one chair smoking a pipe, and I sat in another. We faced each other, but I had a hard time looking at him, because I did not want him to discover that I was basically on a joy ride. I said nothing, and he said nothing. Occasionally, we exchanged one-syllable trivialities. I recall making several appointments with him, but none of them went anywhere beyond what I have just described. There was not much talking in that version of the talking cure.

On the same unit, a civilian psychologist who had been driving down the coast to the Esalen Institute to train in gestalt therapy with Fritz Perls was conducting a "gestalt group." I was assigned to work with that group as a support to the psychologist, and I observed a lot of talking, but I also observed enactment as people were asked to "be your foot," "let your hand speak," and so on.

These were two ways of doing psychotherapy. In each case, a theory guided the method used, and the combination of theory and method produced a distinctive praxis. *Praxis* is the process by which a theory becomes animated in the actions of its adherents. Thus, the praxis of gestalt therapy is different from that of cognitive behavioral therapy (CBT), even though the gestalt therapist and the cognitive behavioral therapist may at times be doing what looks, to any reasonable observer, like the same thing. This would be the case in both approaches' use of mindfulness:

> Gestalt therapy, influenced by Zen Buddhism and Eastern thought since its inception, has always understood the importance of awareness and subjective experience (phenomenology), and understood the value of the experiential "felt sense" (as opposed to thinking and the conceptual), both important aspects of mindfulness. These concepts as well as gestalt therapy's understanding of the change process, and the importance of the acceptance of "what is" have recently been incorporated into other systems such as CBT and ACT. The mindfulness-based therapies (MBSR, MBCT) would therefore have some overlap with aspects of gestalt therapy, as there has now been a change in these approaches from cognition and behavior change to being with and acceptance of "what is." (E. Gold, personal communication, April 5, 2009 [used by permission])

Mindfulness is mindfulness, but gestalt therapy and cognitive behavioral therapy are two different theoretical systems.

Corsini and Wedding (2007), in their book surveying a number of approaches to psychotherapy, have claimed that, in general, the praxis of any form of psychotherapy is a learning process that concerns the way people think, feel, and act:

> All psychotherapies are methods of learning. All psychotherapies are intended to change people: to make them think differently (cognition), to make them feel differently (affection), and to make them act differently (behavior). Psychotherapy is learning. It may be learning something new or relearning something someone has forgotten; it may be learning how to

> learn, or it may be unlearning; paradoxically, it may be learning what one already knows. (p. 6)

Gerald Corey (2009) disagreed that a psychotherapist's chief goal is to change people, but he admitted that people come to psychotherapists in order to change and that change takes place. He further identified the relational aspects of psychotherapy that are integral to change:

> Psychotherapy is a process of engagement between two persons, both of whom are bound to change through the therapeutic venture. At its best, this is a collaborative process that involves both the therapist and the client in co-constructing solutions to concerns.... Therapists are not in business to change clients, to give them quick advice, or to solve their problems for them. Instead, counselors facilitate healing through a process of genuine dialogue with their clients. The kind of person a therapist is remains the most critical factor affecting the client and promoting change. (Corey, 2009, p. 6)

Writing in a practical way for those contemplating the services of a psychotherapist, Elaine Klonicki (2002) described psychotherapy as being in a relationship with a person specially trained to listen in a supportive and nonjudgmental fashion so as to guide one's personal discovery to relieve pain and restore emotional balance. She also asserted that psychotherapy teaches practical skills that help people become more successful. She contrasted and compared three similar activities—counseling, psychotherapy, and psychoanalysis—which she described as increasingly more involved and aimed at in-depth work with patients/clients/consumers: Counseling offers short-term opinion or advice, psychotherapy offers help for ongoing dysfunctional or ineffective patterns of behavior one has not been able to change on one's own, and psychoanalysis helps those whose patterns are so stubbornly reinforced outside of their awareness that they need several sessions a week to go deep enough to understand themselves.[1]

Psychotherapy takes place in dyads (the traditional one-to-one therapy), triads (what many call "couples" or "marital therapy"), small groups, and families. Therapeutic principles are also employed by organizational consultants working with large groups and complex systems. Sometimes therapists work together in teams, especially when conducting group therapy. Sometimes a therapist will have an observing group of "consultants," who remain behind a mirror and call by phone to affect the process.

As mentioned previously, all psychotherapists are guided by a psychotherapeutic theory that can be thought of as a cognitive system defining how things are related and how things happen (Crocker, 2008). Even so-called eclectic or integrative psychotherapists use such cognitive systems, usually ones based on some form of personalized pragmatism and/or positivism. The theories that have found most allegiance and support, however, are cognitive behavioral, psychoanalytic, person-centered (or interpersonal), existential, and experiential. These systems include many subcategories, and elements of several of them can be reformulated into still other theories. Two examples are multimodal therapy and gestalt therapy. Gestalt theory is a revision of psychoanalysis (Freudian theory) that includes (but is not restricted to) elements of cognitive, behavioral, existential, and interpersonal theory. Gestalt theory is described more completely in chapters 4 through 8, but the point here is that therapists need some kind of theory to guide them, to avoid just wandering around in the client's story, trying different techniques, and giving advice in a loosely and intuitively subjective fashion.

FACTORS COMMON TO DIVERSE FORMS OF PSYCHOTHERAPY

All major approaches to psychotherapy share some characteristics—things that contribute to the effectiveness of psychotherapy in one way or another. These factors also help define psychotherapy. Thus, whether a psychotherapist follows a cognitive behavioral approach, a psychodynamic perspective, an interpersonal approach, transactional analysis, rational emotive behavioral therapy, reality therapy, a Jungian approach, or gestalt therapy, he or she will engage the client and some common factors will influence the outcome.

In the *Handbook for Theory, Research, and Practice in Gestalt Therapy*, I described the factors inherent to all approaches to doing psychotherapy, relating them to gestalt therapy as follows (an experienced gestalt therapist would immediately recognize these features as belonging to gestalt therapy theory and practice):

- **Client and Extra-Therapeutic Factors:** This is the field—all things having affect, especially the view of the field most associated with the life spaces of both client and therapist. These factors include what the client brings to therapy that bear on the process of therapy and the issues to be visited during that process. They include the client's cognitive-intellectual capacities and those elements of culture, history, financial resources, and legal impact that affect the course of therapy.
- **Therapist Qualities:** This relates to the therapist as an authentic person, the capacity of the therapist for contact, and his or her training and experience. It includes the life space of the therapist.
- **Relationship:** This concerns the relational qualities of the working alliance, and it relates directly to the gestalt therapy concepts inherent to dialogue—presence, inclusion, commitment to dialogue, and the creation of conditions permissive and conducive to dialogue.
- **Specific Method:** Certainly, this encompasses the aspects of theory referred to earlier, but more specifically it relates to gestalt therapy's reliance on a phenomenological method and experiment, for gestalt therapy is decidedly phenomenological and experiential.
- **Expectancy:** This relates to faith in the paradoxical theory of change; it is a faith position more generally as well, in that gestalt therapists trust the field will supply what is necessary (Brownell, 2008, pp. 98–99).

The most salient features of psychotherapy are those extra-therapeutic events and factors that the client and therapist bring to therapy. Some studies suggest these factors account for about 40% of positive outcomes, so what are they more specifically?

In Bermuda, where I write this, the extra-therapeutic factors affecting psychotherapy include the economic conditions. A slowdown in construction of new homes is the result of the dwindling workforce, as major companies have let some of their workers go. Extra-therapeutic factors in this case include tension between guest workers and Bermudians; race; the systemic dysfunction within some organizations which, like stubborn mold, keeps coming back no matter what you do; and clients' developmental, physical, and intellectual characteristics.

This is not an exhaustive list, but it will suffice. It illustrates how psychotherapy needs to deal with relevant factors in a current situation, which is a mix of spatial, environmental, and social contexts. At times it might be necessary to revisit one's childhood, but the current context is a more salient ingredient in psychotherapy; psychotherapy is therefore some kind of process, verbal and/or experiential, that in some way addresses the current experience of the client, the person who comes for help.

Psychotherapy is also an agreement between two people in which one is seeking help and will pay for it, and the other has wisdom, training, and experience to offer in facilitating the seeker's quest for answers, solutions, skill building, insight, and/or awareness. Thus, a contract is formed in which the provider gives informed consent about what he or she has to offer, its limits, and the conditions under which the psychotherapeutic process will be conducted.

All these things are involved in "the talking cure," no matter how much or how little actual talking takes place.

DOES PSYCHOTHERAPY "WORK"?

If something "works," then it attains an expected effect or outcome. It functions in a desired fashion. A bucket can be used to carry water, for example, but if it is riddled with holes, all the water flows out and the bucket does not "work." The question often asked (not so much any more, actually) is, "Does psychotherapy work?" Or is psychotherapy so riddled with holes that it cannot carry water? That question has been answered,[2] but there are facets to the answer, and they concern the basic issues of justification (is a certain type of psychotherapy—or even psychotherapy itself—warranted), types of outcomes research, evidence-based practice, and practice-based evidence. These concepts are treated only briefly here, but the reader may want to explore these issues in more depth at some other time.

Efficacy, Effectiveness, and Warrant

For the last 50 years or so, people have been concerned with the question of whether or not, or how much psychotherapy works. In the late 1980s and 1990s, the pace of outcomes research in the practice of psychotherapy picked up, and it was dominated by the term *efficacy*. Efficacy is a concept that grew out of the randomized trials used to test the cause-and-effect relationships between taking a medication and symptom reduction. The greater the desired effect, the greater the efficacy. In the late 1990s, some psychologists began to investigate the patient satisfaction associated with various kinds of treatments, not just medications, and their studies became associated with the term *effectiveness*. The greater the patient's/client's/consumer's satisfaction (in one form of such study), the greater the effectiveness. In addition to these concepts, the question of a methodology's efficiency also became increasingly of concern. Haynes and Johnson (2009) provide a succinct summary of all three concepts:

> *Efficacy* is the degree to which interventions result in positive outcomes in ideal settings. Ideal settings are often research laboratories or experimental conditions providing studies with a high degree of internal validity. … *Effectiveness* is the extent to which treatments provide positive patient outcomes in real-world settings. … *Efficiency* is the extent to which one treatment provides relatively better outcomes than other treatments. (Haynes & Johnson, 2009, pp. 302–303)

The term efficacy is usually reserved for statements of causality associated with randomized and controlled studies of manualized treatments and the systematic review of such clinical research using meta-studies of effect sizes. Effectiveness usually refers to feasibility in studies with measurable positive effects across broad populations in clinical situations. Efficacy studies emphasize internal validity and replicability, but effectiveness studies emphasize external validity and generalizability (Nathan, Stuart, & Dolan, 2003). Although randomized, controlled studies have become the standard for research providing evidence, their applicability to psychotherapy research has been questioned, and the issues intrinsic to this concern over their appropriateness further illustrate how psychotherapy contrasts with medical treatments:

> The controlled clinical trial method was initially designed by medical science for use in studies of medications. A physician administers a specific medication knowing it is the only medication being administered to compare the results with a placebo or standard of care condition. Unlike medication, psychotherapy cannot be administered in such pure form, and adherence is much more difficult to measure. The social nature of the interaction must be considered. The controlled clinical trial methodology is effective in investigating medical interventions for comparing psychotherapy to pharmacotherapy or their combination. It is limited however, when imposed on psychotherapy alone, which is an entirely different enterprise because of the complex and dynamic nature of social interaction. (Ablon & Marci, 2004, p. 667)

Warrant, on the other hand, is a philosophical and general term. It refers to the level of justification for any given action and has various bases (Brownell, 2008). Warrant, as a philosophical construct, stands behind all assertions and arguments pertaining to efficacy, effectiveness, and efficiency.

For instance, warrant can be based on personal experience and assertion. In this situation, a psychotherapist claims to know what he or she does is effective, because the therapist has seen the results in the clients' changed lives and general satisfaction.

A person might say, "I don't need research to tell me this works; I know it works from watching my clients." A person's esteemed trainer might say, "Believe me. This stuff works!" Either statement would be a low level of justification, but a valid method of ascertaining whether or not warrant exists.

Warrant can also be based in *foundationalism*; that is, one belief is based on another more "foundational" belief. For instance, early analysts believed they should remain unobtrusive (and they believed they could actually do that) so as to present a blank slate on which the client could project in the therapy room; this was based on their belief that free association was the avenue to the unconscious and was obscured by transference, and that the unconscious is where the intrapsychic and psychosexual conflicts of neurosis lay. Foundationalism is usually rejected because it results in an infinite regress of beliefs, none of which, perhaps, can be independently supported.

Somewhat related is the *coherency* view of warrant, in which justification is achieved through a web of beliefs and the warrant is not subject to a linear regress but stands or falls as a unity. This view can be compared to a ship at sea that requires constant upgrading and maintenance to remain afloat. In the same way, a web of meaning is in a perpetual state of construction. Related to coherentist warrant is the web of factors and theoretical tenets created through the consilience that unites them.

Consilience is a unity of knowledge. A good theory unifies data and laws from diverse domains; one classic example is the successful unification of Kepler's laws and Galileo's laws by means of Newton's theory (Niiniluoto, 2007). Newton established a larger category that accounted for the observations of Kepler and Galileo, thus assimilating them into his theory. William Whewell asserted that coherence is a type of consilience, in that coherence extends the hypothesis to colligate a new class of phenomena without having to adjust the hypothesis to make it fit (Snyder, 2006).

For example, if the cognitive approach of imaginal desensitization is shown to be effective and that approach shares the characteristics of the gestalt use of imagination in experimental enactment (a consilience of praxis between the two perspectives, CBT and gestalt), then part of a coherent web forms, and the fact that people coming at a phenomenon from two different perspectives arrive at virtually the same procedure, construct, theory, and so on suggests they have independently discovered the same approach. In this case, not only would the research support both the CBT and gestalt versions of the shared intervention, but the consilience between the theories would also suggest warrant on the basis of coherence.

Another basis for warrant is in evidence. *Evidentialism* in psychotherapy claims that unless there is conclusive evidence for the efficacy of a certain practice, one lacks warrant and should not engage in that practice. Stated more positively, warrant is attained through conclusive evidence. Unfortunately, all evidence is partial; evidence is inconclusive, even though it can sometimes be quite compelling. There is always error. Effect sizes fall short of perfection. Only relative evidence is available and therefore only relative certainty is attainable.

Even so, warrant is linked to evidence-based practice of psychotherapy through concern for efficiency and effectiveness. The use of any particular approach to psychotherapy is warranted on the basis of the various kinds of evidence different types of research generate. If an approach is said to be evidence-based, it is deemed to be warranted on the basis of evidentialism. It may be that more can be said about warrant based on coherentism and consilience in the future, but that remains to be seen. Finally, if the evidence supporting one approach indicates it is more effective than another approach, then the more effective approach is more efficient and relatively more warranted.

Evidence-Based Practice

The concerns for efficacy, effectiveness, and efficiency are at the heart of the movement for evidence-based practice in psychotherapy. The two considerations that loom largest in any particular intervention or approach to psychotherapy are "does the treatment work—a question of its efficacy, which is most related to internal validity, and does it generalize or transport to the local setting where it is to be used—a question of its effectiveness, which is most related to external validity" (Brownell, 2008).

According to the American Psychological Association, evidence-based practice in psychology is the integration of the best available research with clinical expertise in the context of patient characteristics, culture, and preferences (APA, 2006). That task force identified multiple forms of support as "evidence." The range of research designs that contribute to the body of knowledge relevant to evidence-based practice includes:

> ... clinical observation, qualitative research, systematic case study, single-case experimental designs to examine causal factors in outcome with regard to a single patient, process-outcome studies to examine mechanisms of change, effectiveness studies in natural settings, random controlled treatments and efficacy studies for drawing causal inferences in groups, and meta-analysis for observing patterns across multiple studies and for understanding effect sizes. (Brownell, 2008, p. 94)

In addition to this list, some have argued for the need to remain sensitive to, and make a place for, the clinical judgment of experienced clinicians (Zeldow, 2009) and to make the clinical setting a natural laboratory (Borckhardt et al., 2008; Brownell, 2008; Fago, 2009; Westen & Bradley, 2005) for the production of practice-based evidence. Clinical judgment and reasoning have been defined by Shapiro, Friedberg, and Bardenstein (2006) as a mix of informed analysis and decision making leading to case planning based on such things as research findings, client observation, consideration of etiology, credible clinical theories, compelling authors and trainers, as well as past experience in the use of various techniques.

Practice-Based Evidence

Practice-based evidence has been characterized as a bottom-up process of gathering data that relies on the experience of practicing clinicians to inform treatment (Dupree, White, Olsen, & Lafleur, 2007). Practice-based research networks (PBRNs) have been used among clinician-researchers across diverse organizations in preventive medicine, because these PBRNs increase external validity and the generalizability of results. They are useful.

Psychotherapists who track the quality of their own work and who use sound research methodology, such as single-case, timed research designs, to do so provide themselves with evidence that surpasses assertion based on personal experience and declaration based on foundationalism. They also produce a form of evidence that is critical to the evidence-based movement, and that is practice-based evidence. It is precisely what is in question in studies of the effectiveness of psychotherapy or any particular kind of psychotherapy, and it qualifies as a valid form of research design that many believe rightfully stands beside random, controlled trials (Borckhardt et al., 2008). Among the factors making this approach appealing is the fact that it can be carried out at the clinical level without a major cost and relatively nonintrusively. It is a psychotherapist-friendly method of generating outcomes research that can then be analyzed to assess typical patterns for an individual therapist's practice, including the effectiveness of the psychotherapy that therapist used.

CONCLUSION

Psychotherapy is a general term referring to a process of treating psychological pain and functional ineffectiveness. Thus, it is related to one's individual, subjective experience and focuses on such forms of distress as depression, anxiety, disruptions of thinking, dissatisfaction with one's body, compulsive repetition that seems out of control, psychosis, and extreme mood disturbance. Psychotherapy addresses one's functional effectiveness, taking into consideration such factors as organizational capacity, conscientiousness, agreeableness, and openness to experience, and it has been shown to be a warranted response to pain and dysfunction with a relatively high degree of effectiveness.

The term psychotherapy is often used interchangeably with "counseling." It represents the meeting of two people, one of whom is trained and asserts competence and the other who comes to address pain or discomfort and functional decline. These two individuals form a therapeutic or professional agreement in which the therapist offers services for which the client agrees to pay. Because of the nature of this relationship, ethical and legal guidelines and parameters have been formulated over time to assist the therapist and to protect the patient/client/consumer. That is because the therapist has heightened influence with regard to the patient/client/consumer, and that person's level of vulnerability intensifies when a therapeutic relationship is deeply rooted.

Psychotherapists are guided by clinical and theoretical systems. They typically learn these in formal, academic graduate programs or postgraduate training institutions, and they are supervised in their practical experience by trained, competent, and licensed clinical supervisors. Often, their practices are regulated by certification and licensing boards in the jurisdictions in which they practice.

The various systems of psychotherapy (psychoanalytic, psychodynamic, cognitive, behavioral, cognitive behavioral, humanistic and existential, etc.) all have their literature bases. This book focuses on gestalt therapy, providing a practical guide for the mental health professional who would become competent to practice as a gestalt therapist.

NOTES

1. Corisni and Wedding (2007) would disagree that this kind of distinction can be made between psychotherapy and counseling, claiming the overlap is too great. Along the same lines, it is difficult to see much real difference between counseling and coaching; coaching, counseling, and psychotherapy now overlap extensively.
2. In the middle of the 20th century, several prominent researchers/writers questioned whether the benefits of psychotherapy exceeded what occurred naturally over time without treatment. Since then "thousands of well-controlled outcome studies ... have been completed, reviewed, and meta-analyzed," resulting in the evidence that psychotherapy does, indeed, work; in fact, the evidence is so massive that the question now is which forms of therapy work better than others and under what conditions (Kazdin, 2008, p. 146).

REFERENCES

Ablon, A. S., & Marci, C. (2004). Psychotherapy process: The missing link: Comment on Westen, Novotny, and Thompson-Brenner (2004). *Psychological Bulletin, 30*(4), 664–668.

American Psychological Association. Presidential Task Force on Evidence-based Practice. (2006). Evidence-based practice in psychology. *American Psychologist, 61*(4), 271–285.

Bankart, C. P. (1996). *Talking cures: A history of western and eastern psychotherapies.* Belmont, CA: Wadsworth.

Borckardt, J., Nash, M., Murphy, M., Moore, M., Shaw, D., & O'Neil, P. (2008). Clinical practice as natural laboratory for psychotherapy research: A guide to case-based time-series analysis. *American Psychologist, 63*, 77–95.

Brown, C. (1976). *Dictionary of New Testament theology* (Vols. 1–3). Grand Rapids, MI: Zondervan.

Brownell, P. (2008). Practice-based evidence. In P. Brownell (Ed.), *Handbook for theory, research, and practice in gestalt therapy* (pp. 90–103). Newcastle, UK: Cambridge Scholars Publishing.

Corey, G. (2009). *Theory and practice of counseling and psychotherapy* (8th ed.). Belmont, CA: Thompson Brooks/Cole.

Corsini, R., & Wedding, D. (2007). *Current psychotherapies* (8th ed.). Belmont, CA: Thompson Brooks/Cole.

Crocker, S. (2008). A unified theory. In P. Brownell (Ed.). *Handbook for theory, research, and practice in gestalt therapy* (pp. 124–150). Newcastle, UK: Cambridge Scholars Publishing.

Cushman, P. (1992) Psychotherapy to 1992: A historically situated interpretation. In D. K. Freedheim, H. Freudenberger, J. Kessler, S. Messer, D. Peterson, et al. (Eds.), *History of psychotherapy: A century of change.* (pp. 21–64). Washington, DC: American Psychological Association.

Dupree, J., White, M., Olsen, C. and Lafleur, C. (2007) Infidelity treatment patterns: A practice-based evidence approach. *American Journal of Family Therapy, 35*(4), 327–341.

Fago, D. (2009). Comment: The evidence-based treatment debate: Toward a dialectical rapprochement. *Psychotherapy Theory, Research, Practice, Training, 46*(1), 15–18.

Freud, S. (1950/1978/1994). *The interpretation of dreams*. New York: Random House.

Haynes, W., & Johnson, C. (2009). *Understanding research and evidence-based practice in communication disorders: A primer for students and practitioners*. Boston: Pearson.

Kazdin, A. (2008). Evidence-based treatment and practice: New opportunities to bridge clinical research and practice, enhance the knowledge base, and improve patient care. *American Psychologist, 63*(3), 146–159.

Klonicki, E. (2002) *Thinking about therapy? What to expect from "the talking cure."* Lincoln, NE: Writer's Showcase.

Nathan, P., Stuart, S., & Dolan, S. (2003). Research on psychotherapy efficacy and effectiveness: Between Scylla and Charybdis? In A. Kazdin (Ed.), *Methodological issues & strategies in clinical research* (3rd ed., pp. 505–546). Washington, DC: American Psychological Association.

Niiniluoto, I. (2007). Scientific progress. In E. N. Zalta (Ed.), *The Stanford encyclopedia of philosophy*. Downloaded April 7, 2009, from http://plato.stanford.edu/entries/scientific-progress.

Shapiro, J. P., Friedberg, R. D., & Bardenstein, K. K. (2006). *Child and adolescent therapy: Science and art.* New York: Wiley.

Snyder, L. (2006). William Whewell. In E. N. Zalta (Ed.), *The Stanford encyclopedia of philosophy*. Downloaded April 7, 2009, from http://plato.stanford.edu/entries/whewell.

Westen, D. & Bradley, R. (2005). Empirically supported complexity: Rethinking evidence-based practice in psychotherapy. *Current Directions in Psychological Science, 14*(5), 266–271.

Winick, B. J. (1997). *The right to refuse mental health treatment*. Washington, DC: American Psychological Association.

Zeldow, P. (2009). In defense of clinical judgment, credentialed clinicians, and reflective practice. *Psychotherapy: Theory, Research, Practice, Training, 46*, 1–10.

2 What Is Gestalt Psychotherapy?

In this chapter, gestalt therapy is briefly contextualized in terms of theoretical development. The existential, phenomenological, and behavioral aspects of gestalt therapy are identified, and the complexities of gestalt therapy theory are briefly expressed in ordinary language. What gestalt therapy is and what it is not are clearly defined so that the reader might distinguish it from other approaches; it is also compared and contrasted with other major clinical perspectives.

Some people think of gestalt therapy as an existential field theory. Others think of it as a combination of existential phenomenology and phenomenological behaviorism. Broadly, gestalt therapy fits in the category of humanistic approaches. However, gestalt therapy developed as an expression of the revolutionary science that led to the paradigm shift from positivism to postpositivism—or to what many understand as postmodernism or deconstructionism. Thus, it is not simply a quirky version of person-centered therapy or an embodiment of Maslow's ideas. Gestalt therapy shares concepts with Rogerian and existentialist approaches, and it points to many of the same philosophers in the foundational and ideological development of its theory; but it is a complete theoretical and clinical system of its own. It was birthed in a unique mix of continental philosophy and German science and conceived of as a revision of Freud's psychoanalytic approach. Its theory has been developed extensively since Frederick and Laura Perls started the first gestalt therapy training institute, and certainly since the time when Fritz Perls demonstrated gestalt therapy at the Esalen Institute at Big Sur, California. Today, gestalt therapy is a growing theory that is applied diversely by various therapists all over the world.[1] Its principles have also been adapted by consultants working with organizations and, most recently, by coaches helping individual executives.

To grasp more fully what gestalt therapy is, reading a description of its theory or practice is not enough. One must sense what led up to it, how it took form in the lives of the people who became gestalt therapists, trainers, thinkers, and writers, and what the chief interests are in the work of its contemporary theorists. This chapter provides a prelude to gestalt therapy, and chapter 3 outlines the history of its growth in the world as well as offering a glimpse of some of its contemporary leaders.

BACKGROUND

The background to gestalt therapy can be organized into an Eastern influence and a Western influence. A general description of a few prominent individuals and philosophical currents provides a sense of the developmental ground from which gestalt therapy emerged.

Eastern Influence: Zen and Tao

Buddhism is an Asian religion, or philosophy, founded in India by Siddartha Gautama during the 5th century B.C. Buddhism advocates the eightfold path, which is a subset of the four noble truths: life is suffering, the cause of suffering is craving or desire, suffering ceases only at nirvana (the extinction of desire), and nirvana may be achieved by following the eightfold path. The eightfold path consists of understanding, thinking, speech, action, livelihood, effort, mindfulness, and concentration. "Thus Buddhist teaching provides a set of beliefs about reality, a theory of the human mind and behavior, and recommendations on how to live (Kelly, 2008); these all involve the way a person navigates life, and thus are also process in nature" (Brownell, in press a, np).

One of the more important emphases of Buddhism is on mindful awareness.

> The most common Buddhist method of awareness training is mindfulness of breathing. Two classical Buddhist texts deal with this in detail: The Sattipathana Sutta (Anãlayo, 2003) and the Anapanasati Sutta (Rosenberg, 1998). They both explore awareness under four headings: Awareness of the body; Awareness of feelings; Awareness of mind, Awareness of phenomena. (Kjønstad and Halvorsen, in press)

Zen Buddhist spirituality is

> not about thinking about God when one is peeling potatoes; it is being fully engaged in peeling the potatoes. Indeed, Zen teaches that all daily activities can be done with the same kind of undivided presence in the moment, where we give ourselves wholly to whatever we do, without second-guessing ourselves, without self-consciously observing how we are doing what we are doing, without being double-minded. (Crocker & Philippson, 2005, p. 75)

In very brief summary, Eastern spirituality largely concerns the *way* in which a person lives. It is practical. It is concerned with method and action, with attention to the current flow of experience and awareness, and it is characterized by acceptance of whatever is currently happening, trusting in the natural flow of events that will bring about wholeness and healing.

Taoism is a Chinese philosophy based on the writings of Lao-tzu, who lived somewhere between the 6th and 4th centuries B.C. Taoism has a naturalistic ethos that promotes a process approach for understanding life. It emphasizes a "way" that allows it to encompass many movements and local belief systems, avoiding conflict with their tenets–the "what" or the content of those belief systems–by emphasizing the manner of the process of living with that content. As such, it can be assimilated today as a harmonic complement to the contents of belief systems and clinical perspectives.

The Tao, or the "way," refers to direction, movement, and method in thought, while living in and with nature. Spontaneity and naturalness are its chief virtues, and when reflected in a clinical setting, the task of the therapist is to "engage the client in ways that allow nature to do the healing and the growing" (Crocker, 2005, p. 74; cf. also Dahlsgaard, Peterson, & Seligman, 2005).

In summary, the Eastern thought that influenced gestalt therapy was not something the founders of gestalt therapy studied in depth, but it was "in the air" in their spheres of influence as gestalt therapy was being formed. Eastern thought was a useful metaphor in their thinking. Eastern influence concerns the way in which a person lives. It focuses on method and action, "with attention to the current flow of experience and awareness, and it is characterized by acceptance of whatever is currently happening, trusting in the natural flow of events that will bring about wholeness and healing" (Brownell, in press a, np).

Western Influence: Judaism, Christianity, Philosophy, and Science

The Western influence in the ground of gestalt therapy, by contrast, is huge. It starts in ancient Greece and concludes in post-World War II France and North America.

Most Western systems of thought can be traced back to the Greek philosophers Socrates, his student Plato, and Plato's student Aristotle. Aristotle tutored Alexander the Great and started his own school of philosophy, the Lyceum, in Athens. His writings on logic, physical science, and metaphysics have had a strong influence on subsequent thinkers, especially on medieval and Renaissance writers. Sylvia Crocker (1999) described gestalt therapy as Aristotelian, and her description is a good starting point for tracing the Western influences in the development of gestalt therapy:

> While Aristotle was interested in coming to an understanding of the general nature of the processes of change which are everywhere apparent, he was particularly interested in those functions of living organisms which explain both their morphology and their behavior. Plato's vision looks *away from* nature to those universals which are imperfectly exemplified there, while Aristotle's vision looks *into* nature to find the organizing principles which govern its processes. For Plato, knowledge comes primarily from rational thought, while Aristotle's approach to knowledge begins with experience, which is processed by rational thought and is then applied back to experience. (Crocker, 1999, p. 111)

Among the various concerns that Aristotle considered was his observation that there is a process and a faculty to living things: "[S]hould the process of thinking come first or the mind that thinks, the process of sensation or the sensitive faculty?" (Aristotle, 2006, p. 4). This logical ordering is echoed today in curiosity about wave and particle, field and organism, and the emergent properties of self. In terms of gestalt therapy the question is, "Should the individual come first or the field of which he or she is a part?"

There was a long period in which common reference to thinkers such as Plato and Aristotle were almost lost. The Greek texts suffered as familiarity with the Greek language waned and all but disappeared; however, a few people advanced Aristotle's ideas. Peter Abelard, John Buridan, John Duns Scotus, Thomas Aquinas, and William of Ockham, among others, developed medieval philosophy focused on metaphysics, natural philosophy, science, and epistemology (Spade, 2004).

Fast forward to the 18th century. Immanuel Kant was born in 1724 in East Prussia (now Kaliningrad, Russia). His productive philosophical life extended from 1745 to 1802. His ideas continue to be studied all over the world for their relevance to science, culture, religion, and philosophy proper.

One of the more relevant issues for gestalt therapy is the way Kant defined the terms *noumenon* and *phenomenon*. He used noumenon to refer to an object itself, as it exists in the real world apart from any person's experience of it, and he used phenomenon to refer to how that object appears to a given subject. This is a distinction between what is independent of the mind and what is dependent on it (Langton, 1998), a distinction congruent with Kant's assertion that knowledge is contingent on experience. Kant argued that

> there is no such thing as "bare perception," that we never experience the raw data of experience, that our processes of sensation and perception always filter and organize the data according to the mind's own innate rules. According to Kant, we can never know what, if anything, the resemblance is since we can never escape our own way of perceiving. (Crocker, 1999, p. 137)

In terms of culture, Kant was influenced by Taoist and Confucian thought, which were disseminated in continental Europe by Jesuits based in China and popularized by Leibnitz, Wolff, and their students. One example is the idea of dialectics that Bulfinger found in the Chinese classical literature and Kant encountered in the Russian academy. "Kant was unaware of the Far Eastern roots of the notions that influenced him, and the historical irony is that he dismissed nonwestern cultures while being deeply influenced by their insights." (Schonfeld, 2007, np)

The belief that knowledge is contingent on experience was picked up by Friedrich Schleiermacher, a second-tier philosopher in a world more at home with theism than the current age. Although comfortable with German idealism, Schleiermacher was a contemporary and rival of G. W. F. Hegel in academic circles, and the two ended up quite at odds with one another.

Schleiermacher is significant for two reasons, one of which was his development of the concept of religious "feeling." He is often contemplated along with William James, Søren Kierkegaard, and Jonathan Edwards regarding religious emotions; however, to lump Schleiermacher's term "feeling" into a simple affective category would be to miss his point. He was talking about what today would be called spiritual experience.

Schleiermacher grew up in a part of the world dominated by theism and Lutheran Pietism, the latter of which promoted an experiential knowledge of God (Jones, Wainwright, & Yarnold, 1986). Schleiermacher referred to himself as a Pietist of a higher order, for in his world philosophy often pivoted off religious issues. Thus, Schleiermacher became a renowned philosopher-theologian, who was considered the father of liberal Protestant theology because he sought to incorporate philosophy and science into his thinking about God.

Schleiermacher described individual experience as a "starting point in understanding religious life (McGrath, 2004). Although he revered Plato, he was also a student of Aristotle and understood religious experience as the feeling (Crouter, 2005) of absolute dependence on God, '... identical with the consciousness of being in relation with God'" (Brownell, in press b, np; Feinberg, 2001, p. 112) Thus, for him the ongoing flow of one's experience became a crucial focus of life. He had a great influence on Rudolph Otto (1923/1958), who distinguished between the experience of the *mysterium tremendum* (awe and fear) and that of *mysterium fascinans* (fascination and attraction), when it came to contact with divinity, the experience of the numinous.

Schleiermacher had a tremendous influence on Willhelm Dilthey's work in hermeneutics. Dilthey studied under two of Schleiermacher's students at the University of Berlin, and in 1859 he was asked to complete the editing of Schleiermacher's letters. That year the Schleiermacher Society organized an essay competition, and Dilthey's submission titled "Schleiermacher's Hermeneutical System in Relation to Earlier Protestant Hermeneutics" (1860) won. Subsequently, he was commissioned to write Schleiermacher's biography. Dilthey then wrote his dissertation on Schleiermacher's ethics (Makkreel, 2008). In Dilthey's final productive period, he broadened hermeneutics to include a method for the recovery of meaning out of experience, and thus applied an essentially theological process to social sciences. He is well known for proposing two models of psychological investigation: a natural science that seeks causal explanations and is examined by experimentation and a cultural science that seeks an understanding of psychological phenomena and is examined by hermeneutics (Kashima & Haslam, 2007).

This leads to the second significance of Schleiermacher, which is, for some, the most important impact of his work—his influence on hermeneutics. In the development of the rules for literary interpretation, the question, "How do we read this text?" in his hands became "How do we communicate at all?"

> Without such a shift, initiated by Friedrich Schleiermacher, Willhelm Dilthey, and others, it is impossible to envisage the ontological turn in hermeneutics that, in the mid-1920s, was triggered by Martin Heidegger's *Sein und Zeit* and carried on by his student Hans-George Gadamer. (Ramberg & Gjesdal, 2005)

Schleiermacher was nearing the end of his life as Søren Kierkegaard was entering his most productive period. Rather than Kierkegaard being a disciple of Schleiermacher, it is more likely that Schleiermacher provided Kierkegaard an intellectual and theological anvil against which to hammer out his own thinking on such issues as religious experience, being, and the dialectics of life. Thus, whereas Schleiermacher held dialectic to be conversation and the art of knowing, Kierkegaard viewed it as the contradictory nature of existence and the art of paradox leading to existential earnestness (Crouter, 2005).

On June 10, 1836, Kierkegaard wrote in his journal

> An ambulant musician played the minuet from Don Giovanni on some kind of reed-pipe (I couldn't see what it was as he was in the next courtyard), and the druggist was pounding medicine with his pestle, and the maid was scouring in the yard, and the groom curried his horse and beat off the curry-comb against the curb, and from another part of town came the distant cry of a shrimp vendor, etc., and they noticed nothing and maybe the piper didn't either, and I felt such well-being. (Rhode, 1960/1988, p. 13)

This is the quality of existential wonder in the mundane flow of life, of being alive and mindful of the lives of others in the hum of the community. However, it was Kierkegaard's investigation of the individual person—the individual's experience of such community rather than of community itself—that marked him as the father of existentialism.

In the liturgical ecclesia of his day, stale and rigid in its religious routines and its dogmatic creeds, the individual's subjective experience, to Kierkegaard, was more true, more valuable, than simple adherence to ethical norms and rational precepts (Crowell, 2008). This led to the development of the construct of authenticity in 20th-century existential philosophy and to what gestalt therapists would later understand as spontaneity and fluidity in responding to novel figures.

In regard to religious experience, Kierkegaard expounded faith, personal and passionate entrusting of oneself, animated by acts in which one made faith a living contrast to the relatively dead, Hegelian rationalism he often criticized. It was not a matter of the object of belief, nor what was said about that object, as much as it was about the quality of believing or the way in which one expressed one's faith (Amesbury, 2005).

> Kierkegaard lived in a time similar in some ways to our own. He objected to a prevailing contempt for the individual. He observed a search for science and objectivity motivated by Kant and Hegel, but in place of that Kierkegaard substituted "subjective truth," choice and passion, and he turned attention back to the individual, away from the idea of the collective (Solomon, 2004). His ground was his own Christianity and his rejection of Hegel and the Church as burdens imposed on free people. He lived as an *existing individual*, and he propagated both the concept and the lived experience of *existence* in a way that directly influenced Brentano, Husserl, Heidegger, Sartre and Jaspers. With this influence, he became the ground for European existentialism. (Brownell, 2008a, pp. 214–215; Gaffney, 2006)

Franz Brentano was born in 1838 in Germany. He belonged to a family of intellectuals who were deeply given to German Romanticism. His family were devout Catholics, and their home was a constant meeting place for intellectuals. Brentano obtained a classical European education, and during his final years in school his interests ranged from philosophy to mathematics and geometry, but it was his reading of Aristotle that became the foundation and impetus for his choice of philosophy as a focus for his life's work. He studied for the priesthood and took orders with the understanding from his bishop that he could continue his studies and teach. Eventually, he renounced the priesthood because he could not abide the doctrine of the infallibility of the Pope, but he remained a devout theist. Among his students were Stumpf, Erenfels, Husserl, and Freud (Albertazzi, 2006).

Brentano is credited with reviving the medieval construct of intentionality and using it in his conception of act psychology. Intentionality addresses the "aboutness" of experience. Everything we think, feel, value, imagine, perceive, and experience is about something. Each of these mental acts takes an *intentional object.*

> Franz Brentano considered the qualities that characterize mental acts, or phenomena, and is credited with the first serious inquiry into phenomenology. Reaching back to the Scholastics for a term, he re-introduced "intentionality," placing it into phenomenological vocabulary. In the discourse of philosophy, intentionality is the aboutness of mental phenomena. To think is to think *of* something. All thought has an object, either inexistent (for example, a unicorn) or actual (for example, a house). The name most associated with phenomenology is that of Brentano's student, Edmund Husserl. With Husserl, phenomenology became a philosophical movement.... [I]ntentionality describes the relationship of the knower, the process of knowing, and that which is known, and it is comprised of the quality of knowing, or *noesis*, and the content of knowledge, or *noema.* (Burley & Bloom, 2008, pp. 152–153)

It is Husserl, rather than Brentano, who is considered the founder of phenomenology. He was a prolific theorist who wrote on many subjects and passed through various stages in developing his own thinking. With regard to gestalt therapy, his form of phenomenological inquiry, called the *phenomenological method*, has become most influential. Its adaptation to a therapeutic process is one of the factors that makes gestalt therapy a phenomenological perspective (D. Bloom, personal communication, May 7, 2009a. Throughout his career, Husserl assumed that the best way to approach knowledge was to focus on the meaning-making acts of consciousness and that the best way to do that was by concentrating on what was given or apparent to an individual in immediate experience. Thus, both phenomenology and gestalt therapy begin with the appearance of phenomena to consciousness (Moran, 2000).

The scientific roots of gestalt therapy can be traced largely to two individuals, Kurt Goldstein and Kurt Lewin. They are representatives of the school of gestalt psychologists that arose in Germany just before World War II. Both immigrated to the United States, where each influenced American psychology.

Kurt Goldstein was both a scientist and a philosopher. As such he was particularly heartened by what he believed to be consilience between his findings, through his work with brain-injured people, and the phenomenological philosophy of Edmund Husserl. In particular, it was Husserl's concept of the *lebenswelt* (lived world) in the natural attitude that corroborated Goldstein's philosophy of science. The interest of phenomenologists such as Aaron Gurwitsch and Maurice Merleau-Ponty in his conceptions of abstract and concrete processes provided him with a satisfying affirmation toward the end of his career.

Each person comes by a system of thought or a practical solution in the context of other people. Just so, Goldstein credited contemporaries as well as predecessors who have since become obscure influences in his development of a holistic approach. He was a physician and neurologist, and he is most noted for his work treating and investigating the effects of brain damage in soldiers following World War I. He wrote about his findings and his approach in *The Organism*, which remains one of the classic works of psychological literature and was reprinted in 1995. Interestingly, Skinner (1940) reviewed that book and criticized Goldstein for being metaphysical instead of scientific. It may be that Skinner was picking up on Goldstein's conviction that there is something about the human being that is not reducible to reflex arcs, atomization, and simple association—materialities to which Skinner was committed.

Contrary to Skinner, Goldstein asserted:

> Security needs the material world, that is, a product of the application of natural science by which the spiritual side of man is intentionally by-passed. Existence in the living world presupposes qualitative experience, not simple "order." To understand how we can move from the quantitative results of natural science to the qualitative activity of life is a problem that has always caught the imagination of man. (Goldstein, 1967, p. 155)

Goldstein had been working some time and developed his thinking before he found confirmation in Claude Bernard's[2] assertion, "Living is a contact between the organism and the outer world, if one suppresses the one or the other of the two conditions, life ceases." In 1938–1939, Goldstein delivered the William James lectures at Harvard, which he entitled "Human Nature in the Light of Psychopathology."[3] In these talks he described the conclusions for which he found support in Bernard:

> the biological knowledge we are seeking is akin to this phenomenon in which the capacity of the organism becomes adequate to environmental conditions. This is the fundamental biological process by virtue of which the actualization of the organism, and with that its existence, is made possible. Whenever we speak of the nature of the organism, of the idea, the picture, or the concept of the organism, we have in mind the essentials for the occurrence of an adequate relationship between the organism and its environment. From these, in principle, that picture arises which we have to grasp in determining the nature of man. In doing so we are subjected to practically the same difficulties of procedure as the organism is learning: we are obliged to discover what the relationship is between concept and reality. (Goldstein, 1940, pp. 25–26)

With regard to the relationship between a person and the world, Goldstein claimed that

> The mentioned behavior forms have usually been considered as the effect of the use of the mental capacity of a subject.

> I came to the conclusion that they are not determined by consciousness and that it would be meaningless to call them unconscious. They represent living events and are not the result of intellectual activities. I could no longer accept the assumption that experience is the product of mind or brain functions alone, especially after it became my conviction that the external world is always connected with it.…The study of the world of the brain-injured proved to be no less important to our knowledge than the study of the disturbance of the performance. Indeed, though the patient's behavior is certainly determined by the brain defect, it can only be understood as a phenomenon going on in the totality of his modified personality in relation to the world. The holistic approach induced me to bring psychophysical relationship into the foreground. It became obvious that it was directed by the tendency to come to terms with the world in which the individual feels he lives. There are two different behavior forms in his being in the "man-world" entity.…Sickness cannot be understood correctly if one assumes that it is something that befalls the individual from the outside. Our task is not simply to eliminate the disturbance or fight the effect of the sickness. Sickness seen from a higher aspect has to be considered as a disturbance of the relation between man and world, a disorder involving both. The patient primarily experiences his overt distress, but what is more important is that he is so much incapacitated to come to terms with the world in an adequate way that he becomes unable to realize himself. (Goldstein, 1967, pp. 161–163)

This situated existence, this relationship between the organism and the world, is something that was most thoroughly explored by Kurt Lewin. Gordon Allport described Lewin as a genius, claiming that he possessed the traits inherent to genius: intellectual solitude, originality, periods of fallowness and confusion, hard work, situational factors (World War I, political conditions in Germany, opportunity to observe and live in the United States where democracy was working), and tenacious devotion to one or more nonhedonistic values (Allport, 1947).

Kurt Lewin contributed to the understanding of personality, learning, social psychology, and group dynamics and was identified with the gestalt school of psychology, maintaining that any given response is governed by all the forces in the field of behavior (Brown, 1929; Hartmann, 1935; Westerhof, 1938). Regarding his philosophy of science, he asserted, "Structural properties are characterized by relations between parts rather than by the parts or elements themselves." His overall theoretical approach was composed of three emphases: the interconnection of person and environment, relational rather than object concepts, and systematic rather than historical concepts of causation (Deutsch, 1992).

Lewin was also given to the study of the interaction between theory and practice. He believed basic laws and dynamics of human behavior could be used to effect social change, and for him, theory and application were entirely compatible. He was convinced that social psychology could make the world a better place in which to live (Fong, Hammond, & Zanna, 2006), and that was important to him, coming out of the German society of World War II.

Lewin's ideas have variously been called dynamic theory, topological theory, vector psychology, and field theory. He is most associated with the last of those categories. By the 1960s, his field theory had become one of several phenomenological approaches to understanding personality—along with Henry Murray's needs and press formulation, Goldstein's organismic theory, Carl Rogers' theory of self, and the biosocial-eclectic point of view of Gardner Murphy (Lazarus, 1961). Hall and Lindzey (1957/1959) identified the three principal features of Lewin's field theory as behavior as a function of the field, which exists at the time the behavior occurs; analysis that begins with the situation as a whole, from which contributing parts are differentiated; and the concrete person in a concrete situation, represented mathematically. The most salient description of the field, however, came from Lewin himself, who described it as "the totality of coexisting facts which are conceived of as mutually interdependent" (Lewin, 1951, p. 240).

In summary, the Western influence on gestalt therapy originated with Aristotle's emphasis on empirical data achieved from direct experience, took a phenomenological turn through Kant's depiction of experience as represented and his distinction between the objective world and the presentations made manifest to our perception, and eventually resulted in the thinking of Brentano and Husserl. Meanwhile, Schleiermacher had affirmed spiritual experience as opposed to propositional affirmation, and Otto followed up with his contention that religious experience constituted direct contact with divinity, the experience of the numinous. All this, along with the philosophical reaction to Kant and Hegel, and the condition of the church in his day, brought Kierkegaard to develop his emphasis on faith as a means of actualizing one's existence. Thus, firmly embedded in the philosophical ground of gestalt therapy were emphases on experience, the phenomenological basis for understanding that experience, and the existential call to put one's beliefs to the test of living. As science and philosophy began to differentiate, gestalt therapy was preceded by Kurt Goldstein and Kurt Lewin. Goldstein emphasized holism and the relationship between any given organism and the world, whereas Kurt Lewin applied the concept of a physical force field to the world of social science in order to explicate the nature of the relationship between an organism and its environment. He argued that a person's behavior and personality could be understood as a function of the field.

Aristotle and Schleiermacher spoke of experience. Kant claimed all experience is interpreted through what is presented rather than through what actually and objectively exists. Kierkegaard claimed that only authentic responses of faith to what life presents are worth one's existence. Brentano claimed all experience takes an object of awareness, an intentional object. Husserl provided a phenomenological method in his attempt to get back to the objects themselves, Goldstein spoke of the organism that experiences, and Lewin spoke of the field in which experience takes place.

THEORETICAL OVERVIEW

Gestalt therapy is not a supernova shining alone in the darkness. It is built from an assimilation of ideas, and it shares some similarities with other approaches. Indeed, a consilience exists between gestalt therapy and various aspects of cognitive behavioral therapy, contemporary psychoanalysis, and neuropsychology. Today's gestalt psychologists, for instance (following in the tradition of Goldstein), are investigating consciousness, perceptual-motor relationships, mirror neurons, decision making, executive functioning, and self-regulation. Gestalt therapy theorists today are attempting to integrate science and the phenomenological and existential philosophies that continue to evolve in Europe, and exploring how these developments might apply to the clinical processes in gestalt praxis. Gestalt therapy is not a dead language that one can find only in ancient texts; it is alive, thriving in various parts of the world, and continuously evolving.

Following is a general overview, or forecast, of the more in-depth exploration of gestalt therapy's chief theoretical tenets and practices in the chapters to follow.

Phenomenological Method

The use of the phenomenological method makes gestalt therapy a phenomenological approach. That is what a person observing a gestalt therapist at work would notice, but actually it is the commitment to phenomenology that drives the utility of the phenomenological method. Consequently, the developing thought in phenomenology—starting with Brentano and continuing with Husserl, Heidegger, Merleau-Ponty, Levinas, and the more contemporary French phenomenologists such as Jean-Luc Marion, Michel Henry, and Jean-Louis Chretien—remains a major resource in the ongoing development of gestalt therapy theory and practice. For the practicing therapist, the question is, "How does the client make meaning out of experience?" In that respect, gestalt therapy is consilient with much of the constructivism and mindfulness found in contemporary cognitive behavioral therapy and with any approach using the hermeneutical thinking of Heidegger and Gadamer.

Dialogical Relationship

The dialogical relationship in gestalt therapy is most notably associated with the thinking of Martin Buber. For many years following the turn from awareness of an individual's experience in contacting in the environment to the contact possible between two individuals, Buber's way of conceptualizing relationships served as the backbone of the gestalt therapeutic alliance. Today, matters of alterity, in the thinking of Emmanuel Levinas, have an increasing influence. All in all, the question for a therapist is, "How do I forge a connection, a meaningful relationship with this client?" Because of the common concern with intersubjective process, gestalt therapy is consilient with interpersonal psychotherapy, client-centered integrations such as emotion-focused therapy, and with relational, or contemporary, inter-subjective systems psychoanalysis.

Field Theoretical Strategy

Field theory in physical science was adapted by Kurt Lewin to describe the systemic operations at various levels of the environmental surround in which we live. Field theorists following Lewin, especially among gestalt therapists, have spent a lot of time and energy describing how field forces and dynamics affect current processes. In this respect, gestalt therapy is consilient with systemic family systems and multisystemic interventions in social psychology. For the therapist, the question that moves philosophical speculation to the pragmatic level is "So what?" "How can I use it?" "What must I do if I am going to be appreciative of the field and if I am going to become strategic in my work with the client?"

Experimental Freedom

Gestalt therapy is not based on a cause-and-effect, linear theory of change. Thus, it does not really follow the medical model of simple symptom reduction by means of critical interventions. Rather, the gestalt therapy model makes mystery virtuous and open systems, in which many things are always possible, adventuresome. Gestalt therapy is essentially experimental. The gestalt therapist asks, "What might happen if…?" Something is thrown into action to create an experience that can be mined and used to increase awareness and understanding, and the experienced gestalt therapist finds his or her own stride in just how to craft novel and clinically relevant experiments.

CONCLUSION

Gestalt therapy is a contemporary system of psychotherapy. It is a relevant and effective theoretical approach that has also been adapted for organizational work and for coaching. Gestalt therapy is one of the established ways in which psychotherapy can be conducted, and it comes with ever-increasing evidence for its practice. Gestalt therapy is associated historically with the "Third Wave" in clinical psychology, but it is best conceived of as a holistic and assimilating approach capable of integrating essential tenets of cognitive behavioral, psychoanalytic, systems, and body-oriented modalities. It is experiential. It is existential. It is phenomenological, and it is behavioral. Gestalt therapy provides a therapist with a natural way of being with clients, but it defies easy mastery or simplistic reduction.

NOTES

1. See chapter 3 for a description of the growth and application of gestalt therapy world wide.
2. In autobiographical statements, Goldstein stated, "I was still more encouraged when I learned that my basic concept was much in accordance with the theoretical interpretation of the French physiologist Claude Bernard, as published in *An Introduction to the Study of Experimental Medicine* (1866). Claude Bernard, as famous as he was in Germany for his medical discoveries, was to me and most other physicians there completely unknown for his theoretical interpretation, which he had developed from his practical work" (Goldstein, 1967, p. 158).
3. These lectures have since been published in book form under the same title.

REFERENCES

Albertazzi, L. (2006). *Immanent realism: An introduction to Brentano*. Dordrecht, Netherlands: Springer.

Allport, G. (1947). The genius of Kurt Lewin. *Journal of Personality, 16*, 1–10.

Amesbury, R. (2005). Fideism. In E. N. Zalta (Ed.), *The Stanford encyclopedia of philosophy*. Accessed April 26, 2009, from http://plato.stanford.edu/entries/fideism/#2.2.2.

Anãlayo. (2003). *Satipatthana: The direct path to realisation*. Cambridge, UK: Windhorse.

Aristotle. (2006). *De anima*. New York: Barnes & Noble.

Barber, P. (2006). *Becoming a practitioner researcher: A gestalt approach to holistic inquiry*. London: Middlesex University Press.

Boring, E. G., & G. Lindzey, G. (Eds.). (1967). *A history of psychology in autobiography, Vol. V. The century psychology series* (pp. 145–166). East Norwalk, CT: Appleton-Century-Crofts.

Brown, J. (1929). The methods of Kurt Lewin in the psychology of action and affection. *Psychological Review, 36*(3), 200–221.

Brownell, P. (1998). Renewing our roots in neuropsychology: A gestalt perspective on the work of Joseph LeDoux. *Gestalt! 2*(1). Downloaded May 14, 2009, from http://www.g-gej.org/2-1/ledouxreview.html.

Brownell, P. (2008a). Faith: An existential, phenomenological, and biblical integration. In J. Harold Ellens (Ed.), *Miracles: God, science, and psychology in the paranormal, vol. 2, Medical and therapeutic events* (pp. 213–234). Westport, CT: Praeger/Greenwood.

Brownell, P. (Ed.). (2008b). *Handbook for theory, research, and practice in gestalt therapy*. Newcastle, England: Cambridge Scholars.

Brownell, P. (2009a). Executive functions: A neuropsychological understanding of self-regulation. *Gestalt Review, 13*(1), 62–81.

Brownell, P. (2009b). Gstalt-L: A virtual, electronic community. In B. O'Neill (Ed.), *Community, psychotherapy and life focus: A gestalt anthology of the history, theory, and practice of living in community*, pp. 171–191. Wollongong East, Australia: Ravenwood Press.

Brownell, P. (in press a). Spirituality in the praxis of gestalt therapy. In J. Harold Ellens (Ed.), *The healing power of religion*, np. Westport, CT: Greenwood.

Brownell, P. (in press b). Spirituality in gestalt therapy. In T. Levine Bar-Yoseph (Ed.), *From the here and now to the future—Advancing gestalt theory and practice,* np. New York: Routledge.

Brownell, P. (in press c). Intentional spirituality. In J. Harold Ellens (Ed.), *The healing power of religion*, np. Westport, CT: Greenwood.

Burley, T., & Bloom, D. (2008). Phenomenological method. In P. Brownell (Ed.), *Handbook for theory, research, and practice in gestalt therapy* (pp. 151–183). Newcastle, England: Cambridge Scholars.

Crocker, S. F. (1999). *A well-lived life: Essays in gestalt therapy*. Cambridge, MA: Gestalt Institute of Cleveland Press.

Crocker, S.F. & Philippson, P. (2005) Phenomenology, existentialism, and Eastern thought in gestalt therapy. In A. Woldt and S. Toman (eds.) *Gestalt therapy history, theory, and practice,* pp. 65-80. London, UK: Sage Publications.

Crouter, R. (2005). *Friedrich Schleiermacher: Between enlightenment and romanticism.* Cambridge, MA: Cambridge University Press.

Crowell, S. (2008). Existentialism. In E. N. Zalta (Ed.), *The Stanford encyclopedia of philosophy*. Downloaded April 26, 2009, from http://plato.stanford.edu/entries/existentialism.

Dahlsgaard, K., Peterson, C., & Seligman, M. (2005) Shared virtue: The convergence of valued human strengths across culture and history. Review of general psychology, 9(3), 203-213.

Deutsch, M. (1992). Kurt Lewin: The tough-minded and tender-hearted scientist. *Journal of Social Issues, 48*(2), 31–43.

Feinberg, J. (2001). *No one like him: The doctrine of God.* Wheaton, IL: Crossway Books.

Fong, G., Hammond, D., & Zanna, M. (2006). Bridging to evidence-based public health policy. In P. A. M. VanLange (Ed.), *Bridging social psychology: Benefits of transdisciplinary approaches* (pp. 333–338). Mahwah, NJ: Lawrence Erlbaum Associates.

Gaffney, S. (2006). On being absurd: Søren Kierkegaard 1813–1855. *British Gestalt Journal, 15*(1).

Goldstein, K. (1940) *Human nature in the light of psychopathology*. New York: Shocken Books.

Goldstein, K. (1967). Kurt Goldstein. In K. Goldstein, W. Riese, E. Hall, C., & Lindzey, G. (1957, 1959). Lewin's field theory. In *Theories of personality* (pp. 206–256). Hoboken, NJ: John Wiley & Sons.

Goldstein, K. (1995). *The organism: A holistic approach to biology derived from pathological data in man*. Brooklyn, NY: Zone Books.

Hartmann, G. (1935). *Gestalt psychology: A survey of facts and principles* (pp. 202–240). New York: Ronald Press.

Jones, C., Wainwright, G., & Yarnold, E. (Eds.). (1986). *The study of spirituality*. New York and Oxford: Oxford University Press.

Kashima, Y. & Haslam, N. (2007) Explanation and interpretation: An invitation to experimental semiotics. *Journal of theoretical and philosophical psychology*, 27–28(2–1), 234-256.

Kelly, B. (2008). Buddhist psychology, psychotherapy and the brain: A critical introduction. *Transcultural Psychiatry, 45*(1), 5–30.

Kjønstad, & Halvorsen. (In press) *Gestalt therapy and Buddhism: Sources of inspiration and common ground.*

Langton, R. (1998). *Kantian humility: Our ignorance of things in themselves*. Oxford, England: Clarendon Press.

Lazarus, R. (1961). Personality from a phenomenological point of view. In *Adjustment and personality. McGraw-Hill series in psychology* (pp. 104–136). New York: McGraw-Hill.

Lewin, K. (1951). *Field theory in social science*. Chicago: University of Chicago Press.

Makkreel, R. (2008). Wilhelm Dilthey. In E. N. Zalta (Ed.), *The Stanford encyclopedia of philosophy*. Downloaded May 18, 2009, from http://plato.stanford.edu/entries/dilthey.

McGrath, A. (2004). *The science of God*. London: T & T Clark/Wm. B. Eerdmans.

Moran, D. (2000). *Introduction to phenomenology*. New York: Routledge.

Otto, R. (1923/1958). *The idea of the holy: An inquiry into the non-rational factor in the idea of the divine and its relation to the rational*. Oxford, England: Oxford University Press.

Perls, F. (1947/1969). *Ego, hunger and aggression*. New York: Vintage Books/Random House.

Perls, F. (1969). *A life chronology*. Downloaded on May 3, 2009, from http://www.gestalt.org/frtiz.htm.

Perls, F., Hefferline, R., & Goodman, P. (1951). *Gestalt therapy: Excitement and growth in the human personality*. New York: Julian Press.

Perls, L., & Rosenfeld, E. (1977). *An oral history of gestalt therapy—part one: A conversation with Laura Perls*. Downloaded May 3, 2009, from http://www.gestalt.org/perlsint.htm.

Polster, E., & Polster, M. (1973). *Gestalt therapy integrated: Contours of theory and practice*. New York: Vintage Books/Random House.

Ramberg, B., & Gjesdal, K. (2005). Hermeneutics. In E. N. Zalta (Ed.), *The Stanford encyclopedia of philosophy*. Downloaded April 25, 2009, from http://plato.stanford.edu/entries/hermeneutics.

Rhode, P. (Ed.), (1960/1988). *The diary of Søren Kierkegaard*. New York: Citadel Press/Kensington.

Rosenberg, L. (1998). *Breath by breath: The liberating practice of insight meditation*. Boston: Shambala.

Schonfeld, M. (2007). Kant's philosophical development. In E. N. Zalta (Ed.), *The Stanford encyclopedia of philosophy*. Downloaded April 18, 2009, from http://plato.stanford.edu/entries/kant-development.

Skinner, B. F. (1940). Review of the organism: A holistic approach to biology derived from pathological data in man. *The Journal of Abnormal and Social Psychology, 35*(3), 462–465.

Solomon, R. (2004). *Existentialism* (2nd ed.). New York: Oxford University Press.

Spade, P. (2004). Medieval philosophy. In E. N. Zalta (Ed.), *The Stanford encyclopedia of philosophy*. Downloaded April 18, 2009, from http://plato.stanford.edu/entries/medieval-philosophy.

Westerhof, A. (1938). The Gestalt psychology of Kurt Lewin. In *Representative psychologists* (pp. 44–53). Union Bridge, MD: Pilot.

Woldt, A., & Brownell, P. (2005). Appendix A, digital gestalt: Online resources for the discipline of gestalt therapy, a comprehensive international listing. In A. Woldt & S. Toman (Eds.), *Gestalt therapy: History, theory, and practice.* London: Sage.

Wulf, R. (1996). The historical roots of gestalt therapy theory. *Gestalt dialogues: newsletter for the integrative gestalt centre*, np. Downloaded May 3, 2009, from http://www.gestalt.org/wulf.htm.

3 The Growth of Gestalt Therapy

This chapter outlines the beginnings and growth of gestalt therapy from a historical standpoint. To understand what gestalt therapy is requires not only comprehension of its theoretical base—the what—but also an understanding of the people who were taken by its relevance and what attracted them to it in the first place. In the foreground of the history of gestalt therapy are Frederick (Fritz) and Laura Perls, Isadore From, and Paul Goodman, but in the background are all the people who preceded them. In addition, this history is still being written, so there is a horizon that stretches out from the recent past, through the present moment and into the things that will come about in the near future.

In light of this, the following divisions in the history of gestalt therapy are an organization after the fact. The actual events and development were much messier, with generations overlapping and people moving out from training under the originators to train still more gestalt therapists, and then returning for more training themselves without ever having written much or established long-lasting training institutes; thus, gestalt people exist all over the world, with many more waves, cycles, and generations of training than can be described in detail here. This chapter includes the genealogies of trainers and trainees to illustrate the connections among these cycles and generations. This is a broad-stroke approach, but it does provide a general and relatively valid understanding of what gestalt therapy developed from and how it is still evolving.

If a drop of ink falls onto wet paper, it spreads out in all directions at the same time. That is what happened after the first training groups were established in New York, Cleveland, Los Angeles, and San Diego. The people discussed in the following section are representative of that movement. This chapter offers one description of what happened, with one list of individuals; many perspectives would configure the story with other players, but the general drift is accurate and would still be evident in any other version of the story.

THE FIRST CYCLE: ORIGINATORS AND THEIR TRAINEES

Gestalt therapy was not forced on people by academic regulation; it grew because people found it attractive and in harmony with what they already sensed, a pathway for them to travel in a direction they were already headed.

Frederick and Laura Perls

As a young man, during the period immediately following World War I in Germany, Frederick (Fritz) Perls worked as an actor, learning about the emphasis on nonverbal communication from Max Reinhard. Later, he would adopt elements of psychodrama from the work of Jacob Moreno. Perls was part of the left-wing, creative and artistic Bauhaus school in Germany, which emphasized harmony between an object's function and its form or design. At this time, Perls was also influenced by the thinking of Salomon Friedlander, with his concept of polarities and the neutral point between two poles (Wulf, 1996). In 1925, he began what would become 7 years of psychoanalysis with Wilhelm Reich and then Karen Horney. In 1926, he was exposed to Kurt Goldstein's organismic theory, and gleaned ideas of homeostasis, contact and withdrawal, and figure and ground; but it was not until he had moved to South Africa and was exposed to Jan Smuts's thinking on holism that he developed a more robust concept of the organism as a whole, embedded in its environment (Perls, 1969). By that time, he had married Lore Posner (later to be known as Laura Perls), a woman he had met in Goldstein's lab. Together they embarked on the project that later became known as gestalt therapy, but which they always conceived of as a revision of Freud in the light of their continental philosophical and scientific influences.

Laura Perls was born and educated in Germany. As a young girl, she was influenced by Elsa Gindler, who taught her to be at home in her body and to attend to movement; she studied dance from the age of 8 (Perls & Rosenfeld, 1977). She was 12 years younger than her husband and had a more formal base of training. For instance, she had studied with Goldstein for years before she obtained her analysis (whereas Frederick had obtained his analysis and then assisted Goldstein for only a few months). Laura also read the existentialist thinkers, and she studied for a time with both Paul Tillich and Martin Buber. When it came time to name the new approach they were developing, she was outvoted by her husband and others, wanting to call it "existential therapy" instead of "gestalt therapy." Laura's way of working in gestalt therapy was more dialogical, more patient, much less given to experiment, as contrasted with Frederick's demonstrations of gestalt therapy that used vivid enactments to achieve quick "breakthroughs." More concerned that a breakthrough not become a breakdown, Laura developed a balance between contact and support in all her work and mentoring. She also took a back seat to her husband, allowing him the credit for such things as writing *Ego, Hunger, and Aggression* (Perls, 1947/1969), when she had actually been an equal partner in its conception and production. She abstained entirely, however, from the production of *Gestalt Therapy: Excitement and Growth in the Human Personality* (Perls, Hefferline, & Goodman, 1951), because she was busy raising her two children, conducting her practice, and helping to organize the first gestalt therapy institute in New York.

While Frederick Perls was living at Big Sur, California, Laura was in New York. While she acted as a single parent to their two children, Frederick ignored them, living like a showman, a sort of guru, during the late 1960s, often sleeping with women who came to train with him. Laura lived the professional and ethically sound life of a psychotherapist and became the center of gravity for the activities of the New York Institute for Gestalt Therapy.

Paul Goodman

Paul Goodman is credited with writing the theoretical half of the book *Gestalt Therapy: Excitement and Growth in the Human Personality* (referred to as PHG, for the names of its three authors). Goodman (1911–1972), was a sociologist, writer, and poet. Though he was married and had three children, he was an avowed homosexual. His anarchist values and lifestyle cost him several teaching jobs. He is best known for his book, *Growing Up Absurd*.

Goodman was part of the group that started the first gestalt institute in New York. At a pivotal moment, Frederick Perls asked him to write up some notes about gestalt therapy, and Goodman used his understanding of the new approach, along with his knowledge of Otto Rank, to craft the theoretical half of PHG. Goodman is better known for his other writings than for his work as a gestaltist; still, within the field, he is appreciated for his efforts in early training of new converts to gestalt therapy, and he became enshrined as a theoretical mastermind.

> Paul Goodman's contribution to gestalt therapy theory in PHG has not been precisely identified. Without question, several of its chapters had been previously published as essays written by him in critical journals such as *Dissent*. Goodman's later writings also reflected his continuing use of the gestalt therapy principles first articulated in PHG, while Fritz Perls famously distanced himself from PHG. Goodman's exact contribution notwithstanding, he brought a Walt Whitmanesque Americanism to gestalt therapy, reflecting not only his natural exuberance but also his free-ranging intellectual knowledge, both of which complemented Fritz Perls's own personality. Increasingly, the influence of American pragmatism is being identified in gestalt therapy. This would be from Goodman's, and not Perls's, background.

> Many gestalt therapists continue to identify Goodman's influence in gestalt therapy and teach gestalt therapy in his name. (D. Bloom, personal communication, May 17, 2009b)

Isadore From

In 1945 Isadore From came to New York to attend the New School for Social Research. He soon felt in need of psychotherapy and sought the services of an analyst. Because he did not have much money, he ended up asking Frederick Perls, who had newly arrived in the United States from South Africa. Perls, who believed From knew something about phenomenology, took him on as a patient. When Perls learned what From wanted from him, he referred him to Laura for therapy.

From was a friend of Paul Goodman, having known him in Chicago, and he was an early reader for the PHG text. From eventually apprenticed as a therapist with Frederick. He also became the therapist "in residence" for trainees at the Gestalt Institute of Cleveland, meeting with its first cohort twice a month for 10 years and then once a month for another 10 years (From & Rosenfeld, 1978). From became one of the central leaders of the New York institute, and he was instrumental in training early gestalt therapists in Europe, Cleveland, and Portland, Oregon. While in Europe, he influenced many people, including Therese Tellegen, a Dutch therapist who later immigrated to Brazil, and Jean-Marie Robine. Unfortunately, From was not a writer, so his influence, though great, was not captured directly in the gestalt therapy literature.

In the immediate years following the deaths of Frederick Perls and Paul Goodman, gestalt therapy began its global expansion. In New York, Isadore From, Laura Perls, and Richard Kitzler maintained the integrity of the New York institute, and Joe Wysong began to organize conferences and publish the first journal devoted to gestalt therapy; he called it *The Gestalt Journal*.

Edwin and Sonia Nevis

Edwin and Sonia Nevis were among the first group of gestalt trainees outside of New York. They joined with others in the training group

Frederick Perls and Paul Weisz had started in Cleveland, and, together with Elaine Kepner, Bill Warner, Rennie Fantz, Miriam Polster, Erving Polster, Joseph Zinker, Cynthia Harris, and Dick Wallen, they helped to create the Gestalt Institute of Cleveland. Later, in the 1970s, Edwin and Sonia created the Gestalt International Study Center (GISC) in Cape Cod, Massachusetts. In a personal communication, Edwin Nevis recalled the sequence of events:

> I went to graduate school at Western Reserve University in Cleveland, from 1949 to 1953, with people like Erving Polster, Elaine Kepner, Marjorie Creelman, Rainette Fantz, and Bill Warner. Richard Wallen was one of our teachers. After working in Chicago for 18 months I returned to Cleveland in 1955 to find that these folks had started to invite Fritz Perls to do workshops for them and other psychologists. I started taking workshops immediately at the suggestion of Richard Wallen and helped organize an association which became the Ohio Center for gestalt therapy in 1956. I soon took over the administration and became President of what became the Gestalt Institute of Cleveland in 1957 or 1958. Shortly afterwards, Joseph Zinker, Sonia Nevis, Cynthia Harris, and Miriam Polster became part of our core group. I remained as President until 1972.
>
> I trained with Fritz Perls, Laura Perls, Paul Goodman, Isadore From, Virginia Satir, Carl Whitaker, Paul Weisz, and Richard Wallen.
>
> I participated in about 10 training workshops a year for 6 years (1956–1962). I also did individual and group therapy with Erving Polster (1959–1962) and training therapy with Isadore From (1959–1963).
>
> The people listed in the first paragraph above began to conduct our own workshops and training programs in the early 1960's—when we concluded that we had enough training to do this. (Keep in mind that most of us had PhD degrees before we discovered GT, and some were practicing for several years).
>
> In 1979 Sonia and I created the Gestalt International Study Center (GISC) as an independent yet sister research and development organization.

> After getting GISC established in its home on Cape Cod (2002), I gave up being president (2007) and chairman of the board (2009). I now do some teaching and help in planning and implementing specific new programs. I do some coaching of organization consultants and maintain a consulting relationship with one long-term client.

In 2002, GISC built its meeting house on the Cape. In addition to their training programs, they support various annual or biennial international conferences, and they publish *Gestalt Review*, edited by Susan Fischer and Joseph Melnick.

Joseph Melnick

Joseph Melnick was finishing his studies at Cincinnati as his supervisor was completing the training program at the Gestalt Institute of Cleveland (GIC). He returned with stories about his work with Erving and Miram Polster, Joseph Zinker, Elaine Kepner, and Edwin and Sonia Nevis, stimulating Joe to read about gestalt therapy. For a graduation gift, he gave himself a weekend lab at GIC, and that is when he "got hooked" (J. Melnick, personal communication, May 22, 2009). Melnick continued training in Cleveland, taking a 6-week course and then advanced courses in couples, family, and individual therapy. His trainers included Maurice Creelman, Sonia Nevis, Joseph Zinker, and Elaine Kepner. He became active in the workings at GIC, and he became a member of the board. Today, he exemplifies the continuing exploration of diverse issues that gestalt therapists undertake. "Edwin and I are just finishing an edited book of social change, and I have become fascinated with the concept of contempt. As soon as the book is done, I will start focusing on this topic, and I am halfway through writing a book with Sonia on the 'Cape Cod Model'" (J. Melnick, personal communication, May 22, 2009).

Erving Polster

Erving Polster's early training in gestalt therapy was principally under Frederick Perls, complemented by workshops by Paul Weisz,

Laura Perls, and Paul Goodman. The original cohort at Cleveland formed itself into an organization in about 1955, and they immediately began creating training experiences. In their first workshops they invited Frederick Perls to work weekends with the groups, preceded by three evenings of theory and clinical demonstrations with Erving and Dick Wallen. After a time, the Cleveland group brought Isadore From in from New York on a biweekly basis for more extensive and more individuated training. As a group, they also trained themselves, in leaderless weekly meetings over an extended period of time (E. Polster, personal communication, May 11, 2009). At first, these trainings were directed to members, but before long they started training programs for the larger psychological community.

Erving and Miriam Polster moved to San Diego, where they opened their own training center. In 1973, they wrote what became the best statement of gestalt therapy theory[1] in the three to four decades following the publication of PHG. It established "contact" of a person with environmental "other" as central to gestalt therapy. Reminiscing about how he became exposed to gestalt therapy in the first place, Erving Polster said:

> I was invited by some friends to come to a workshop Fritz Perls was going to be conducting in Cleveland. I had heard that gestalt therapy had created some exercises which people could do on their own and I was intrigued by the idea of therapy outside the guidance that office therapy provided. That didn't turn out to be true about gestalt therapy, but I did find that it was hospitable to some of the populist ideas I had about therapy and I was enthralled with Perls' magical entry into each person's psyche and the communal setting in which people revealed their deep feelings. It was very unusual in those days for therapy to be conducted among peers. (E. Polster, personal communication, May 11, 2009)

This interest in therapeutic, or growth, experience outside the confines of formal psychotherapy led him time and again to study congregations of people, and that eventuated the development of his concept of life focus groups, in which people blend the therapeutic aspects of both psychotherapy and religious community.[2]

In thinking about the course his work has taken over more than 50 years, Polster said:

> My only concerns are with the relevance, clarity, sensitivity, effectiveness, illuminations or inspirational effects my work may offer. If these are lacking, I am being deficient. I follow "principles" of gestalt therapy because of all theories I like them best to guide my mind. But none of these principles are so sacrosanct as to replace common sense, the reconciliation of human complexity and simplicity, and the invitation we face to enter each other's minds and make strong and thematically timely human connectedness. (E. Polster, personal communication, May 11, 2009)

Jean-Marie Robine

In 1975, Jean-Marie Robine attended gestalt trainings conducted in Belgium, at an institute called Multiversité, in collaboration with the French-speaking trainers from the Gestalt Institute of Cleveland—Janine Corbeil, Lois Meredith, Gordon Wheeler, Bill Warner, and others. Following that, Robine attended several groups with Erving and Miriam Polster, Sonia Nevis, and some others from the Cleveland orientation. About 1980, he met Isadore From during one of From's European periods and joined his training and supervision group, working with them until Isadore stopped teaching. He began coordinating other trainings with his wife and with Jean-Marie Delacroix, a French colleague who returned to France after several years in Quebec, Canada. He also collaborated with Ed Lynch, Michael Vincent Miller, and colleagues from Belgium. As the French gestaltists began to organize into training institutes, Robine facilitated the cooperation among those with conceptualizations close to his own (and with foreign institutes as well), exchanging trainers and organizing summer universities together. This effort culminated in an international, postgraduate training for professionals called the Gestalt Therapy International Network, involving Michael Vincent Miller, Gary Yontef, Philip Lichtenberg, Peter Philippson, Margherita Spagnuolo Lobb, Lilian Meyer Frazao, and himself. They completed two summer programs—one near Montpellier, France, and the other in San Miguel de Allende, Mexico.

Today, Robine considers his vocation to be the continuity of Goodman's and From's work in developing the theory of gestalt therapy and the sustenance of a clinical practice grounded in that theory. Robine has widely taught the gestalt therapy theory of self and its clinical usefulness (in France, Russia and Ukraine, South America and Mexico, Africa, Belgium, and Spain). He has also developed the field perspective, the concept of the "id of the situation," psychotherapy as aesthetics, and other fundamental concepts in gestalt therapy. In order to broaden gestalt therapy ideas, he created two French journals,[3] functioning as editor in chief for 20 years, and served as associate editor of many other journals (i.e., *Gestalt Review*, *International Gestalt Journal*, *Studies in Gestalt Therapy*). He wrote six books about gestalt therapy,[4] published in seven languages. Robine describes his interests as "the clinical work and theoretical deepening of our theory… supporting human psychic suffering and in teaching young therapists this art" (J-M. Robine, personal communication, May 8, 2009).

Serge Ginger

Serge Ginger had practiced psychoanalysis and psychodrama when he attended trainings in gestalt therapy at Esalen in 1970 and later at the fledgling Gestalt Institute of San Francisco. He went on to receive training from Erving and Miriam Polster, Alberto Rams, Jean-Marie Robine, George Thomson, and Joseph Zinker. Ginger and his wife, Anne, have been part of the cooperative movement for training in France. They were the founders, in 1980, of the Paris School of Gestalt Therapy (*École Parisienne de Gestalt*, or EPG). In 1991, he founded and became the president of the International Federation of Gestalt Training Organizations (FORGE), gathering 30 training institutes from 20 countries.

Malcolm Parlett

In 1975, Malcolm Parlett attended a gestalt workshop conducted by Carolyn Luckensmeyer, part of the gestalt community in Cleveland.

He was smitten with the gestalt approach, and 2 years later started training at the Cleveland institute. His trainers included Edwin and Sonia Nevis, Bill Warner, Rainette Fantz, Isobel Frederickson, Marjorie Creelman, Elaine Kepner, and subsequently Rich Borofsky. Back home in England in 1986, he founded the Gestalt Psychotherapy and Training Institute with Petruska Clarkson and Gestalt SouthWest with Marianne Fry. He was the founding editor of the *British Gestalt Journal*, which had its inaugural issue in 1991. He has since retired from clinical work, but he maintains his interests, which he describes as consulting, in writing, "and in the application of our approach to social, political, and ecological questions, and the relation of gestalt to spirituality" (M. Parlett, personal communication, May 8, 2009).

Robert Resnick

Robert Resnick studied with Frederick Perls and Jim Simkin at Esalen and in Los Angeles. Along with Bob Martin, Perls, and Simkin, he was one of the founding members of the Gestalt Therapy Institute of Los Angeles (GTILA), a training group that was started in 1969. GTILA has since divided into two training organizations—Gestalt Associates Los Angeles (GATLA) and the Pacific Gestalt Institute (PGI)—and exists today as a membership organization. In 1969, Frederick Perls selected Resnick to respond to an invitation by Nels In de Vid in the Netherlands to introduce gestalt therapy to Europe. He has been training gestalt therapists in Europe ever since, through summer residentials sponsored by GTILA and GATLA.

Gary Yontef

In 1964, Gary Yontef attended a training workshop given by Frederick Perls at the Metropolitan State Hospital in Los Angeles. Arnold Beisser[5] was director of psychiatrist training at that time, and Gary was a psychiatric social worker. When Perls came to the hospital, Yontef was amazed at how he could get to staff members. Yontef recalled one Horneyian training analyst who came to Los Angeles to semi-retire. "Fritz reduced him to tears. I did not know what to make of that. But was curious" (G. Yontef, personal communication, May 15, 2009). Perls also talked about Chinese thought, and that attracted Yontef. It was partially because he detected errors in Perl's thinking on Chinese thought that Yontef imagined there might be a place for him in the group associated with what Perls was doing.

Yontef eventually went to Esalen for an advanced workshop with Fritz Perls and Jim Simkin. At the workshop, he felt *met*, understood, and guided by the experiential work. He joined a group for training and therapy led by Simkin, and because of his experience of feeling accepted and understood, including his growing understanding of himself through the process of gestalt therapy, he pursued a career in gestalt therapy. He joined the faculty of GTILA in 1972 and became head of its training program for 18 years. When GTILA became a membership-only organization, he cofounded the Pacific Gestalt Institute with Lynne Jacobs. They were joined by Jan Ruckert, who was also, and is still, part of the fundamental planning and administration.

Leaders in Other Countries

In 1969, Walter Kempler visited New Zealand, where he presented the first demonstration of gestalt therapy for New Zealanders. In 1982, Fred Grosse continued attending regularly, and in 1991, together with Anne Maclean and Gill Caradoc-Davies, he formed the Gestalt Institute of New Zealand (Maclean, Levien, & Jarosewitsch, 1997).

Meanwhile, gestalt therapy arrived in Australia in 1971, when William Schutz taught the "Esalen Spirit" to students at the University of New England at Armidale. In 1974, James Oldham arrived from Toronto, Canada, having completed a 3-year training at the Gestalt Institute of Toronto, and he established training groups in Melbourne and Perth. In 1976, Patti Oliver-Nolan and Peter Mullholland began sharing their training with Miriam and Erving Polster. Associated in this was Barry Blicharski. In 1978, Yaro Starak arrived, having completed his training in Toronto and after serving as part of the training faculty there for 4 years. He established a formal, 3-year training program in Brisbane (Starak, 1997).

In 1976, Bob Martin met Therese Tellegen, Tessy Hantschel, and Raquel Vieira da Cunha at a gestalt workshop led by Erving and Miriam Polster in San Diego, and they invited him to Sao Paulo, to conduct workshops and supervision. After that, other trainers came to offer workshops in Brazil, including Janette Rainwater, John Wood and Maureen Miller, Gary Yontef, Violet Oaklander, Richard Hycner, Michael Vincent Miller, Jean-Marie Robine, Serge and Anne Ginger, and Joseph Zinker. In 1980, due to the interest shown by students and professionals, Abel Guedes, Jean Clark Juliano, Therese Tellegen, and Lilian Frazao were invited to offer a brief course in gestalt therapy at the Institute Sedes Sapientiae, in which several approaches to psychotherapy were taught. Due to student demand, it turned into a 3-year, weekly course involving 8 hours each week. Lilian Meyer Frazao has been teaching at the Psychology Institute of the Sao Paulo University, where gestalt therapy has been part of the minimum curriculum for psychology students since 2005 (L. Frazao, personal communication, May 7, 2009).

The Chilean psychiatrist, Claudio Naranjo studied with Fritz Perls and Jim Simkin at Esalen, and returned to Chile in the early 1970s to teach gestalt there. In 1974, the gestalt practitioners and psychiatrists Dr. Adriana Schnake and Dr. Francisco Hunneus began coming once a month from Chile to lead seminars and workshops in Buenos Aires. Myriam Sas de Guiter was one of their students. At that time, the dominant theory in Argentine psychotherapy was psychoanalysis, but these students were looking for new approaches. Drs. Schnake and Hunneus continued coming for several years until, in 1980, they joined with Myriam and the other students to create the Asociacion Gestaltica de Buenos Aires. Other trainers who influenced Myriam Guiter and her colleagues were Dr. Norberto Levy, Claudio Naranjo, Joseph Zinker, Philip Lichtenberg, Theo Skolnik, Jean Clark Juliano, and Margherita Spagnuolo Lobb. The Asociacion Gestáltica de Buenos Aires took shape in 1982 with a 3-year training program that still continues. In 1997, Myriam Guiter organized the Colloquium of Gestalt in

Buenos Aires to enhance training and attract international teachers. Zinker, Lichtenberg, Skolnik, Juliano, and Lobb became frequent contributors.

SECOND CYCLE: TRENDS IN GESTALT THERAPY'S DEVELOPMENT

Contemporary gestalt therapy is marked by the thinking and influences of various persons and organizations. Some of them are described below, but many of the people and ideas mentioned previously are still active as well. These trends help answer the question, "What is gestalt therapy?" by pointing to some of its growing edges and what it is becoming.

Gordon Wheeler, Field Theory, and the Esalen Institute

For many people, the initial attraction to gestalt therapy has not been the impact of its theory but the sense that they have met an unusually fascinating and competent person doing something novel and intriguing. This is what happened for Gordon Wheeler. He attended a training given by Carolyn Lukensmeyer and Bill Warner at the National Training Laboratory and was so taken by them that he went to the Gestalt Institute of Cleveland for training in gestalt therapy. In the late 1980s, Edwin Nevis founded Gestalt Press and handed it over to James Kepner and Wheeler. Gordon went on to become a prolific writer and the head of Gestalt Press.

In the 1990s, Wheeler moved to the West Coast and joined the community at the Esalen Institute, eventually to become its president (Wheeler, 2009). The Esalen Institute was founded in 1961–1962, and the communal aspects of the Esalen Institute are heavily infused with a gestalt spirit. That is because Richard Price, cofounder of Esalen, became associated with the form of gestalt work demonstrated at Esalen by Frederick Perls, and he continued for years to conduct gestalt work after Perls, Simkin, and others had left. Wheeler's influence has been one of building on what was already there to develop the field perspective more fully at Esalen.

Margherita Spagnuolo Lobb

Margherita Spagnuolo Lobb has been a gestalt therapy trainer since 1979. She has served as president of the European Association for Gestalt Therapy (EAGT) for 6 years, president of the Italian Umbrella Association for Psychotherapy (FIAP) for 2 years, and president of the Italian Association for Gestalt Therapy (SIPG) for two decades. She founded the European Conference of Gestalt Therapy writers and has served as editor of the Italian journal *Quaderni di Gestalt* since 1985. She is co-editor of the journal *Studies in Gestalt Therapy—Dialogical Bridges*. Her writings, which cover both epistemological and practical issues, have been published in many languages.

When Lobb was 23 years old, she was attending university in Rome. One of her teachers had just trained with Erving and Miriam Polster in California, and gave a demonstration of what he had learned. Lobb was so fascinated by this approach that she wanted to go to La Jolla, California, to train with the Polsters as soon as she completed her degree. In addition to Erving and Miriam, she trained with Isadore From in Europe and New York; he also became her therapist. She trained with many other psychotherapists as well, from both the gestalt therapy field and other approaches, including Daniel Stern. As with many gestalt therapists, the peer exchange she enjoys in communities of her colleagues has been a strong and formative experience for her in recent years—the New York Institute for Gestalt Therapy, the European Association for Gestalt Therapy, and the Association for the Advancement of Gestalt Therapy. These are "homes" where she continues to learn (M. Lobb, personal communication, May 21, 2009).

Lobb started to work as a trainer in Italy in 1979. At that time no school of gestalt therapy existed there, just sporadic training events. She invited those who had trained her, as well as other gestalt psychotherapists, to teach regularly in Italy. Gradually, a group of local colleagues was formed, subsequently becoming the resident trainers in her institute.

This Italian group of trainers and clinicians developed their own, original theoretical and clinical application of gestalt therapy.

The model of Lobb's institute became well known around the world and was accredited by the Italian minister for universities as a postgraduate school of psychotherapy.

Over the years, Lobb has elaborated two basic ideas evident in gestalt therapy literature and clinical work. One is the concept of the contact-boundary as a practical perspective on basic psychotherapeutic "events" such as transference and countertransference, and the relational meaning of therapeutic dialogue. She views events in the psychotherapy setting as "a co-creation of the contact-boundary between therapist and client, where emotions, relational patterns, values and personal styles interweave in a beautiful dance which brings forward the intentionality of contact for each of them" (M. Lobb, personal communication, May 21, 2009). This perspective overcomes the traditional individualistic, one-mind perspective in psychotherapy, and it allows gestalt therapists to describe psychotherapy as the art of improvising a real relationship rather than of analyzing the mind of the client. The other idea is that of supporting aesthetic experience as a guide for the psychotherapist. She developed clinical tools to "help the client to do better what he already does, to support the beauty of his process. This view on psychotherapeutic aim changes a lot the traditional epistemology of psychotherapeutic work, that is to make explicit what is implicit" (M. Lobb, personal communication, May 21, 2009). Lobb believes that gestalt therapy epistemology requires the therapist to support the positive process that presents itself in the client, the aesthetic of the client's process, rather than to dichotomize that process into good and bad.

The European Association for Gestalt Therapy

In 1985, 13 people representing gestalt institutes and regional associations in Europe, involving 11 countries, met in Germany to found the European Association for Gestalt Therapy (EAGT). The aim of the EAGT is to promote gestalt therapy in Europe, to combine and exchange knowledge and resources, to foster a high professional standard for the discipline of gestalt therapy, and to promote research. The founders set high standards leading to a certification that is commensurate with a European certificate to practice psychotherapy.

One of the current governing board members for the EAGT is Daan van Baalen. Like Lobb, van Baalen practices the European approach to gestalt therapy, infused with the need to certify qualified gestalt psychotherapists and to approve their credentials. The EAGT is not just an advocacy and membership group for gestalt therapists, but also a regulatory body. To that task van Baalen brings his background in gestalt therapy and his own interests. He was a general practitioner in Rotterdam, where his patients were considered socially depraved; they were immigrants, criminals, prostitutes, and social dropouts. Being newly trained as an MD in a teaching hospital, he was not prepared for these kinds of clients; by coincidence he took a course titled "MDs and Gestalt Therapy," where he found an approach that worked with the type of people he had been seeing. In 1976, he started functioning as a trainer at the Dutch Instituutt voor Comunicatie (IVC), and in 1986, in Norway, he cofounded the Norsk Gestaltinstitutt. He has developed training programs in gestalt psychotherapy, coaching, and organizational development in Norway, the Netherlands, and Belgium and is a visiting trainer in several European countries. While a university lecturer at the Erasmus University, the Netherlands, he also engaged in research investigating chronic diseases and psychotherapy. He has written articles in several languages and is co-editor of the *European Journal for Qualitative Research in Psychotherapy*. Van Baalen is the external relations officer for the EAGT and chair of the Norwegian Association for Psychotherapy. He is a member of the board and recognized expert for the European Association for Psychotherapy, a member of the International Federation of Gestalt Training Organizations (FORGE), and serves on the editorial board of *Gestalt Review*.

Lynne Jacobs, Relational Psychoanalysis, and Gestalt Therapy

Lynne Jacobs is a gestalt therapist and a training and supervising psychoanalyst. She is a pioneer in what has become known as *relational gestalt therapy*, a movement that deemphasizes individuality and instead emphasizes relationship and community.

Jacobs was introduced to gestalt therapy by a teacher and counselor at the university where she earned her undergraduate degree, who showed her the book *Gestalt Therapy Verbatim*. She was immediately drawn to the person-to-person, emotionally honest encounter. "That seemed like a life-saver to me, since in my home I felt like I was speaking into an empty darkness. Perls' responsiveness gave me hope" (L. Jacobs, personal communication, May 14, 2009). She then moved to Los Angeles to attend graduate school and took up training at the GTILA. There, she was exposed to several trainers over time. The two most important were Bob Martin and Gary Yontef, who were attractive to her because of their focus on contacting. Jacobs entered a long-term therapeutic relationship with Yontef.

By 1984, Jacobs had joined the faculty of GTILA. In 1998, when GTILA became a membership-only organization, she suggested to Yontef that the two of them form their own training institute. "That was a very easy decision in that we were still both actively interested in training, and our philosophies of gestalt therapy were very similar (close attention to the relational dimension that is the ground for contacting)" (L. Jacobs, personal communication, May 14, 2009).

Jacobs's current work as a leader in the field of gestalt therapy is an extension of what led her into gestalt therapy to begin with. "I am invested—as are so many others—in carrying gestalt therapy thinking into a consistent, radical, post-Cartesian worldview, which I believe is an inevitable outgrowth of conceiving of all experience as relationally-emergent" (L. Jacobs, personal communication, May 14, 2009).

Peter Philippson, Neuropsychology, and Gestalt Therapy

Peter Philippson went to a gestalt workshop in 1979 at a group work conference and fell in love with it—the immediacy, the sense that things and he himself could change. The therapist was Beverley Edwards, who offered "Taoist Gestalt," which suited Philippson well, as one of his abiding interests is martial arts. Philippson went on to train with Petruska Clarkson, and he also attended workshops with Gary Yontef, Erving and Miriam Polster, Bob Resnick, Malcolm Parlett, Marianne Fry, Maria Gilbert, Sue Fish, and Hunter Beaumont. Eventually he collaborated on the establishment of two training organizations, the Gestalt Psychotherapy and Training Institute (GPTI) and the Manchester Gestalt Centre.

Philippson is a prolific influence in gestalt therapy and his expanding work focuses largely on the assimilation of neuroscientific research into a gestalt understanding of both psychotherapy, including body process, and the functioning of groups. His most recent book, *The Emergent Self: An Existential-Gestalt Approach* (2009) is a synthesis of these interests, and it illustrates a "coming home" of sorts for the field of gestalt therapy.

This coming home is a full expression of the interest in neuropsychology that has consistently been a subtle influence among gestalt therapy thinkers, harkening back to Kurt Goldstein and his study of brain function (Brownell, 1998, 2009). It is also seen in the assimilation of the thinking of Antonio Damasio, which has been underway in gestalt therapy ever since his book, *Descartes' Error: Emotion, Reason, and the Human Brain* (1994). Others who attract the attention of gestalt therapists to neuropsychology include Joseph LeDoux, Warren Brown, Elkonen Goldberg, Vilayanur Ramachandran, Muriel Lezak, and Oliver Sacks.

Dan Bloom and the Association for the Advancement of Gestalt Therapy

In the mid-1970s, Dan Bloom was fresh from 7 years of psychoanalysis. Armed with what he thought to be an abundance of enlightenment, Bloom moved to New York City in the hope of offering himself as a volunteer counselor to the gay community. At that time, gay-affirmative counseling was a radical notion. Counseling and psychotherapy for the most part was still aimed at encouraging lesbians and gays either to make a heterosexual adjustment, or, failing that, to make the best of a bad situation. This was changing, however, and Bloom was looking for the edge in that change.

He found it in Identity House, a volunteer peer counseling not-for-profit center in Greenwich Village. He became a peer counselor, and, unknowingly began his training as a gestalt therapist.

> Identity House had been formed by gestalt therapists a year or so prior to my joining. Peer counselors were trained with a gestalt therapy model that emphasized the social field, relationship, and authenticity. We all met in regular supervision groups facilitated by gestalt therapists who attended to figure/ground, contact interruptions, and used 1970s-ish gestalt therapy techniques. The organization was committed to a non-hierarchical and emergent structure.
>
> This was all new to me. I challenged it, of course. My new friends started to describe gestalt therapy to me and urged me to read *The Gestalt Therapy Book* (Latner, 1974). I argued with each page of the book. But I increasingly became engaged by counseling and drawn to the gestalt therapy method of being with another person in a helping way. The community became an important part of my life. (D. Bloom, personal communication, May 7, 2009a)

His curiosity led him to a gestalt therapy practicum led by Patrick Kelley, but it lacked depth, and at the same time he was feeling the need to consult with a therapist of his own, so he decided to try a gestalt therapist. He was referred to Richard Kitzler. "Richard had depth, education, respect for intelligence, respect for words and attention to feeling. He brought it all together and made gestalt therapy a complete modality for me. Up until then, gestalt therapy had a side-show quality" (D. Bloom, personal communication, May 7, 2009a).

> Sometimes I think of myself as an intellectual conservative with a radical temperament. By this I mean that from my earliest approach to gestalt therapy, I questioned its assertions, challenged its basis, and subjected all its principles to ongoing reevaluation as I practiced gestalt therapy. Some of us may do this more scientifically than I, but I am content to pursue this with an historical and philosophical method. I am studying American pragmatism, phenomenology (especially Husserl

> and most especially Heidegger. Merleau-Ponty, and Levinas are next, of course), and their contemporary proponents. Currently, I am exploring the sufficiency of the organism/environment field as a means to describe human experience. Can it account for human relationship? Personal values? I've been experimenting with a supplement to the organism/environment field—the self/world—field to account for this.
>
> How can we further develop our notion of the person as a function of the phenomenal field, of the world, and of the therapy itself?
>
> What are the implications of this for our practice?
>
> How can we understand "dialogue" within gestalt therapy and, more importantly, situated within the sequence of contact?
>
> I am turning the lens of my interest on the actual meeting at the heart of the therapy session—therapeutic contact—to see if we can learn even more about our process. What is emergent? What is disclosed in contact?
>
> Is our traditional understanding of "contact" sufficient, or must it be retooled as our sense of our work has developed—as we've come to appreciate the implicit ethics of the human relationship?
>
> I have no doubt that gestalt therapy has changed over its 60 or so years. The world has changed. Our core theory may be intact, but a core is only the center that can support stability. We must continue to teach and train from this core, but we must also radically address the changing world around us. That is, in fact, one of the core values of gestalt therapy. (D. Bloom, personal communication, May 7, 2009a)

After his training, Bloom eventually became president of the New York Institute for Gestalt Therapy, serving for two terms. In addition, he is currently executive editor of the international journal *Studies in Gestalt Therapy: Dialogical Bridges*, which fosters cross-pollination among clinical paradigms for the field of gestalt therapy.

As of this writing, Bloom is the president of the Association for the Advancement of Gestalt Therapy (AAGT), an international community. The AAGT's philosophy is that advancement of the field of gestalt therapy can best be accomplished by association of gestalt-minded people, who spontaneously generate ideas, collaborations, and other creative responses to the needs in the field when they gather. The association has grown from mostly U.S.-based meetings to a truly international organization, with regional representation in Scotland, England, Denmark, Germany, the Netherlands, Belgium, Spain, Italy, eastern Canada, western Canada, Japan, the Philippines, the southeastern, southwestern, and midwestern United States, Bermuda, Turkey, Australia, and New Zealand. Brian O'Neill, of Australia, is a past president of the AAGT who currently heads its regional contact network, which meets regularly for teleconferencing. The organization views itself as an experiment and is constantly reforming its identity. One thing is clear however: it is not a certifying body. Its abiding interest is the theory and practice of gestalt therapy itself and advancing the clinical discipline known as gestalt therapy, but it is not interested in regulating its members. Indeed, it has no structures by which to accomplish such a thing.

Talia Levine Bar-Yoseph, Cross-Cultural Dialogues, and Gestalt Therapy

Talia Levine Bar-Yoseph became interested in gestalt therapy while doing her master's study at Hebrew University, and enrolled in formal training through GTILA. In 1997, she and Hanan Gur-El founded the Jerusalem Gestalt Institute. Bar-Yoseph is currently active with a training group in Greece as well. In 2005, she edited *The Bridge, Dialogues Across Cultures* (Gestalt Institute Press), and in 2009 completed her doctoral work while editing a book on advanced concepts in gestalt therapy and another on organizational development.

Bar-Yoseph is increasingly recognized as someone who transcends many cultural boundaries. In Israel, where she grew up, the grocer counted in Polish, the green grocer in Arabic, their neighbor was Hungarian, her grandfather and grandmother yelled at one another in Russian, but when things were peaceful they all spoke in Hebrew. She claims that

> Gestalt therapy enables a dialogue across the divide by means of the value it gives to heritage, subjective experience,

> difference, and context. The bridge it builds across the divide is composed of meeting through separateness, listening, trust, interest in the other, and conviction of the ther's [*sic*] right to exist no more or less than one's own. (Bar-Yoseph, 2005, p. 17)

Alan Meara, Complexity, and Gestalt Australia and New Zealand

Alan Meara came to gestalt therapy through practicing Chinese medicine. As a new graduate, he discovered that he was not equipped in that modality to process the emotional reactions of his clients. A quick search through his bookshelf unearthed a copy of PHG, and a scan of that book intrigued him. Subsequently, he found a course that was starting within a few weeks, and he has gone on to establish a long-term relationship as assistant trainer with GATLA. Meara described his training and practice as follows:

> Of course, the personal learning and confronting of my own habits was challenging, as well as exciting and humbling. My main trainers were Yaro Starak, Bill and Eileen Wright, and Mac Hamilton. My practice has been a mix of OD, individual clients, couples, and supervision. The OD component is mainly process facilitation, where I can introduce gestalt processes in facilitating dialogue that opens new possibilities in relating, goal redefinition and achievement. It was also the ground for my interest in researching and applying complexity theory to group work and change theory within gestalt, and more recently the potential contribution of Merleau-Ponty to this field. My overriding interest is linking theory to practice—guiding what happens in the therapy relationship. (A. Meara, personal communication, July 28, 2009)

Meara became involved with the professional association in his region (Gestalt Australia and New Zealand—GANZ) and has served as president since 2002. In Australia, gestalt (like all other psychotherapies) is not recognized by the health system for employment or medical insurance. GANZ is a member of a larger body (Psychotherapy and Counselling Federation of Australia—PACFA), which is lobbying for recognition in providing services within the health care system in which, ironically, clients cry out for services that include gestalt therapy.

Jungkyu Kim and Growth in Asia

Dan Rosenblatt led training groups in Japan for several years. Paula Bottom taught gestalt therapy in Japan and China during the 1980s and 1990s and was instrumental in starting the Gestalt Network of the Pacific Rim (GNPR). Today, the Gestalt Network of Japan is an outgrowth of that work, but it is in Korea where gestalt therapy has most flourished in Asia thus far.

Jungkyu Kim was exposed to gestalt therapy by attending a gestalt therapy group in Bonn, Germany, in 1986, while studying at the University of Bonn. Afterwards, he attended a gestalt therapy group at the Fritz Perls Institute in Germany, in 1993 and again in 1997. For 3 years, starting in 1994, he trained with the Polsters in San Diego, and in 2001 he joined the gestalt training group with Lynne Jacobs and Gary Yontef at PGI.

Kim was the first person to introduce gestalt therapy to Korea. He founded the Korean Gestalt Therapy Research Association in 2002, with over 200 affiliates, many of whom are licensed psychologists. In collaboration with the Korean Gestalt Therapy Research Association, he has been translating gestalt therapy books into Korean, teaching gestalt therapy by means of workshops and academic meetings, and offering supervision to trainees. As of this writing, there are seven private gestalt therapy counseling centers run by his former students and many more counseling centers where gestalt therapists now work in Korea (for example, the university student counseling center, company counseling centers, public counseling and social welfare centers, civilian or religious counseling centers, and school counseling centers). Gestalt therapy is quite well known in Korea, ranging in the middle stratum of preferred modalities.

Research in Gestalt Therapy

In 1992, Eleanor O'Leary published her book *Gestalt Therapy: Theory, Practice, and Research*, and in 2006, Paul Barber published

Becoming a Practitioner Researcher: A Gestalt Approach to Holistic Inquiry. In 2007, I organized a number of established gestalt practitioners to produce a new volume on research and gestalt therapy (Brownell, 2008b). The *Handbook for Theory, Research, and Practice in Gestalt Therapy* presented a philosophy of science, a call for research specifically focused on gestalt therapy, a review of the chief methods in the praxis of gestalt therapy, and a challenge for gestalt therapists to collaborate in practice-based research networks. At the 2009 annual meeting of the AAGT, I became co-chair, along with Christine Stevens, of the Research Task Force for the AAGT and began consulting with established researchers, among whom was Leslie Greenberg at York University in Toronto.

Leslie Greenberg first became aware of gestalt therapy while reading PHG during a graduate course in psychotherapy, and then trained in gestalt therapy at the Toronto Institute with Harvey Freedman and Jorges Rosner. He later collaborated with Dolores Bate in Vancouver to found the Gestalt Experiential Institute. His greatest contributions to gestalt therapy have been in his research. His studies emphasize the processes of change working with emotion in both individual and couples therapy. He conducts psychotherapy process and outcome research, and has developed an evidence-based approach that integrates the person-centered relationship with gestalt therapy methods, including chair dialogues, embedding these in a dynamic systems and emotion-theory framework.

In May of 2009, the research task force identified five possibilities for the AAGT to support research involving gestalt therapy:

- Start a collaborative research project.
- Create a team of research-oriented trainers to help existing training institutes augment their programs with regard to research.
- Collaborate with existing research projects at university laboratories.
- Create a research resource "barrel" where gestalt researchers might use tests, scales, designs, and tools for data assessment.
- Hold periodic conferences focused on research.

Spirituality and Gestalt Therapy

My own practice as a gestalt therapist has also been influenced by my first career in Christian ministry. I am an ordained clergyman who completed a Master of Divinity from Western Seminary in Portland, Oregon, taught New Testament Greek at Simpson College, served as a minister of children in a large, multistaffed church in central California, and then pastored two small, rural churches before going back to school for a doctorate in clinical psychology.

I had been exposed to gestalt therapy while in the navy during the Vietnam war. As a neuropsychiatric technician, I was assigned to cofacilitate "the gestalt group" with Evan Wolf, a civilian psychologist who was part of the San Francisco Gestalt Institute and who, with colleagues such as Cyndy Sheldon, had been driving down to Esalen to train with Frederick Perls and returning to practice on the psych wards. I liked what I was seeing, and I seemed to pick it up quickly and get into step with Dr. Wolf. So, I started learning by doing before I really knew what gestalt therapy was. Then, in my doctoral program, the faculty kept telling us we had to choose a clinical orientation. I saw a notice about a local gestalt therapy training institute, and it all clicked into place for me. I ultimately committed to what became a 6-year formal training with Carol Swanson and Maya Brand. Other trainers were Bob and Rita Resnick, Todd Burley, Jan Ruckert, Lynne Jacobs, Philip Lichtenberg, Steve Zahm, and Nan Narboe.

I still remember the day I invited Maya Brand to demonstrate gestalt therapy for a class I was taking on experiential therapy. After her work with one of the students, the entire class of about 20 people broke out in spontaneous and enthusiastic applause. Gestalt therapy had always just felt right to me, and the chance to be around such accomplished, broadly influenced, well-educated people who were outside my usual circle of associates was stimulating; that my cohort would sense the value in what Maya did in front of them was satisfying and confirming. I made every one of my papers into an intellectual exploration of gestalt therapy and became nauseatingly predictable to my friends; I was the lone "gestalt guy" among a sea of budding cognitive behavioral therapists.

My current work in the psychology of religion includes the integration of Christian thought in gestalt therapy praxis. In 2008 and 2009 I contributed several chapters to a series of books exploring miracles, gestalt therapy, and the healing power of spirituality, and in each of them I contributed to an integration of gestalt theory and theology.[6] I continue to develop an integration of Christianity and gestalt therapy, including an exploration of the implications of the turn toward theology in French phenomenology. In the process, I have become one of a few people investigating spirituality in gestalt therapy from a theistic perspective.[7]

CONCLUSION

Gestalt therapy grew in the minds of its originators from a consilient brew of many influences, and this is how it continues to evolve. Gestalt therapists, consultants, and coaches will no doubt assimilate whatever presents itself on the horizon. Already, some fertile influences are evident: neuroscience and neuropsychology, spirituality (including theology and theistic spirituality), philosophy, developmental psychology, kinesiology, experimental psychology, and psychotherapy research.

NOTES

1. *Gestalt Therapy Integrated: Contours of Theory and Practice* (1973, Simon & Schuster).
2. These ideas are more fully developed in Erving Polster's *Uncommon Ground: Harmonizing Psychotherapy and Community to Enhance Everyday Living* (2006, Zeig, Tucker, and Theissen) and Brian O'Neill's edited volume titled *Community, Psychotherapy and Life Focus: A Gestalt Anthology of the History, Theory, and Practice of Living in Community* (2009, Ravenwood Press).
3. *Gestalt*, starting in 1990, published by Société Française de Gestalt; *Cahiers de Gestalt-thérapie*, starting in 1996, published by Collège Européen de Gestalt-thérapie de langue Française.
4. *Formes pour la Gestalt-thérapie* (1989, Bordeaux: Presses de l'IFGT); *La Gestalt-thérapie*, Essentialis, Ed. (1994, Paris: Bernet-Danilo); *Pli et dépli du self*, (1997, Bordeaux: Presses de l'IFGT; reprinted as *Gestalt-thérapie, La construction du soi*, Ed. Paris: L'harmattan); *Contact and relationship in a field perspective*, (2001,

Bordeaux: L'exprimerie; reprinted in *International Gestalt Journal*, *31*(1), 2008); *S'apparaître à l'occasion d'un autre*, (2004, Bordeaux: L'exprimerie); *La psychothérapie comme esthétique*, (2006, Bordeaux: L'exprimerie).

5. Arnold Beisser's chapter on "The Paradoxical Theory of Change" has become a classic of gestalt therapy literature and one of the "givens" in its theoretical base. That chapter first appeared in a book edited by Joen Fagan and Irma Lee Shepherd titled *Gestalt Therapy Now: Theory, Techniques, Applications* (1971, Harper Collins College Division).
6. These chapters include. Intentional spirituality, in *The Healing Power of Spirituality: How Religion Helps Humans Thrive, vol.1, The Healing Power of Personal Spirituality*, J. Harold Ellens (Ed.) (in press, Praeger/Greenwood); Healing potential of religious community, in *The Healing Power of Spirituality: How Religion Helps Humans Thrive, vol. 2, The Healing Power of Religion*, J. Harold Ellens (Ed.) (in press, Praeger/Greenwood); Spirituality in the praxis of gestalt therapy, in *The Healing Power of Spirituality: How Religion Helps Humans Thrive, vol. 3, The Psychodynamics of Healing Spirituality and Religion*, J. Harold Ellens (Ed.) (in press, Praeger/Greenwood); Spirituality in gestalt therapy, in *From the Here and Now to the Future—Advancing Gestalt Theory and Practice,* Talia Levine Bar-Yoseph (Ed.) (in press, Routledge); Personal experience, self-reporting, and hyperbole, in *Miracles: God, Psychology, and Science in the Paranormal, vol. 3, Para-psychological Perspectives*, J. Harold Ellens (Ed.) (2008, Praeger/Greenwood); Faith: An existential, phenomenological, and biblical integration, in *Miracles: God, Psychology, and Science in the Paranormal, vol. 2, Medical and Therapeutic Events*, J. Harold Ellens (Ed.) (2008, Praeger/Greenwood).
7. Others include Brian O'Neill, Sylvia Crocker, Christine Stevens, Tilda Norberg, Ed Harris, and Des Kennedy.

REFERENCES

Bar-Yoseph, T. L. (2005) Introduction–making a difference. In T.L Bar-Yoseph (Ed.) The bridge: Dialogues across cultures, pp. 17-34. Metairie, NO: Gestalt Institute Press.

Barber, P. (2006). *Becoming a practitioner researcher: A gestalt approach to holistic inquiry*. London: Middlesex University Press.

Brownell, P. (1998). Renewing our roots in neuropsychology: A gestalt perspective on the work of Joseph LeDoux. *Gestalt! 2*(1). Downloaded May 14, 2009, from http://www.g-gej.org/2-1/ledouxreview.html.

Brownell, P. (Ed.). (2008). *Handbook for theory, research, and practice in gestalt therapy*. Newcastle, England: Cambridge Scholars.

Brownell, P. (2009). Executive functions: A neuropsychological understanding of self-regulation. *Gestalt Review, 13*(1), 62–81.

Damasio, A. (1994). *Descarte's error: Emotion, reason, and the human brain*. New York: Putnam.

From, I., & Rosenfeld, E. (1978). A conversation with Isadore From. Downloaded May 3, 2009, from http://www.gestalt.org/fromint.htm.

Latner, J. (1974). *The gestalt therapy book*. New York: Bantam.

Maclean, A., Levien, B., & Jarosewitsch, R. (1997). Gestalt in New Zealand. *Gestalt!*, *1*(3), np. Downloaded July 19, 2009, from http://www.g-gej.org/1-3/histories.html.

O'Leary, E. (1992). *Gestalt therapy: Theory, practice, and research*. New York: Chapman & Hall.

Perls, F. (1969). *A life chronology*. Downloaded on May 3, 2009, from http://www.gestalt.org/fritz.htm.

Perls, F. (1947/1969). *Ego, hunger and aggression*. New York: Vintage Books/Random House.

Perls, F., Hefferline, R., & Goodman, P. (1951). *Gestalt therapy: Excitement and growth in the human personality*. New York: Julian Press.

Perls, L., & Rosenfeld, E. (1977). An oral history of gestalt therapy—part one: A conversation with Laura Perls. Downloaded May 3, 2009, from http://www.gestalt.org/perlsint.htm.

Starak, Y. (1997). Gestalt in Australia. *Gestalt!*, 1(3), np. Downloaded July 19, 2009, from http://www.g-gej.org/1-3/histories.html.

Wheeler, G. (2009). Intention, boundary, and shadow: Forty years of gestalt community life and practice at Esalen. In B. O'Neill (Ed.), *Community, psychotherapy and life focus: A gestalt anthology of the history, theory, and practice of living in community, pp. 87–108.* Wollongong, Australia: Ravenwood Press.

Wulf, R. (1996). The historical roots of gestalt therapy theory. *Gestalt dialogues: Newsletter for the integrative gestalt centre*, np. Downloaded May 3, 2009, from http://www.gestalt.org/wulf.htm.

PART II

How To Do Gestalt Therapy

4 Deal With Personal Experience

This chapter describes the phenomenological method as applied to psychotherapy. The method was initiated out of the act psychology of Franz Brentano, including his construct of intentionality, and developed by Edmund Husserl as a tool for philosophy. It has since been used in qualitative research, but as a method in psychotherapy it is a valuable way of observing and describing the cognitive, affective, physical, and spiritual experience of the client. The method is used to increase awareness leading to insight and change.

Cognitive science has two faces. With one face it gazes at nature and sees cognitive process as behavior, but with the other it looks at the life world of human beings and sees cognition as experience (Varela, Thompson, & Rosch, 1991). These are two pictures of the same thing. This observation is the open door of consilience between gestalt therapy and cognitive behavioral therapy, neuropsychology, and phenomenology. Neuropsychology and phenomenology both belong in gestalt therapy's conceptualization of the situated individual and his or her being in the world, because neuropsychology studies the physiological correlates of behavior and phenomenology studies the mental correlates of experience.

Because gestalt therapy has traditionally been located in the third wave of humanistic approaches, it has not been recognized for its own cognitive perspective; however, it is just as much a cognitive approach as cognitive behavioral therapy. Compare cognitive behavioral's baseline principles[1] below with gestalt therapy's consilient understanding of each one, as shown in Table 4.1.

Gestalt therapy's perceptual and conceptual gestalts, shifting between foreground and background, the hermeneutics of experience, the nonreductive relationship between mind and brain, and the self-regulation in executive functions all involve cognitive processes. They are embodied cognition (Gallagher & Zahavi, 2008) and occur in the whole person; the gestalt therapist is thus not concerned just with a mind that thinks, dissociated from the phenomenal experience of the whole person, but also with a body that feels and a spirit that aches with ultimate concern.

Table 4.1

COMPARISON BETWEEN COGNITIVE BEHARIORAL THERAPY AND GESTALT THERAPY

COGNITIVE BEHAVIORAL PRINCIPLES	GESTALT THERAPY CONSILIENT PRINCIPLES
Interaction between cognitions, affect, and behavior	Holistic approach weaves together every level of functioning
Experiences evoke cognitions, explanation, and attributions about the situation	Immediate, situated and pre-reflective experience gives rise to interpretation for relevance and meaning
Cognitions may be made conscious, monitored, and altered	Awareness of holistic function can be heightened through experiment, dialogue, and phenomenological inquiry, leading to creative adjustment
Emotional and behavioral change can be achieved through cognitive change, just as cognitive change can be altered by actions or emotions	Change is multidirectional, contextual, idiographic, and paradoxical; it emerges from supported contact, acceptance, and heightened awareness

AWARENESS AND CONSCIOUSNESS

Consciousness and awareness closely approximate one another in meaning. If someone is conscious of the fan twirling around above on the ceiling, then that person is aware of it. If a person is aware of his or her posture, then that person is conscious of it. Interestingly, a person can be aware of a state that is not itself a conscious state. One can be conscious of one's posture, but posture itself is not a conscious state (Kim, 2006). If I am awake, I am in a conscious state; however, if I am in a coma, I am not in a conscious state, but I may be aware, at some level, of what people are saying in my presence. To be aware is to shine the light of interest and personal investment into one's state of consciousness. Awareness in gestalt therapy consists of the first person perspective of self-conscious experience in which one "owns" his or her experience.

Antonia Damasio (1999) suggested that consciousness is a matter of generating sensory data, the qualia that come from sensory experience, into a coherent flow (like making a movie from a series of snapshots), and of producing the sense of self in which a person tells himself or herself that this movie is *his* or *her* movie—it is part of the story of his or her life. In fact, it *is* his or her life currently taking place, currently being "filmed." Using a different metaphor, consciousness is the improvisational music of one's existence, currently being played, and the self is the artist currently creating the improvisation.

The First-Person Agent of Experience

In Greek, the personal pronoun used to designate the first person is *ego*. Freud used it to point to the subject in view in such statements as, "I did this" or "I want that." Gestalt therapy turns the ego into a function, pointing to the "capacity of the self in contact: the capacity to identify oneself with or alienate oneself from parts of the field" (Lobb & Lichtenberg, 2005, p. 30), while maintaining the sense of ego as the agent of experience. Consequently, conceptions of the *self* are analogous to the ego in action. Whether it is the ego as function, the ego as agent of experience, or the self and self-experience, what one is talking about is a person's sense of being alive and existing in a world with others—of the relationship between oneself and everything else, which constitutes "other."[2]

The self in gestalt therapy is both the system of contacting and the agent of experience (Crocker, 1999). "The self is the experiencer and organizer of contact at the boundary between self and other and plays the crucial role of organizing our perceptions of people and circumstances and making meaning out of the perceived world in which we live" (MacKewn, 1997, p. 74). Self is both process and concept—the process of contacting and the enduring sense of identity. This is what John Searle pointed to when he said,

> We do not just have disordered experiences; rather, all of the experiences I have at any instant are experienced as part of a single, unified conscious field. Furthermore, the continuation of that conscious field throughout time is experienced by the possessor of that conscious field as a continuation of his or her own consciousness. (Searle, 2004, p. 201)

Contact, Emergence, and Self-Experience

Contact is what happens when people move about in the world. In a very rudimentary way contact is what happens when a person bumps into a wall. There is a sudden meeting between soft, sensitive face and hard, resistant wall. They touch. Contact in the gestalt vernacular involves a bit more. There is a meeting, but this meeting constitutes the awareness of the relationship between self and other and makes explicit the way in which self and other touch. It, too, gets one's attention, because contact is exciting. "Primarily, contact is the awareness of, and behavior toward, the assimilable novelty; and the rejection of the unassimilable novelty" (Perls, Hefferline, & Goodman, 1951/1972, p. 230). Erving Polster and Miriam Polster (1973) described contact as the lifeblood of growth and the means by which a person changes himself or herself and the experience of the world.

Contact takes place at a boundary, conceived metaphorically as an organ or membrane connecting oneself to one's environment. The contact boundary is the point at which a person experiences

"me" as opposed to "not me." It is not a place lo
space, but its physiological correlate can be loca
lobes and prefrontal cortex (Brownell, 2009a), wl
tion of a person's "touch" with the world comes t
conscious responding, and involves the executive functions
regulation.

> The choices we make are not inherent in the situations at hand. They are a complex interplay between the properties of the situations and our own properties, our aspirations, our doubts, and our histories. It is only logical to expect that the prefrontal cortex is central to such decision making, since it is the only part of the brain where the inputs from within the organism converge with the inputs from the outside world. (Goldberg, 2001, p. 78)

That is a good description, from a neuropsychological perspective, of the contact boundary at work. It could be said that the self is drawn to the contact boundary where something of interest or concern in the environment is met, *but actually*, the whole person is involved in the environment and various features of the self take shape at the boundary of the organism and the environment. The human being is *of* the environment and not a separate entity from the environment with only a potential for meeting it. The whole person is always in some kind of contextual situation, and it is the emergent and supervenient activity of the mind that continually forms and reforms at the boundary, contributing to the overall self (Brownell, 2009a).

In gestalt therapy, the self is one whole system integrating various capacities of the whole person. The self has three operative means by which it works, serving as the subject, and they are identified as *functions*: Id function tells the person what he or she is feeling and sensing, ego function distinguishes between self and other, and personality function tells the person what kind of person he or she happens to be (Lobb & Lichtenberg, 2005; Perls, Hefferline, & Goodman, 1951/1972). With the id function, a person becomes aware of needs, curiosities, desires, excitement, and disaffectedness. With the ego function, a person makes choices, identifies with ures of interest or alienates them, and navigates contact at the boundary. With personality function, the person constructs the ongoing story of one's life in a characteristic style of responding, forms a history that orients the person with regard to a way of life, including a world view, and uses the residue of experience to make as efficient a way as possible for the person to live among others in the world.

That said, some attention needs to be paid to the concept of emergence, because "the self is not constructed by something more potent; it comes into being as the most potent aspect of the person, exercising will and providing downward causation on everything from which it emerges, and the best word for that process *is* 'emergence'" (Brownell 2009a, p. 72). So, what is this thing called emergence and how does it work?

Emergence is the process by which properties or substances arise out of more fundamental entities but are distinct from them and irreducible to them (O'Conner & Wong, 2006). Emergence relates to gestalt therapy in that gestalt therapy maintains an emergent theory of self, and therein resides a problem. Gestalt therapists face a conundrum in attempting to integrate neurophysiological evidence with the gestalt therapy theory of self, because this boils down to the issue of how the brain (or the nervous system) is related to the mind. Gestalt therapists adhere to substance monism but property dualism. That is, they believe the immaterial self arises from the functioning of the material brain as the organism contacts the environment. Property dualism occurs when "the ontology of physics is not sufficient to constitute what is there" (Robinson, 2007, np). When a gestalt therapist encounters a client, there is more *there* than a simple firing of synapses, the reflecting chorus of mirror neurons, and the memory of emotionally laden experience stored in the amygdala. Nonreductive physicalism maintains that mind emerges as the brain engages; the working of the fundamental nervous system generates a complex order of properties, a mind, that is distinct from, but dependent on the working of the brain.[3] No brain; no mind (Stoeger, 2002). Thus, the gestalt therapy experience of self belongs in discussions of the theory of mind, because it is so similar to the properties of mind as to be synonymous. Conversely, gestalt therapists enhance their understanding of a client when they assess that person's neuropsychological capacities, because self depends on the individual's neurological capabilities.

The triangulation of sensory perception yields the experience of being in the world of objects. When I sit at a table, look down and see its wooden pattern of browns, tans, and even yellows and at the same time feel its hardness with my elbow and its cold smoothness with my fingers, and tap on it and hear the solid sound, I get a triangulated sense, through multiple streams of perception, of the nature of this object. I am situated, contextualized, and I exist as a being in triangulation with other beings. That produces an experience that is both encountered directly and constructed internally. This, by the way, is near the crux of couples work, for in a dyadic relationship both people attempt to reconcile the fact that they each directly share the same situation, yet internally construct or interpret it differently. This gestalt structuring is

> not only a matter of organizing our perceptions into coherent wholes, but within the entire conscious field, we make a distinction between the figures that we are perceiving and the ground on which they are perceived. So, for example, I see the pen against the background of the book, the book against the background of the desk, the desk against the background of the floor, and the floor against the rest of the room, until I reach the horizon of my entire perceptual field. (Searle, 2004, p. 100)

Self-experience can be thought of as self-conscious in nature. As such, it amounts to the awareness of one's self in situ or in vivo. When a biologist examines a phenomenon where it occurs, without moving it to a Petri dish, that is in situ. However, it is not necessarily in vivo. When a biologist examines a cell in an organ that is still part of the living organism, that is in vivo, or "within the living." When gestalt therapists work with clients they work in situ and they work in vivo; that is, they are working with the client's experience of a part of life extracted from the whole context of life. They do not go home, eat dinner, go to bed, wake up, and have breakfast with their clients. Similarly, they do not extract the thinking part of the whole person and isolate it in its own "Petri dish" (in vitro). Rather, gestalt therapists work with their clients' sense of being caught up in some kind of situation in which they carry elements of their ongoing life, intact, into each session, and the gestalt therapist works with the whole person in situ, "in the place," often moving from the transplanted situation to the lived experience of the client in session (in vivo).

For example, one client came for therapy because he felt lonely, isolated, and depressed, and he complained that he could not keep conversations with other people moving. He would inevitably reach a point at which it all stopped. He would exhaust himself following a script of questions he had devised, and then not have anywhere to go from there. It seemed to him that others would lose interest in him, and he would then drift apart from the group and find himself alone in a crowd, looking for some way to escape. Through a phenomenal exploration of his narrative of one specific event like this, the therapist attempted to slow down the sequence to more closely examine that situation. The client described the situation, and the therapist listened and asked clarifying questions about what was happening, what happened next, how the client had been feeling, and what he had been thinking. Finally, he stated that while listening to the client he got a sense of the client drifting, diffuse, in a cloud and not connecting with people. The client agreed; that is what it felt like to him. The therapist asked what the connection taking place at that moment between himself and the therapist felt like to the client, and the client stated that it felt the same as the others; the gestalt therapist then moved to a phenomenal exploration of that moment-by-moment interaction. Together, they moved from an in situ to an in vivo phenomenal investigation.

INTENTIONALITY

Franz Brentano retrieved the term *intentionality* from the scholastics' development of the concept in medieval philosophy. As suggested in chapter 2, intentionality in phenomenology does not mean *purpose*; it signals the aboutness of experience, and it is the starting point for a phenomenological approach to anything. How is intentionality, this aboutness, related to gestalt therapy? It is the dynamic factor in figure formation, in which interest, need, or curiosity brings to mind a focus. It is the move from diffuse and vague sensory perception, a kind of awareness, to the clarity that intensifies general awareness into a signal indicating what that sensory experience is about. It's the move from an empty feeling in the pit of one's stomach to the realization, "I am hungry." As such, intentionality has three facets worth considering: voice, attitude, and horizon.

Voice

The subject thinking or feeling is connected by the act of thinking or feeling to the thought being contemplated or the feeling being experienced. In admiring, something is admired. In fearing, something is feared. There is a subject acting, and there is an object intuited, represented, or perceived. Thus, the object in question is called an intentional *object*. It is the object of one's *a*ttention and *in*tention. In the work of Edmund Husserl, the object became known as a *noema* and the process of intending became known as a *noesis* (Spinelli, 2005). The noema is an enduring mental representation of either tangible things existing in the world, such as an apple, or constructs of contemplation, such as "justice." Although the apple might grow brown and rot away, the noema constituting the apple cannot be destroyed, because the mental act at the center of intentionality creates an enduring image (Moran, 2000).

Willhelm Dilthey described this relationship of the subject to the intentional object:

> I only *appear* to live among things that are independent of my consciousness; in reality, my self distinguishes itself from facts of my own consciousness, formations whose locus is in me....The system of my representations extends as far as these objects which appear to me. Whatever is encountered in objects—the hardness that demolishes, the glowing heat that melts—is to its very core a fact of my consciousness, and

> the thing is, so to speak, a synthesis of just such mental facts. There are no distinct objects to which my representations refer; the object simply *is* the representation....Existence itself, reality, being—these are only expressions for the way in which my consciousness processes its impressions and its representations. (Dilthey, 1991, pp. 245–246)

The aboutness of the experience makes intending a transitive process as the person creates his or her own experience. As described earlier, then, the grammatical construct of "voice" stands for the implicit relationship between subject and the action of intending.

Voice is a grammatical feature in verbal systems; it "is that property of the verbal idea which indicates how the subject is related to the action" (Dana & Mantey, 1927/1955, p. 155). The active voice describes the subject as producing the action or representing the state intrinsic to the object, the passive voice shows the subject receiving the action, and the middle voice describes the subject as participating in some way in the results of the action; it relates the action more intimately to the subject (Dana & Mantey, 1927/1955).

> The active voice emphasizes the action, but the middle voice emphasizes the agent, thus is more immediately relevant to *self* experience. Hindu grammarians described the active voice as *parasmai padan* (word for another), while they described the middle voice as *atmane padan* (word for one's self). (Brownell, in press, np)

The middle voice has several nuances of meaning indicating how the subject participates in the action, but the three most salient are the following:

1. The direct middle in which the results of the action are referred directly to the agent with a reflexive force, that is, "I found myself."
2. The indirect middle in which sometimes the stress is on the agent as producer of the action rather than participant in its results and the action is related to the agent in some special way, that is, "I, myself, found myself."

3 The permissive middle in which the agent voluntarily yields self to the results of the action or seeks to secure those results for his or her own self-interest, that is, "I found myself for myself."

> Thus, I intend—think, feel, experience in some way some "thing," some aspect, some feature of my phenomenal landscape—in the middle voice. It is this reflexive self-reference, this self-interest that connects the subject *to* his or her intentional object, and it is an immediate action. That is, the first-personal givenness of experiential phenomena is accounted for by a pre-reflective self-consciousness, which is present whenever a person is living through an experience; that is, whenever one is consciously perceiving the world, thinking a thought, feeling an emotion or sensing a sensation (Zahavi, 2006). One is *having* an experience, not noticing oneself having an experience. However, if one begins to attend, on a meta level, and thinks about oneself having an experience, then the pre-reflective self-consciousness, the middle voice of intentionality, shifts to another intentional object, but the flow of intentionality keeps moving in that same middle voice (Brownell, in press, np).

In gestalt therapy the middle voice is prominent in such statements as "the self is the agent of experience," or "the self is the artist creating one's life." However, voice has not been developed as a useful construct by gestalt therapists, even though grammatical voice is inherent in the gestalt ideas of self, responding, and spontaneity. Paul Goodman attempted to explicate the concept of voice in PHG, but he mixed up Greek grammar and referred to a "middle mode." There is no such thing in Greek grammar, but the context of his comments clearly indicates he was working the idea of voice:

> In English we have mostly only active or passive verbs.... Greek has a regular middle mode [*sic*] ... But we must make a careful distinction: just what the middle is not is action *on* the self—this we shall later call "retroflection," often a neurotic mechanism. The middle mode means, rather, that whether the self does or is done to, it refers the process to itself as

> a totality, it feels it as its own and is engaged in it. (Perls, Hefferline, & Goodman, 1951/1972, footnote, p. 376)

Attitude

Attitude is the tint coloring one's identity and the flavor in one's interest that influences one's relational stance toward the world. Attitude is the parameter in which one reaches out to the world.

Saying one has a "bad" attitude is a common expression; it means that one is rancorous, vitriolic, irritable, or even hostile in one's stance toward the world, and if a person is like that, then the manner in which he or she meets others influences the kind of experience all will have. This is understandable, but it is not exactly the kind of attitude involved here.

The attitude in which one engages his or her intentional objects influences the experience one has of those objects. That is true. However, the emphasis is not so much on one's affective stance as it is on one's identity and interest and the bearing or the pose one assumes as an expression of them. Attitude can be thought of as a measure and a description of one's openness in any given situation. It also includes the direction of such openness (toward, away, beside, etc.).

For instance, if I walk through a shopping mall with a designer's attitude, then I will gravitate to clothing and furniture stores but perhaps away from sporting goods, and I will stop to admire the colors and the composition in various displays.

It is a natural way of approaching whatever one is experiencing, and it takes percepts as they come without questioning whether or not objects are actually there—or how they are there. Such a designer's attitude would be a subset of the natural attitude.

On the other hand, if I walk through the same mall with a phenomenological attitude, then I throw relevant percepts into relief and assume a detached, observing, and critical posture—a meta-level cognition—with regard to them.

In the natural attitude, I see a painting, and as the designer I may evaluate its color scheme and theme for an appropriate fit in some project I am doing, but I approach the painting in the course of my everyday life and do not notice myself thinking about the painting as painting. In the phenomenological attitude, however, I do think about the painting as painting. I think about how I am perceiving and thinking about the painting; if I see that same painting, I am observing its features in order to conclude what it actually is, its essence, but I am not actually incorporating it *into* the mundane flow of my life.

> My specific interest in a certain entity, my situation in other words, is always embraced or surrounded by an attitude. The attitude is like a halo (or an aura) around a certain act of interest. Being in the attitude of the businessman, let me call it the "business attitude," my intentional rays of interest will be carried out according to this attitude. Likewise, I can shift my attitude, as an act of my free will, to the architectural attitude, or I can shift to an aesthetic attitude and view the selfsame thing, the house in my example, as a work of art. Strictly speaking, my active life is always already carried out in a certain attitude of which there are many, some of which may still be unknown to me. (Luft, 1998, p. 157)

In phenomenology the two main attitudes of interest are the natural attitude and the phenomenological attitude (see below for more on these). The first comes with a measure of naiveté that accepts beliefs about the world as given without much question, the chief of which is that the objective world actually exists. It is this belief, this basic ontological naiveté, that even undergirds the scientific method, and it illustrates how, at the core, all other attitudes arise from the natural attitude. This is because all attitudes assume the universe exists and move on from there in some way (Luft, 1998).

In gestalt therapy a therapist may move in and out of several subsets of the natural attitude, one of which could be called the therapeutic attitude. In this attitude the stance in relation to the client is a felt experience as the therapist is aware of clinical issues and procedures. The therapist does not adopt a false persona of professionalism and force himself or herself to maintain professional distance, but the therapist does realize an identity (the therapist self) and he or she does follow clinical interests (open to the client for clinical purposes). What is important to understand, and is addressed below, is that the therapist, even though using a modified phenomenological method, does *not* assume a philosophical attitude and conduct a phenomenological reduction. This has been confused and misunderstood in many treatments of gestalt therapy methodology, and this is one difference between gestalt psychotherapy and phenomenological psychotherapy (they are sisters but not identical twins).

Horizon

The openness one has toward potential objects encountered in any given attitude is called the horizon that correlates to that attitude, and for each horizon there is a corresponding world. Thus, for the business attitude there is a horizon and world of business. For the designer's attitude, there is a horizon and world of design. The objects encountered in these attitudes and worlds exhaust a person's attention so that one is unaware of the given attitude or the given world as such, even as they act like channels that steer one's considerations. In gestalt therapy, this is called identifying with one's figure of interest. In addition, the total influence of one's culture and society create a grand horizon and its corresponding world, and that is called the individual's *homeworld*; the homeworld is what provides one's sense of normalcy such that objects and experiences are considered either normal or alien by virtue of their relationship to the homeworld.

In gestalt therapy, the therapist seeks to meet the home world of the client in the natural attitude. There is no attempt to achieve a realization of things as they exist absolutely. The attempt is to understand the experience of the client, and in order to do that the therapist may take a therapeutic stance with regard to the client, but it is a posture that is actually subsumed in the natural attitude of the therapist as well. Therapist and client, in order to meet and have contact, must share the common medium of experience that is accepted for what it is rather than objectified and thematized.

PHENOMENOLOGICAL METHOD IN PSYCHOTHERAPY

The situated individual is what psychotherapists deal with. The experience of the client itself is phenomenal, and the study of that experience is called *phenomenology*. Gestalt therapy is a phenomenological discipline, building on the thinking of philosophers in the phenomenological tradition, but gestalt therapists are not philosophers; they are psychotherapists who find just as much interest in behavior as they do in experience. When gestalt therapists practice their professions, therefore, they work within the phenomenal field, not the phenomenological field. The insights of phenomenological philosophy must be "bent" somewhat to support a therapeutic process.

Adapting a Philosophical Method for Use in Psychology

Edmund Husserl's project was to retrieve philosophy from what he saw as an overwhelming capitulation to naturalism—the empirical exploration of consciousness (Jennings, 1986). Ironically, it sometimes seems as if gestalt psychotherapy has surrendered to philosophy, not just settling for the guidance philosophy can provide any endeavor, but also introjecting Husserl's philosophical method to suffice for a psychological process. Giorgi and Giorgi commented on experimental psychology's use of the phenomenological method, and a similar criticism could be lodged against some gestalt therapists, because they both use

> [Husserl's] description of the steps of the method without modification without realizing that such a description is in the service of a philosophical project. Thus, Moustakas (1994) also provided an independent interpretation of Husserl's philosophical method, and he used Husserl's transcendental articulations as a guide. However, our perspective is that the transcendental perspective is wholly philosophical and should not be a guide for psychological analyses. (Giorgi & Giorgi, 2003, p. 245)

Toward that end, Sylvia Crocker wrote about, and she and Peter Philippson (2005) discussed, the nature of the phenomenological method as developed by Edmund Husserl and then adapted to the existential process inherent in gestalt therapy. Todd Burley and Dan Bloom (2008) struggled with the same task and became a bit more explicit in defining the ways in which the "bending" of Husserl's philosophical method takes place. Crocker and Philippson indicated that the goal of Husserl's phenomenological method is knowledge, but the goal in gestalt therapy is a practical one—healing and growth. The concern in gestalt therapy "is not to find out whether the client is telling the truth as she tells her story but to understand the *meanings the client gives* to the people and events in her life. The therapeutic task thus becomes, in part, *hermeneutic*" (Crocker & Philippson, 2005, p. 68). The gestalt therapist is interested in how the client's beliefs and understandings of experience function as the ground for her cognitive, emotional, and behavioral responses to the people and ongoing events in her or his life. This is accomplished in part by "turning this philosophical method back on itself, that is, 'doubling back' to the natural attitude ... and not taking the reduction into the phenomenological (and philosophical) attitude" (Burley & Bloom, 2008, p. 155). By this turning back,

> the phenomenological method returns to the sensuous, concrete experiencing of the lived-body. By returning to the lived-body and not moving toward the non-empirical eidetic realm, gestalt therapy's perspective prepares for the emergence of those forms of experiencing, gestalt forming and destructuring, that are the hallmarks of its method. (Burley & Bloom, 2008, p. 160)

The Adapted Phenomenological Method

Three rules apply in a phenomenological process: (1) epoché, (2) description, and (3) horizontalization (Brownell, 2009b; Crocker & Philippson, 2005).

> In the rule of epoché, one sets aside his or her initial biases and prejudices in order to suspend expectations and assumptions. In the rule of description, one occupies himself or herself with describing instead of explaining. In the rule of

> horizontalization, one treats each item of description as having equal value or significance. (Brownell, 2009b)

These are all conducted in the therapeutic attitude. What gestalt therapists do in therapy is all done in the natural attitude; however, the therapeutic attitude is a subset of that. This is so because the therapist does not leave behind the normal flow of experience, and therapists track the client in terms of the real world in which both therapist and client live. The meta-stance is a watered down version of the meta-cognizing of the transcendental reduction, but it does not take a philosophical posture. Thus, the designer mentioned above does see the painting with the everyday eyes of a designer, but according to the homeworld of that person, and in the same way the therapist does see the client with the everyday eyes of the therapist, according to his or her familiar homeworld.

Here is another example. In a discussion of Heidegger's "new" phenomenology, James K. A. Smith (2002) contrasts "the ontic, or positive science (theology), and the ontological field of research (phenomenology). Theology's field is particular and concrete: one's faith community. In addition, theology functions *within* and makes no *epoché*. A phenomenology of religion, on the other hand, is able to range across religions and communities. . . . Theology, then, would always be particular and concrete—the theology of this particular believing community. A phenomenology of religion, however, brackets such participation and is able to range across religious communities" (p. 101).

This is *exactly* what gestalt therapists do in not using a (philosophically based) phenomenological method in dealing with the phenomenal field of the client. Gestalt therapists are experience near, specific, and concrete. They are not abstracting and theorizing when they use a modified phenomenological method, which amounts to observing, bracketing "noise," and describing what they are observing. As soon as a gestalt therapist starts theorizing, he or she moves from this level to something else, perhaps even to a field theoretical strategy, which Kurt Lewin described as not a theory at all but a method for detecting causal influences.

When the gestalt therapist bends the method created by Husserl, he or she uses it as a paradoxical intervention. By aiming to make as clear as possible the current experience of the client (by observation, bracketing, description, and experiment within the support of a dialogical relationship; see chapters 4 and 6 below), the therapist trusts that the client may seize the opportunity to actualize himself or herself in the moment, leading to adjustment in subsequent moments. It may or may not happen, but whatever takes place, that becomes the ground of the next phase in the process.

In observing, the therapist fine tunes his or her ability to sense the other person. The therapist uses every available perceptual portal and waits on the presentation the client provides. He or she notices clothing, colors, skin tone, musculature, posture, body movement and carriage, facial expressions, grooming, and so on. The therapist tracks shifts in nervous energy and split off body movements, surges or retreats of emotional energy. The gestalt therapist develops skill in observing all that is possible to sense and available to be perceived.

In bracketing, the gestalt therapist puts aside, as much as possible, interpretations, theories, and initial models—even the initial foundations of theories—about the client. The therapist puts them aside with permission to come back to them later, and in a similar manner the therapist puts aside any unfinished personal issues triggered by the client's way of presenting (what is commonly known as countertransference).[4]

In describing, one simply speaks the observation back to the client, introducing with such phrases as, "I see that ..." "I notice you ..." or "Now you are ...." As an extension of this, the therapist might choose to self-disclose what it is like for the therapist to be in the presence of the client. This is not a loss of the therapeutic attitude, in some kind of slip into another dimension of identity, directionality, and interest; that is, this is not using the client to take care of the needs of the therapist. Rather, this kind of self-disclosing is a dialogical disclosure, a description of the total impact of being with the client. In any case, the therapist presents the descriptive statement and then stops.

The potency of the phenomenal intervention is most effective when not watered down by excessive verbiage. Observe carefully, bracket effectively, and describe succinctly. Then stop describing, and wait on the client, while continuing to observe, and to bracket. If necessary, if the client says nothing, continue to describe in accordance with where the process has moved to in time at *that* time.

The phenomenological method is just one among several options available to gestalt therapists, who practice a coherent and unified approach (Brownell, 2009b; Crocker, 2008; Yontif & Philippson, 2008). It is not the be-all and end-all of therapeutic process. As will be seen, gestalt therapists also work dialogically and experimentally with reference to the field, but the phenomenological method is used specifically to clarify and make explicit what the client experiences, what it is like to be him or her and how he or she makes sense of life from his or her unique vantage point in some difficult situation.

CONCLUSION

Gestalt therapy does not address a person's thinking as if it were diseased and needing to be changed by something the therapist does; it approaches a person's thinking and explores it with the client in order for the client to sync up his or her thinking with everything else going on in the whole person who is situated in a psychosocial-environmental surround called "the field" (see chapter 5). It is a growth model of change focused on what the client does, and not a medical model focused on what the therapist prescribes.[5] Gestalt therapy deals with the personal experience of the client, with the quality of the client's contacting and the meaning-making that arises from the flow of the process of the client's life. In order to make clear what the client is going through and the ways in which the client is dealing with that, the gestalt therapist employs a modified phenomenological method as a paradoxical intervention, trusting that the heightened awareness and clarity it engenders will lead the client to his or her own, best creative adjustment. This form of treatment is conducted as one aspect of an overall approach that also includes the relationship between therapist and client, all those extratherapeutic factors the client and therapist bring into session that are affecting the client's life (also known by gestalt therapists as "the field"), and the experimental freedom that turns talking about something that happened somewhere else at some other time into a current and conducive experience.

NOTES

1. Cognitive behavioral basic principles adapted from Freeman and Freeman (2009, p. 304).
2. "Other" is an important technical term in phenomenology. It stands for what is not the same; that is, whatever is not of the self and its thematizations—its cognizing and constructions of meaning—and in some thinkers, such as Emmanuel Levinas, the other is separate, held in the transcendent mystery he called "alterity."
3. This also relates to the concept of supervenience. When the emergent entity supervenes, then:
   a. The two entities are ontologically (i.e., numerically) distinct; B is not simply a further description of A.
   b. A relationship exists between properties in A and B.
   c. Property G in A supervenes on property F in B if and only if x's instantiating G is in virtue of x's instantiating F under circumstances c (Murphy, 2002).

   "That was a tight, logical statement defining supervenience. What it means is that in supervenience there are two entities (A and B). B is distinct from A but related to it. B has properties that correlate with properties in A and supervenes on them because any change in A results in a change in B, under a given, specific set of circumstances. Therefore, supervenience is context specific" (Brownell, 2009a, pp. 74–75). A more detailed explanation of supervenience is beyond the scope of this chapter.
4. Countertransference can be useful, and this putting aside does not mean the gestalt therapist never comes back to it. It just means that in the service of the adapted phenomenological method, the gestalt therapist does not use it at that moment.
5. Which is not to say that the therapist does nothing, but to put the emphasis where it belongs.

REFERENCES

Brownell, P. (Ed.). (2008). *Handbook for theory, research, and practice in gestalt therapy.* Newcastle, England: Cambridge Scholars.

Brownell, P. (2009a). Executive functions: A neuropsychological understanding of self-regulation. *Gestalt Review, 13*(1), 62–81.

Brownell, P. (2009b). Gestalt therapy. In I. Marini & M. Stebnicki (Eds.), *The professional counselor's desk reference* (pp. 399–407). New York: Springer.

Brownell, P. (in press). Intentional spirituality. In J. H. Ellens (Ed.), *The healing power of spirituality: How religion helps humans thrive, vol 1, The healing power of personal spirituality*, np. Westport, CT: Greenwood/Praeger.

Burley, T., & Bloom, D. (2008). Phenomenological method. In P. Brownell (Ed.), *Handbook for theory, research, and practice in gestalt therapy* (pp. 151–183). Newcastle, England: Cambridge Scholars.

Crocker, S. (1999). *A well-lived life: Essays in gestalt therapy*. Cambridge, MA: Gestalt Institute of Cleveland Press.

Crocker, S. (2008). A unified theory. In P. Brownell (Ed.), *Handbook for theory, research, and practice in gestalt therapy* (pp. 124–150). Newcastle, England: Cambridge Scholars.

Crocker, S., & Philippson, P. (2005). Phenomenology, existentialism, and eastern thought. In A. Woldt & S. Toman (Eds.), *Gestalt therapy, history, theory, and practice* (pp. 65–80). Thousand Oaks, CA: Sage.

Damasio, A. (1999). *The feeling of what happens: Body and emotion in the making of consciousness.* New York: Harcourt Brace.

Dana, H. E., & Mantey, J. R. (1927/1955). *A manual grammar of the Greek New Testament*. Toronto, Canada: Macmillan.

Dilthey, W. (1991). *Introduction to the human sciences*, trans. Rudolf Makkreel & Frithjob Rodi. Princeton, NJ: University of Princeton Press.

Freeman, A., & Freeman S. E. M. (2009). Basics of cognitive behavior therapy. In I. Marini & M. Stebnicki (Eds.), *The professional counselor's desk reference* (pp. 301–311). New York: Springer.

Gallagher, S., & Zahavi, D. (2008). *The phenomenological mind: An introduction to philosophy of mind and cognitive science*. New York: Routledge.

Giorgi, A., & Giorgi, B. (2003). The descriptive phenomenological psychological method. In P. Camic, J. Rhodes, & L. Yardley (Eds.), *Qualitative research in psychology: Expanding perspectives in methodology and design* (pp. 243–273). Washington, DC: American Psychological Association.

Goldberg, E. (2001). *The executive brain: Frontal lobes and the civilized mind*. Oxford, England: Oxford University Press.

Jennings, J. (1986). Husserl revisited: The forgotten distinction between psychology and phenomenology. *American Psychologist, 41*(11), 1231–1240.

Kim, J. (2006). *Philosophy of mind* (2nd ed.). Cambridge, MA: Westview Press.

Lobb, M., & Lichtenberg, P. (2005). Classical gestalt therapy theory. In A. Woldt & S. Toman (Eds.), *Gestalt therapy history, theory, and practice* (pp. 21–39). Thousand Oaks, CA: Sage.

Luft, S. (1998). Husserl's phenomenological discovery of the natural attitude. *Continental Philosophy Review, 31*, 153–170.

MacKewn, J. (1997). *Developing gestalt counselling*. Thousand Oaks, CA: Sage.

Moran, D. (2000). *Introduction to phenomenology*. New York: Routledge.

Moustakas, C. (1994) Phenomenological research methods. Thousand Oaks, CA: Sage Publications.

Murphy, N. (2002). Supervenience and the efficacy of the mental. In R. Russell, N. Murphy, T. Meyering, & M. Arbib (Eds.), *Neuroscience and the person: Scientific perspectives on divine action*. Vatican City State: Vatican Observatory; Berkeley, CA Foundation and Center for Theology and the Natural Sciences.

O'Conner, T., & Wong, H. Y. (2006). Emergent properties. In E. N. Zalta (Ed.), *The Stanford encyclopedia of philosophy*. Downloaded May 23, 2009, from http://plato.stanford.edu/entries/properties-emergent.

Perls, F., Hefferline, R., & Goodman, P. (1951/1972). *Gestalt therapy, excitement and growth in the human personality*. London: Souvenir Press.

Polster, E., & Polster, M. (1973). *Gestalt therapy integrated: Contours of theory and practice.* New York: Vintage Books/Random House.

Robinson, H. (2007). Dualism. In E. N. Zalta (Ed.), *The Stanford encyclopedia of philosophy*. Downloaded May 23, 2009, from http://plato.stanford.edu/entries/dualism.

Searle, J. (2004). *Mind, a brief introduction*. Oxford, England: Oxford University Press.

Smith, James K. A. (2002). *Speech and theology: Language and the logic of incarnation.* London: Routledge.

Spinelli, E. (2005). *The interpreted world: An introduction to phenomenological psychology* (2nd ed.). Thousand Oaks, CA: Sage.

Stoeger, W. (2002). The mind-brain problem, the laws of nature, and constitutive relationships. In R. Russel, N. Murphy, T. Meyering, & M. Arbib (Eds.), *Neuroscience and the person: Scientific perspectives on divine action* (pp. 129–146). Vatican City State/Berkeley, CA: Vatican Observatory/Center for Theology and the Natural Sciences.

Varela, F., Thompson, E., & Rosch, E. (1991). *The embodied mind: Cognitive science and human experience.* Cambridge, MA: MIT Press.

Yontif, G., & Philippson, P. (2008). A unified practice. In P. Brownell (Ed.), *Handbook for theory, research, and practice in gestalt therapy* (pp. 257–276). Newcastle, England: Cambridge Scholars.

Zahavi, D. (2006). Phenomenological approaches to self-consciousness. In E. N. Zalta (Ed.), *The Stanford encyclopedia of philosophy*. Stanford, CA: Metaphysics Research Lab, Center for the Study of Language and Information (CSLI), Stanford University. Downloaded January 30, 2009, from http://plato.stanford.edu/entries/self-consciousness-phenomenological.

5 Work the Therapeutic Relationship

This chapter describes the relational aspects of gestalt therapy. The intersubjective philosophy of Martin Buber and the philosophy of alterity as developed by Emanuel Levinas provide the ground for an exploration of the therapeutic relationship. This is understood in gestalt therapy as "dialogue," and the reader is shown how to practice in a dialogical attitude.

This chapter covers four important concepts fundamental to gestalt therapy: (1) alterity, (2) dialogue, and the (3) relational matrix that emerges through (4) contact. The discussion of these ideas explicates gestalt therapy's understanding of the therapeutic relationship. Since outcomes research indicates that the working relationship accounts for approximately 30% of positive results in psychotherapy (Brownell, 2008a, 2008b), an understanding of what this is and how it works is essential. Such an understanding develops by attending to the individual encountered as Other, the contact between self and Other, the concept of relationship itself, and the web of relationships one navigates in dyads, families, groups, organizations, and communities. All four concepts (alterity, contact, dialogue, and relationship) are essential to an ability to use the therapeutic relationship effectively, and each may be in the foreground at any given time.

ALTERITY

Discussions of alterity can become filled with what feels like opaque reasoning and hopeless philosophical jargon; but hopefully this section will not become tediously arcane. To make the discussion more "user friendly," this chapter in no way approximates a rigorous philosophical explanation.

"Alterity" is Emmanuel Levinas's term. Husserl's system of phenomenology concerns how an individual might know—the subjective perspective—but Levinas views phenomenology as an ethic focused on the implications of the *other* in general and the *Other* person, specifically, which concerns how an individual might be—that is, how an individual lives in relation to other individuals. The application is to how the therapist might approach being with and relating to clients.

Alterity as a construct is incompatible with philosophical reduction, because the reduction is understood to be a violence perpetrated against an Other by making immanent what is transcendent. One therefore needs to appreciate what these two terms mean. It is no accident they have a theological ring to them, for Levinas was a believing Jew who also participated in phenomenologically relevant philosophical conferences held by Karol Wojtyla (Pope John Paul II) at Castel Gandolpho (along with Paul Ricoeur and others).

Transcendence and Immanence

Whereas Husserl privileges the individual and his or her immediate experience, Levinas privileges the "face" of the Other and his or her mysterious difference. Therein resides the essential contrast between the terms *immanence* and *transcendence*.

To Levinas the face of another person does more than simply express emotion; it presents an ethical obligation, an imperative, that calls to a subject (Waldenfels, 2002). Transcendence is the trace of a paradox that points to the relation with what is separate. "It is a way for the distant to give itself" (Hayat, 1999, p. ix).

> His main point is that the "other" is not another me, nor is it something defined by its relationship with me, but rather

> something or someone completely other and unique. The other is *incommensurate* with me. Moreover, the other, as that which calls to me, calls for a response from me. (Moran, 2002, p. 337)

Outside of Levinas and those following him, the concept of "other" can indicate someone else quite similar who shares many of one's own traits and tendencies and with whom one might empathize (just another person numerically), but it can also mean someone who is quite strange and so different as to be incomprehensible (another person qualitatively). This distinction is related to the concepts of "same" and "other" and is essential in Levinas. The "same," however, does not mean someone or something similar to oneself, nor does "other" just mean one's concept of someone very different from oneself.

Bear with me and consider a text taken from the New Testament. By contemplating two Greek words, *allos* and *heteros*, and recognizing a grammatical construction used to communicate obvious or strong contrast (such constructions introduced one item with *men* and contrasted it with another item preceded by *de*), one can appreciate what "Other" really means. Although allos and heteros eventually merged in usage to become interchangeable, the contexts in which they occur in ancient texts show that sometimes the Greeks pointed to *another of the same kind*, but at other times they pointed to *another of a different kind*. Both were considered to be "other," but one usage communicated more sameness and the other indicated more difference. So, when Paul wrote to the church in Corinth about the resurrection, he contrasted the earthly body that goes into the grave with the spiritual body that comes out of it, and he used both allos and heteros in that classical, syntactical construction for communicating contrast:

> That which you sow will not be coming to life unless it dies, and you do not sow what is being made alive, but a naked grain.... Not all flesh is the same flesh; quite so, some (*men*) are of human beings while (*de*) others (*allos*) are the flesh of beasts; some (*men*) are flesh of birds, while (*de*) others (*allos*) are of fish. There are heavenly bodies and there are earthly

> bodies; in fact, the glory of the heavenly is one thing (*men*) but (*de*) the glory of the earthly is another (*heteros*). (1 Corinthians 15:36–40)[1]

The religious content of this illustration is irrelevant to the point of contrast—the distinction between another of the same kind and another of a different kind is the distinction between that which is immanent and that which is transcendent. When someone thematizes another person, they make that person into another of the same kind (the same as oneself). One may contemplate a difference, but it is a superficial difference overlaying a meta-level cognition that draws on all one's definitions and previous experiences. The other person is not, obviously, the *same* numerical person as oneself, but in constructing a theory about him or her, even in allowing an "aboutness" to form, a therapist creates a picture that is made from all the raw material of the therapist's own life, and thus, the other becomes another of the "same" kind (*allos*). In order to break clear of that, the therapist must sow that "other" of the same kind into the ground where it can die, and the therapist must let the other of a different kind (*heteros*) rise from the grave of his or her own subjectivity, so to speak, through a novel revelation of the other person, who is not an object of intentionality at that point, but a kind of saturated phenomenon (Smith, 2002).

How Alterity Relates to Gestalt Therapy

Martin Buber believed that to regard the Other in the scope of one's phenomenological knowledge would be to approach the other with an I-It perspective (Zank, 2007). To conduct any kind of phenomenological reduction, then, instantly eliminates the possibility of dialogue. Further, when one constructs a view of the Other, which is what therapists do when they begin to conceptualize the client as a "case" or when they assess and diagnose a person, one cannot help but construct that view out of one's own world, one's own attitude at the time, and the horizon of all possibilities one associates with that world. Thus, the Other's true otherness becomes violated by the first person's conceptualizing—his or her *thematizing*. What makes the Other the same is that through intentionality, one brings the Other within the scope of one's subjective meaning making, and that shreds the transcendence of the Other, making the Other immanent. This is the "violence" to which Levinas points and to which Buber alludes.

> I-Thou is the primary word of relation. It is characterized by mutuality, directness, presentness, intensity, and ineffability. Although it is only within this relation that personality and the personal really exist, the Thou of I-Thou is not limited to men but may include animals, trees, objects of nature, and God. I-It is the primary word of experiencing and using. It takes place within a man and not between him and the world. (Friedman, 2002, p. 65)

What Friedman points to here is what Levinas identified as the "same." It is affirmation that the phenomenological approach to experience is a represented experience that takes place within a person and not between that person and the world. Even though gestalt therapists are concerned for the phenomenal field of the client, there must be a way beyond, a way out of the prison of subjective intentionality, and that way is through dialogue. As soon as one accepts the reality of the Other, and receives the revelation of the Other as saturated phenomenon, then direct contact is possible, and the representationalism of Kant and Husserl drops away. A gestalt therapist encounters, meets, a transcendent Other when he or she dialogues with a client.

When people use clients' diagnostic labels, saying things such as, "Today we had to deal with a borderline," they are referring to their model or representation of the actually existing Other made into an object—an intentional object—by virtue of the aboutness of experience in the phenomenological system. Levinas considers such things unethical, calling them a violence against the Other (the Other being an actually existing and transcendent Other).

Alterity provides an ethical value for one's stance as a therapist in meeting people. Although the dialogic approach in gestalt therapy always advocates acceptance of however the client enters the circle of dialogue, alterity demands, and by implication the therapist owes it to the client, that the therapist hold at bay every meta-level thought about the client in order to not only accept how the client enters the circle, but also to be amazed by the revelation of a transcendent Other.

There are times when clinical business must be carried out, and a gestalt therapist is no different in that respect from a psychoanalyst. If the third-party payer needs a diagnosis, then the therapist needs to do an assessment. If charting and other documentation needs to be accomplished, then it simply does. The trick is to do these tasks with awareness and to make deliberate room for the ethics of alterity wherever one can find professional room to do so.

CONTACT

Directing a musician's gaze toward the audience, so that performers' and audience's eyes meet, increases enjoyment of musical performance as a piece of music (Antonietta, Cocomazzi, & Iannelo, 2009). Having connection to a spiritual world can contribute to the sense of purpose in life among the very old (Hedberg, Brulin, & Aléx, 2009). Putting groups together that are normally prejudiced against one another reduces the prejudice in some ways, but in other ways it reduces their associating (Binder et al., 2009). Simply imagining social proximity between such groups, though, can often lead to more positive intergroup relations (Crisp & Turner, 2009). Introducing skin-to-skin contact during early postpartum can facilitate breastfeeding and help prevent breastfeeding cessation among mothers who desire to sustain it (Chiu, Anderson, & Burkhammer, 2008). Carl Rogers regarded psychological contact between therapist and client as essential to positive outcomes in psychotherapy (Rogers, 2007). Finally, in 2009, as President Barack Obama contemplated closing the detention center at Guantanamo Bay, Cuba, the Pentagon did a study to see how well that prison complied with Geneva Conventions. The study indicated it met criteria for humane treatment of detainees, but it recommended one thing: increasing human contact for prisoners (Glaberson, 2009).

In all the examples listed above some form of touching, proximity, and connection is involved, but what makes contact what it is? *Contact* is a central construct in gestalt therapy, so it needs a closer look.

Definition of Contact

Contact has been described as the central fact of human life, as well as the life of all organisms, and it can be understood as "meetings of various kinds with others" (Crocker, 1999, p. 18). Contact also means being in touch with what is emerging in the moment (Yontef & Jacobs, 2007). Contact is the means for changing oneself and one's experience of the world (Polster & Polster, 1973). In the context of gestalt therapy, contact means "*aware meeting with the other.* Such contact is possible only where there is awareness of difference, of what is not-me" (Crocker, 2008, p. 132).

> The Gestalt therapy interest in awareness in the field leads to a focus on the relation of the elements of the field. Seen from our individual point of view, rather than another position in the field, it is a focus on our relation to the environment. We call this encounter, or meeting, or even dialogue, but primarily we call it contact.... Contact can be described in terms of its distinguishing characteristic, its location, and its primary dimension. Its distinguishing quality is the meeting of differences. Its location we call the contact boundary, and the fundamental organizing quality of contact we call figure/ground. (Latner, 2000, p. 22)

Contact, then, can be rather vague, but it can also be specific and sharp. Being in the physical proximity of another person is a meeting of a kind that may come with a low level of awareness of the nearby individual and his or her differences; it may not be very satisfying, and the figure of that other person might be unclear. At that level, contact is superficial and a poor gestalt. However, on the occasion that someone emerges for me from a crowd, and I introduce myself and start talking with that person about himself or herself, the figure of that other person becomes clear, the contact becomes more bright, and the gestalt takes on heightened quality. The difference between these two experiences is such that many gestalt therapists would say the first is not really contact at all (or at best fore contact—the initial stage in contacting). Others would say that being embedded in some kind of environmental surround provides at least minimal contact without which we could not survive.

Another way of looking at contact, though, is not as an object in itself but more of a process. Contacting consists of connecting, separating, moving, and being aware (Yontef, 1993), and people are always in some stage of contacting with regard to the people and things that inhabit their worlds.

We are built *for* contacting, and we are programmed to learn and grow *through* contact.[3] At a basic developmental and sensory level, the reaching-for and the touching-while-seeing of objects in early infancy (6–9 months or so) lays down an initial neural map for physical contact between a human being and his or her environment that provides a neural capacity for subsequent contactful experience (Corbetta & Snapp-Childs, 2009). Mirror neurons are generated through perceptual-motor activity (for instance as the infant senses himself or herself reaching and grasping), and subsequently, the person is primed to intuit meaning in the observed actions of others (Del Guidice, Manera, & Keysers, 2009), establish meaningful social communication, and understand others' intentions, emotions, and sensations (Gallese, Rochat, Cossu, & Sinigaglia, 2009)—all this at a pretheoretical level. However, this is not a confluence, a blurring of the sense of self and other; rather, it is what provides the subvenient capacity for the supervenient experience of self-and-other.

Mind, or self, is said to emerge from the activity of the brain as the person meets the actual world (or the imagined or remembered world) and the brain is engaged in whatever situation is at hand, even while sleeping. Mind is said to be *supervenient* on brain, which is then understood as *subvenient*. These are two distinct characteristics of a person—a substance monism but a property dualism.

> Emergence has been defined as what happens when entities or processes are combined at a higher level of integration. Some features of the world *emerge out of* others. Not all

> the qualities of these new features are necessarily logical or predictable consequences of the properties of the components (Hefner, 2000). Furthermore, whereas "the emergent property is dependent on the lower-level abilities (i.e., cannot exist in the absence of these lower abilities), the emergent property cannot be understood by close scrutiny of the lower abilities, nor can the behavior in the realm of the emergent property be totally accounted for using the descriptive concepts of the lower-level phenomena." (Brown, 1998, p. 102) Gestalt therapists understand this, because we have long affirmed that the whole is greater than the sum of its parts. Thus, when the organism engages in the process of contacting in the environment, the material components interface at a heightened state of excitement and what emerges is the immaterial experience of self. I claim in this article that the higher level of integration required for emergence takes place in the frontal lobes, where self-regulation takes on aspects of agency and helps form the experience of self. (Brownell, 2009, p. 73)

The sense of the transcendence of the other, which at this pretheoretical level is a saturated phenomenon that surprises and exceeds one's expectation, overwhelming one's horizon (Smith, 2002), is what creates the sense of self-and-other in contact. It is unpredicted, abrupt, and unlooked-for. Gestalt therapists know this flood-of-other experience to be exciting and potentially unnerving. In dialogue (see below), it is the I-Thou moment.

DIALOGUE

If a relationship is contact over time, then dialogue is the discourse of relationship. This is true regardless of what dimension of the field one is talking about. Martin Buber, for instance, originated the philosophy of dialogue by considering his sense of his own dialogic relationship with God (Seltzer, 1952/1988). Maurice Friedman, Buber's biographer, wrote

> The basic paradox of the Hebrew Bible is the dialogue between eternal God and mortal man, between the imageless Absolute

> and man who is created in God's "image." If that dialogue is to take place, it must take place not in eternity but in the present—in the unique situation of a limited man who was born yesterday and will die tomorrow. (Friedman, 1992, p. 5)

Dialogue can take place between one person and another, and it can take place between a human person and the Divine Person. That is the crux of a theistic approach to a spiritual perspective in gestalt therapy, and it underlies therapeutic work with many religious clients (Brownell, 2006, in press a, in press b; Carpenter, 1997; Norberg, 2006). Gary Yontef asserted that a gestalt therapy notion of spirituality included the I-Thou and the I-It: "man's dialogue with God depends on the dialogue of person-to-person and the person-to-person dialogue can exist only against the background of the dialogue between humanity and God" (Yontef, 1993, p. 17).

Dialogue in gestalt therapy is most associated with the work of Martin Buber. However, the intersubjectivity present in dialogue has also been described by psychoanalytic writers such as George Atwood, Donna Orange, and Robert Stolorow (Jacobs, 2002), and many gestalt therapists have begun to identify themselves as "relational" gestalt therapists[2] in the process of following their discussion. Dialogue emerges out of the dialogic attitude in support of presence, acceptance, and commitment to the process.

The Dialogical Attitude

The dialogic attitude is a stance the therapist takes with regard to the client. It is not necessary for the client to return such a stance, although, if the client were to do so, then a dialogic moment might ensue (Hycner & Jacobs, 1995). What is necessary is that the therapist assume this orientation toward the client, such that the therapist practices presence, acceptance, and commitment, as described below. This is not the same thing as unconditional positive regard; this is a process orientation, and it goes beyond a way of thinking about the client as a separate object to orienting the therapist toward the connection that is forming between them.

Presence

Presence is self-disclosure. It is a decision to be real. It is an orientation the therapist takes with regard to the client; the therapist shows up as the authentic person he or she happens to be (Gold & Zahm, 2008). This comes with a relative degree of transparency (Yontef & Bar-Yoseph, 2008). This transparency is both verbal and nonverbal; the therapist cannot help but reveal, and instead of fighting this, or putting on a façade of professionalism, the therapist "sits down" with the client as he or she actually is.

> Authenticity is a matter of living the truth about oneself, which presupposes that a person actually knows him or herself. People have wondered for centuries if there might be a "self" inside somewhere that can be discovered. The classic statement of the mid-life crisis is, "I've got to find myself," but where can one find that? There is no outward trip, no spa, no guru outside oneself that can lead the way. Rather, it's a matter of settling down into the daily process of experiencing in which one finds such things as attraction or revulsion, interest or boredom. (Brownell, 2008b, pp. 216–217)

The interest and respect the therapist has for the client

> shows in gesture, tone, affect as well as in what the therapist says and how he or she says it. The therapist may share how he or she is affected at the moment, associations of emotional experiences, imagery triggered by what the patient is going through, and so forth. (Yontef & Bar-Yoseph, 2008, p. 190)

Therapist presence is not something unique to gestalt therapy (Viederman, 2008), but it has been resident in gestalt praxis from the inception of the gestalt approach. It extends to being courteous in caring for the client's sense of being accepted and considered (Pinkerton, 2008), the use of the body (Avstreih, 2008; Kepner, 2001), and the trust that develops between therapist and client (Barth, 2008). This is a particular kind of trust; it's the belief that the therapist will not deceive or take advantage of the client, that the therapist will "be real."

For example, once a mother brought her young adolescent son to me, because he had instigated an intimidating assault on another boy at school. He lured the boy into an area where others were waiting for him; someone grabbed the boy's arms from behind and held him while others harassed him and my client threatened him. As my client told this story, he smirked gleefully, and I felt anger rising within me. I felt compassion for the boy who had been bullied. I let the anger out enough for it to be evident in my demeanor, and I said to the young client, "That makes me angry! I would not like it if someone did that to you." I said it with congruent affect, and he was startled by my presentation. His own affect changed, and he became more subdued; in subsequent sessions he set aside his aloof and superior attitude, and he began to share more of his own torment at having to be at that school.

Acceptance

Acceptance of what is has been magnified to a form of therapy often used to augment cognitive and behavioral therapies, which is known as Acceptance and Commitment Therapy (ACT) (Roemer, Erisman, & Orsillo, 2009; Roemer & Orsillo, 2009). In ACT, acceptance "refers to the conscious abandonment of a mental and emotional change agenda (when change efforts do not work) and an openness to one's own emotions and the experience of others" (Callaghan, Gregg, Marx, Kohlenberg, & Gifford, 2004). These are things that make ACT consilient with the paradoxical theory of change in gestalt therapy (Beisser, 1970; Yontef, 2007). While these things are not exactly what is meant by acceptance with regard to dialogue, they convey some key ingredients.

Acceptance (also called "inclusion" in gestalt therapy) is a welcoming, a receiving, a tolerating, a confirming, and a trusting decision of the self with regard to an Other. When the therapist adopts a dialogical attitude and attempts to create the conditions that might support meaningful contact and dialogue, he or she accepts the client however that person might enter into fore contact and then proceed through to completed contact without an agenda for change. The therapist extends himself or herself to greet or embrace the client. The therapist then "collects" whatever is given, whatever the client is presenting of himself or herself, and the therapist tolerates (in the sense of bracketing) whatever seems odd, awkward, strange, or offensive. In confirming the presentation of the client, the therapist extends trust in the client, and trust that this tentative meeting will turn out well, trust that the client will respond and further the process, and trust in the process itself—that, come what may, the field will provide what is necessary.

In clinical practice this can be illustrated by contrasting two individuals with whom I worked on the locked unit of a co-occurring disorders psychiatric hospital. The first was schizophrenic and was floridly psychotic, while the other was a sociopathic murderer.

When I sat down with the hallucinating patient, I accepted his presentation *as it was*. He was having a hard time talking with me, because the chorus of voices in his mind made it sometimes impossible to listen to *me*. I did not demand that he blot them out or that we give up talking until his medications had blunted his psychotic symptoms. Rather, I observed that at times he was not responsive to something I had said, and he admitted that it was because he often could not pay attention or could not tell it had been me talking. The effort for him to stay there with me and try to communicate was exhausting for him, and I accepted that as well, observing aloud the various phenomena associated with his presence and the courage and tenacity it required of him to try to communicate.

The sociopathic patient was often sullen and dismissive of staff, if not downright intimidating. He was a large man. If you knew his history, it was difficult not to fear in his presence. I did not demand that he be nice and obey all the rules before I could talk with him. I purposefully determined to practice a dialogical inclusion or acceptance with him. I had come fresh from a training lecture with Lynne Jacobs in which I had raised the issue of antisocial people who do horrible things in my questioning of this acceptance, and she had remarked, "Phil, I think you're still trying to change the person." She meant, change the person in order to make him or her acceptable in some way. So, with my sociopathic patient I determined to accept him as a person who was as much a mystery to me as any other, and to make myself present to him for whatever kind of contact he might be able to muster. It took some warming, some time. Eventually, though, his attending psychiatrist wrote me a note thanking me for my work with the man and remarking that he believed I may have been the only person this murderer had ever trusted with his feelings.

This acceptance of the client by the therapist opens up the possibility of the client's acceptance of himself or herself (Hycner & Jacobs, 1995). When both client and therapist accept their experience of being-in-situation—that is, with one another (which is an in vivo experience), at that instant—then a dialogical moment has arrived.

Commitment

Commitment is a devotion to the process of what is going on between therapist and client. It is a dedication and faithfulness; it is the resolution that one is engaged for the duration. Seen from the perspective of the therapist, commitment means that the therapist will not turn and run from resistance, impasse, his or her own anxiety, boredom, or whatever else presents itself in the process of meeting the client. The therapist is given to abiding *with* the Other to the extent possible (Crocker, 1999).

For example, I once had a young boy who refused to talk with me. His mother brought him to the community mental health center where I was working at the time, but the boy simply refused to talk. We spent several sessions in which I waited on him. We sat in complete silence for an hour each time. Eventually, circumstances changed at home, and he became a ward of the court, at which time he was transferred to a residential facility. That is when he softened with me a bit. As soon as he did that, I engaged him and we began working together looking at truck designs he was interested in and that we could find on the internet. If I had not simply waited on him, being committed to the process, however that process was unfolding, he would not have had a therapist when his family situation became more challenging.

RELATIONSHIP

Relationship can be impersonal or personal. Impersonal relationships could be a causal relationship between two variables or simply a correlation between them. Personal relationships could be a sexual relationship between two people or simply a friendship between them. A relationship is a connection between two or more variables, objects, or subjects. When this connection is between two people, it can be thought of as contact over time.

> Gestalt therapy is thoroughly relational in its philosophy, personality theory, clinical methodology, and practice. The gestalt therapy perspective is that all phenomena are constructed and organized by relational processes. Even inanimate events and configurations that appear to be set by their nature rather than their relationship with contextual forces are viewed as constructed and organized by the relationship of the multiple influences of the entire field of which they are part. (Yontef & Bar-Yoseph, 2008, p. 184)

Martin Buber and Emmanuel Levinas shared the same perspective regarding the importance of the Other, but whereas Buber was focused on the *relationship* between I and Thou, Levinas was focused on the *other person* in an I-Thou relationship. Whether or not it is a human person or the Divine Person, whether the relationship is between one human being and another or between a human being and God, Buber and Levinas regarded the same issues to be relevant:

> Martin Buber (Buber, 1952/1988) asserted that a complete inclusion of the divine within the sphere of the human would effectively abolish its divinity. Levinas would say that it would make the divine Other the "same" as oneself, confining God to one's thematization(Levinas, 1998, 1999). Buber further claimed that if a person were to dare to turn toward God, in a face-to-face meeting, and to call out to Him, then "Reality" would meet him. Levinas would say that this sentient meeting constitutes the enjoyment of God, experienced directly and immediately in the course of embodied living, as opposed to

> an objectification of God through intentional representation (Critchley, 2002). With such a perspective, if a person refuses to limit God to the transcendent, he will have a fuller conception of God than the one who does so limit Him; conversely, if a person limits God to only the immanent, then it is not actually the divine Being one is talking about. (Brownell, in press a, in press b, np; Buber, 1952/1988)

If you insert "another human being" where the preceding quotation refers to God, the same things would apply. In a relationship, if a person refuses to limit the other person to the unknowable and inscrutable (i.e., transcendent), a more complete conception of that person will emerge; conversely, if a person limits the other in a relationship to only what is immediately seen and heard, one will not be considering the actual being of the other person, for we are all more than what is available for others to observe.

Just what a relationship is changes depending on the antecedent in the construction, "A relationship is _______." A relationship is a partnership. A relationship is a romance. A relationship is a friendship. A relationship is a kinship. A relationship is an alliance.

What is in view is some kind of connection between two people. Interestingly, when researchers conduct dyadic data analysis, they admit to one overarching construct in dyadic relationships—nonindependence (Kenny, Kashy, & Cook, 2006). Whatever the descriptive antecedent might be in the statement, "A relationship is _____," nonindependence characterizes the statements and behaviors of each individual in it.

Nonindependence is a technical term that addresses a distinctive feature of the two people involved with one another. Experimental psychologists describe nonindependence as follows:

> If the two scores from the two members of the dyad are nonindependent, then those two scores are more similar to (or different from) one another than are two scores from two people who are not members of the same dyad. The heightened

> similarity (or dissimilarity) of scores from dyads is the critical issue.... Our discussion tends to focus on nonindependence that results from close interpersonal relationships such as friendships, married or dating couples, and roommates. However, similar issues may arise when the two individuals are initially strangers who have just met in the laboratory or on the Internet. Nonindependence can even occur when two people never actually interact but share a common experience; for example, two patients of the same physician. (Kenny, Kashy, & Cook, 2006, p. 4)

Here, in the language of the statistician, is recognition that in a relationship between two people one has left behind the sheer individuality of one-person dynamics. A relationship is a two-person field that may, in turn, be embedded within wider and more comprehensive fields. In a relationship, the contact over time can be understood only as a couple process, and the same is true when the dyad in question is the therapist–client relationship. It is never a matter solely of what the therapist does, nor solely of what the client does. Rather, it is an interaction of nonindependence and a matter of what they do together.

This relational matrix is shown in Table 5.1.

By extension, nonindependence applies to webs of relationships, extending from couples to families, small groups, and communities. In these webs of relationships, one can imagine various matrices like the one in Table 5.1, for they constantly form and dissolve, and reform with different partners, and they are the basis for understanding larger networks in the field.

Table 5.1

THE RELATIONAL MATRIX

	THERAPIST PRESENCE	THERAPIST ACCEPTANCE
Client presence		
Client acceptance		

CONCLUSION

One might say that the developments from the early 1970s to the present around contact and relationship in gestalt therapy parallel those in other approaches to psychotherapy, but gestalt therapists claim that the seminal ideas in Perls, Hefferline, and Goodman (1951) parallel or precede Carl Rogers's interpersonal ideas (both were part of the same humanistic third wave, but gestalt therapy really has a different root in continental philosophy and neuroscience). Indeed, from one perspective, the wider field of psychotherapy is catching up to the revolutionary ideas that were present in gestalt therapy from its beginning. As an example, consider the following list of clinical and theoretical innovations in contemporary psychodynamically oriented psychotherapy:

- A shift from understanding clinical material in terms of a one-person model to understanding these issues through a two-person model or field;
- A similar shift from attributing therapeutic gain to accurate therapist interpretations to attributing improvement to the provision of a collaborative therapeutic relationship;
- A shift from therapeutic neutrality and detachment toward acceptance of the usefulness of overt expressions of the therapist's caring;
- A similar shift from analytic anonymity toward acceptance of the usefulness of therapist disclosure to clients (Farber, 2007, p. 292).

This list indicates that a dialogical relationship is related to the field (see chapter 6), and it identifies the recognition by colleagues outside the discipline of gestalt therapy that therapist presence and authentic self-disclosure are beneficial aspects of a therapeutic relationship. A therapeutic relationship in gestalt therapy is built on contact, a dialogical attitude, presence, acceptance, commitment, and the realization that the dialogic relationship is a two-person field in which both therapist and client are affected and apt to change in some way.

NOTES

1. Original translation from the text of the Greek New Testament (3rd ed.), Stuttgart, Germany: United Bible Societies.
2. The Pacific Gestalt Institute (www.gestalttherapy.org), led by Gary Yontef and Lynne Jacobs, is a central influence for this emphasis in gestalt therapy.
3. The contact cycle consists of four stages: fore-contact, contacting, full contact, and post contact. These are elucidated in a number of texts starting with Perls, Hefferline, and Goodman (1951) and continuing through Seán Gaffney's (2009) useful article comparing the contact cycle with the cycle of experience. The cycle of experience has various versions but usually consists of six stages: sensation, awareness, mobilization of energy, action/contact, assimilation, and withdrawal.

REFERENCES

Antonietta, A., Cocomazzi, D., & Iannelo, P. (2009). Looking at the audience improves music appreciation. *Journal of Nonverbal Behavior, 33*(2), 89–106.

Avstreih, Z. (2008). The body in psychotherapy: Dancing with the paradox. In F. Kaklauskas, S. Nimanheminda, L. Hoffman, & M. Jack (Eds.), *Brilliant sanity: Buddhist approaches to psychotherapy* (pp. 213–221). Colorado Springs, CO: University of the Rockies Press.

Barth, F. D. (2008). Hidden eating disorders: Attachment and affect regulation in the therapeutic relationship. *Clinical Social Work Journal, 36*(4), 355–365.

Beisser, A. (1970). The paradoxical theory of change. In J. Fagan & I. Shepherd (Eds.), *Gestalt therapy now: Theory, techniques, and applications* (pp.77–80). Palo Alto, CA: Science and Behavior Books.

Binder, J., Zagefka, H., Brown, R., Funke, F., Kessler, T., Mummendey, A., et al. (2009). Does contact reduce prejudice or does prejudice reduce contact? A longitudinal test of the contact hypothesis among majority and minority groups in three European countries. *Journal of Personality and Social Psychology, 96*(4), 843–856.

Brown, W. (1998). Cognitive contributions to soul. In W. Brown, N. Murphey, & H. Malony (Eds.), *Whatever happened to the soul? Scientific and theological portraits of human nature*. Minneapolis, MN: Fortress Press.

Brownell, P. (2006). This is what I know—a response to "spirituality and gestalt: A gestalt-transpersonal perspective." *Gestalt Review, 10*(1), 26–32.

Brownell, P. (2008a). Practice-based evidence. In P. Brownell (Ed.), *Handbook for theory, research, and practice in gestalt therapy* (pp. 90–103). Newcastle, England: Cambridge Scholars.

Brownell, P. (2008b). Faith: An existential, phenomenological, and biblical integration. In J. H. Ellens (Ed.) *Miracles: God, science, and psychology in the paranormal, vol. 2, medical and therapeutic events* (pp. 213–234). Westport, CT: Praeger.

Brownell, P. (2009). Executive functions: A neuropsychological understanding of self-regulation. *Gestalt Review, 13*(1), 62–81.

Brownell, P. (in press a). Spirituality in gestalt therapy. In T. L. Bar-Yoseph (Ed.), *From the here and now to the future—advancing gestalt theory and practice*, np. New York: Routledge.

Brownell, P. (in press b). Spirituality in the praxis of gestalt therapy. In J. H. Ellens (Ed.), *The healing power of spirituality, how religion helps humans thrive, vol 3, The psychodynamics of healing spirituality and religion*, np. Westport, CT: Praeger.

Buber, M. (1952/1988). *Eclipse of God: Studies in the relation between religion and philosophy*. Amherst: Humanity Books.

Callahan, G., Gregg, J., Marx, B., Kohlenberg, B., & Gifford, E. (2004). FACT: The utility of an integration of functional analytic psychotherapy and acceptance and commitment therapy to alleviate human suffering. *Psychotherapy: Theory, Research, Practice, Training, 41*(3), 195–207.

Carpenter, D. (1997). Ethical considerations in working with religious clients. *Gestalt!, 1*(2), np. Downloaded June 4, 2009, from http://www.g-gej.org./1-2/religious_clients.html.

Chiu, S-H, Anderson, G. C., & Burkhammer, M. D. (2008) Skin-to-skin contact for culturally diverse women having breastfeeding difficulties during early postpartum. *Breastfeeding Medicine, 3*(4), 231–237.

Corbetta, D., & Snapp-Childs, W. (2009). Seeing and touching: The role of sensory-motor experience on the development of infant reaching. *Infant Behavior & Development, 32*(1), 44–58.

Crisp, R., & Turner, R. (2009). Can imagined interactions produce positive perceptions?: Reducing prejudice through simulated social contact. *American Psychologist, 64*(4), 231–240.

Critchley, S. (2002). Introduction. In S. Critchley & R. Bernasconi (Eds.), *The Cambridge companion to Levinas* (pp. 1–32). Cambridge, UK: Cambridge University Press.

Crocker, S. (1999). *A well-lived life: Essays in gestalt therapy*. Cambridge, MA: Gestalt Institute of Cleveland Press.

Crocker, S. (2008). A unified theory. In P. Brownell (Ed.), *Handbook for theory, research, and practice in gestalt therapy* (pp. 124–150). Newcastle, England: Cambridge Scholars.

Del Guidice, M., Manera, V., & Keysers, C. (2009) Programmed to learn? The ontogeny of mirror neurons. *Developmental Science, 12*(2), 350–363.

Farber, B. (2007). On the enduring and substantial influence of Carl Rogers' not-quite necessary nor sufficient conditions. *Psychotherapy: Theory, Research, Practice, Training, 44*(3), 289–294.

Friedman, M. (1992). *Religion and psychology: A dialogical approach*. New York: Paragon House.

Friedman, M. (2002). *Martin Buber: The life of dialogue*. London: Routledge.

Gaffney, S. (2009) The cycle of experience re-cycled: Then, now . . . next? *Gestalt Review, 13*(1), 7–23.

Gallese, V., Rochat, M., Cossu, G., & Sinigaglia, C. (2009). Motor cognition and its role in the phylogeny and ontogeny of action understanding. *Developmental Psychology, 45*(1), 103–113.

Glaberson, W. (February 21, 2009). Guantanamo meets Geneva rules, Pentagon study finds. *New York Times*, 158(54, 593).

Gold, E., & Zahm, S. (2008). Gestalt therapy. In M. Herson & A. Gross (Eds.), *Handbook of clinical psychology, vol. 1, Adults* (pp. 585–616). Hoboken, NJ: John Wiley.

Hayat, P. (1999). Preface. In E. Levinas, *Alterity and transcendence* (pp. ix–xxiv). New York: Columbia University Press.

Hedberg, P. Brulin, C., & Aléx, L. (2009). Experiences of purpose in life when becoming and being a very old woman. *Journal of Women and Aging, 21*(2), 125–137.

Hefner, P. (2000). Imago dei: The possibility and necessity of the human person. In N. Gregersen, W. Dress, & U. Gorman (Eds.), *The human person in science and theology*. Grand Rapids, MI: Wm. B. Eerdmans.

Hycner, R., & Jacobs, L. (1995). *The healing relationship in gestalt therapy: A dialogic/self psychology approach.* Highland, NY: Gestalt Journal Press.

Jacobs, L. (2002). It's not easy to be a field theorist: Commentary on "cartesian and post-cartesian trends in relational psychoanalysis" In R. Stolorow, D. Orange, & G. Atwood, *Gestalt!*, 6(2), np. Downloaded June 26, 2009, from http://www.g-gej.org/6-2/jacobsreview.html.

Kenny, D., Kashy, D., & Cook, W. (2006). *Dyadic data analysis*. New York: Guilford Press.

Kepner, J. (2001). *Body process: A gestalt approach to working with the body in psychotherapy.* Cambridge, MA: Gestalt Press.

Latner, J. (2000). The theory of gestalt therapy. In E. Nevis (Ed.), *Gestalt therapy: Perspectives and applications* (pp. 13–56). Cambridge, MA: Gestalt Press.

Levinas, E. (1998). *Of God who comes to mind.* Stanford, CA: Stanford University Press.

Levinas, E. (1999). *Alterity and transcendence*. New York: Columbia University Press.

Moran, D. (2002). *Introduction to phenomenology*. New York: Routledge.

Norberg, T. (2006). *Consenting to grace*. Staten Island, NY: Penn House.

Perls, F., Hefferline, R., & Goodman, P. (1951). *Gestalt therapy: Excitement and growth in the human personality.* New York: Julian Press.

Pinkerton, R. (2008). "I apologize for being late": The courteous psychotherapist. *Psychotherapy: Theory, Research, Practice, Training, 45*(2), 273–277.

Polster, E., & Polster, M. (1973). *Gestalt therapy integrated: Contours of theory and practice.* New York: Vintage Book/Random House.

Roemer, L., Erisman, S., & Orsillo, S. (2009). Mindfulness and acceptance-based treatments for anxiety disorders. In M. Antony & M. Stein (Eds.), *Oxford handbook of anxiety and related disorders* (pp 476–487). Oxford, England: Oxford Library of Psychology.

Roemer, L., & Orsillo, S. (2009). *Mindfulness- and acceptance-based behavioral therapies in practice.* New York: Guilford Press.

Rogers, C. (2007). The necessary and sufficient conditions of therapeutic personality change. *Psychotherapy: Theory, Research, Practice, Training, 44*(3), 240–248.

Seltzer, R. (1952/1988). Introduction. In M.Buber *Eclipse of God: Studies in the relation between religion and philosophy*, pp. ix–xxii. Amherst, MA: Humanity Books.

Smith, J. K. A. (2002). *Speech and theology: Language and the logic of incarnation.* New York: Routledge.

Viederman, M. (2008). A model for interpretative supportive dynamic psychotherapy. *Psychiatry: Interpersonal and Biological Process, 71*(4), 349–358.

Waldenfels, B. (2002). Levinas and the face of the other. In S. Critchley & R. Bernasconi (Eds.), *The Cambridge companion to Levinas* (pp. 63–81). Cambridge, UK: Cambridge University Press.

Yontef, G. (1993). *Awareness dialogue and process: Essays on gestalt therapy*. Highland, NY: Gestalt Journal Press.

Yontef, G. (2007). The power of the immediate moment in gestalt therapy. *Journal of Contemporary Psychotherapy, 37*(1), 17–23.

Yontef, G., & Bar-Yoseph, T. L. (2008). Dialogical relationship. In P. Brownell (Ed.), *Handbook for theory, research, and practice in gestalt therapy* (pp. 184–197). Newcastle, England: Cambridge Scholars.

Yontef, G., & Jacobs, L. (2007). Gestalt therapy. In R. Corsini & D. Wedding (Eds.), *Current psychotherapies* (8th ed., pp. 328–367). Florence, KY: Cengage.

Zank, M. (2007). Martin Buber. In E. N. Zalta (Ed.), *The Stanford encyclopedia of philosophy*. Downloaded June 4, 2009, from http://plato.stanford.edu/entries/buber.

6 Use the Context of Life

This chapter describes gestalt therapy's understanding of "the field," a concept brought from physical to social science in the work of Kurt Lewin, as constituting all things having affect through overlapping spheres of influence. Thus, the "life spaces" of both the client and the therapist become relevant to therapeutic process, and the reader is shown how to utilize the field in practice. Comparisons with and contrasts to organizational and family systems are also provided, and the dyadic field constructed in the therapeutic alliance, so in view with intersubjective systems psychoanalysis/relational psychoanalysis, is also considered.

Gestalt therapists have been chewing on field theory since Perls, Hefferline, and Goodman (1951) wrote their basic text. The implications of field theory for gestalt's approach to psychotherapy are still being worked out. Gordon Wheeler introduced a more contemporary discussion of it in *Gestalt Reconsidered* (1996), continued that discussion in *Beyond Individualism* (2000), and added still further to it in his collaborative work with Mark McConville (McConville & Wheeler, 2001; Wheeler & McConville, 2002). Malcolm Parlett is also known for his explorations of field theory in gestalt therapy (Parlett, 1991, 1997, 2005), and Frank Steammler (2006) wrote a wonderful article clarifying the terminology used to refer to the field. Brian O'Neill (2008) and his responders discussed field theory from the perspective of the relativistic, quantum field, and Brian O'Neill and Seán Gaffney (2008) developed their "field perspective" by bringing together Lewin's conception of the field with that of contemporary physics.

In virtually every text on gestalt therapy for nearly the past two decades writers have considered field theory as theory, which is ironic, as the man most closely associated with the development of field theory for the social sciences, Kurt Lewin (Kounin, 1963; Massarik, 2000), did not consider it so much a *theory* as a *method*.

> Field theory, therefore, can hardly be called correct or incorrect in the same way as a theory in the usual sense of the term. *Field theory is probably best characterized as a method:* namely, a method *of analyzing causal relations and of building scientific constructs.* This method of analyzing causal relations can be expressed in the form of certain general statements about the "nature" of the conditions of change. (Lewin, 1943, p. 294)

That field theory is a method is reflected in the title of O'Neill's and Gaffney's (2008) chapter, which refers to a field-theoretical *strategy* in gestalt therapy. Whereas Lewin conceived of field theory as a way of conducting research, gestalt therapists utilize field theory as a way of doing psychotherapy. As such, it shares kinship with the conceptualization of complex, adaptive systems and is consilient with family systems and group therapy as well as with organizational dynamics for people working with large groups or groups within organizational systems.

This chapter will discuss the theory of the field as understood in gestalt therapy in order to talk about how gestalt therapists might use the field perspective in working with their clients.

THE CONCEPT OF FIELD

Kurt Lewin contributed a great deal to the concept of the field, but he was not the only one to do so. Henry Murray spoke of a needs-and-press, Kurt Goldstein spoke of the organism and its relationship to the environment, and Gardner Murphy spoke of the biosocial situation. All four have something to say to gestalt therapists about the field, even though only Goldstein and Lewin were direct influences in the development of gestalt therapy. What this shows, however, is that the developing idea of a field was a widespread phenomenon and one that continues to evolve as the ripples of these various theorists spread throughout clinical psychology.

Goldstein came to his field-theoretical conceptualizations while working with brain-injured patients after World War I and in adopting a holistic view of the human organism. As Richard Lazarus (1961) described Goldstein's thinking,

> Self-actualization requires that an individual come to terms with the environment. It must take place in an environment that impinges upon the organism, disturbing its equilibrium and requiring it to act to restore the balance. To actualize itself, the organism must search in the environment for what it needs. Coming to terms with the environment represents a kind of adaptive interaction between the organism and the environment. The environment provides the means by which self-actualization can be achieved, although it can also obstruct self-actualization by excessive demands or by the scarcity of the means to self-actualization. (p. 120)

In referring to what he called a "man–world entity," Goldstein himself said that he considered the mental capacity of a subject and came to the conclusion that what he observed was not a function of the mind/brain alone. Rather, the behavior he observed represented living events and was not the result of intellectual activities—the brain/mind alone directing the person:

> I could no longer accept the assumption that experience is the product of mind or brain functions alone, especially after it became my conviction that the external world is always connected with it.... The study of the world of the brain-injured proved to be no less important to our knowledge than the study of the disturbance of the performance. Indeed, though the patient's behavior is certainly determined by the brain

> defect, it can only be understood as a phenomenon going on in the totality of his modified personality in relation to the world. The holistic approach induced me to bring psychophysical relationship into the foreground. It became obvious that it was directed by the tendency to come to terms with the world in which the individual feels he lives. (Goldstein, 1967, pp. 161–162)

Kurt Lewin's term for the field was "life space," and to him that meant "the totality of coexisting facts that influence the behavior of an individual at a particular time" (Kounin, 1963, p. 142). Although Lewin spoke of a psychological field, he included as contributing aspects of such a field one's perception, the character of the person, one's motivation, one's cognitive processes, thus one's way of perceiving and making meaning out of experience, and what he called the *stimulus distribution* "by physical processes outside the organism" (Lewin, 1943, p. 307). That sets up a bipolar perspective on the field in which one contemplates a person's experience (one's phenomenal field) and environmental context (one's ontic field).

How to Talk About the Field

Obviously, some time has elapsed since Lewin worked on his ideas. Gestalt therapists do not approach the field by utilizing the mathematical formulas that Lewin did in his topological psychology. Many gestalt therapists do not recognize a separation of the person from the person's various contexts of life. They do not speak of the person *and* the field, or of the field exerting pressure *on* the person; they speak of the person–environment field or of the organism *of* the field. Some gestalt therapists have also begun speaking of the field as if it were alive and sentient. In this way of seeing things, the person becomes the aware agent of the field and a means for the field to choose, change course, and direct itself. For other gestalt therapists, that goes too far and leaves behind the individual.

Frank Steammler (2006) asked that gestalt therapists define what they mean by the term "field" whenever they refer to it, because he observed that usage of the term had become quite sloppy, such that one never was quite sure whether a person meant the field as Lewin (1951) conceived of it, as Perls, Hefferline, and Goodman (1951) conceived of it, or just as a catch-all category for mysterious forces at work in people's lives, and he called for more precision that would also admit that the field is specific to a given person. That is, there is not one giant field that is the same for all people; rather, there is a unified field relative to each person.

I will attempt in this chapter to define further what I mean by "unified" and "relative to each person," for I hold to a field perspective that integrates Lewin's and Goldstein's perspectives on the field, as well as some of the ideas of other field theorists not usually mentioned in the history of the development of gestalt therapy theory. The reason for this approach is that gestalt therapy is a living and evolving praxis; it assimilates wherever helpful concepts and practices can be found that harmonize with its core.

The Situation as Field

The person who comes for therapy is regarded as part of a situation; thus, to observe that person and to understand the direction and force, so to speak, of what is going on with them, a therapist must take stock of the scope of the situation. Thus, another way of conceptualizing the field is to refer to the "situation."

The field consists of "all the complex interactive phenomena of individuals and their environment. Gestalt field theory looks at the total situation, affirming and respecting wholeness and complexity" (MacKewn, 1997, pp. 48–49).

In an early description of field dynamics, Gardner Murphy described the situation by saying that whatever is real at any given moment is part of the interaction of the organism and environment that makes up the situation. In this way of speaking he anticipated the language of contemporary field theorists, but he used the term "situation" to identify the person's field in action.

> The complexities of the environment are specified at the same time that the complexities of organic response are specified; personality is the going concern which is expressed by the interaction of the living system with the outer world.... But this seems to grant a good deal; hence the bewildered

> psychologist decides next to ask whether perceptual habits as well as emotional habits are part of the situation. When you speak of a situation, he says, do you mean the situation as *you* see it or as *your subject* sees it? Does not each stimulus field have a different stimulus value for each person? Does not each person experience the situation differently, selecting certain aspects of it, remaining blind to the others, and making his own personal organization of its attributes? Is not each situation, as a functionally real thing, determined in part by the individual who confronts it?...the situation is an expression of the full organism-environment relation; the individual's own perceptual habits are part of the situation. The situationist has had to grant the importance of much that goes beyond the question of roles played. Although the psychologist could hardly have wanted more, he asks a final question: Is not the present situation, then, a projection into the present of the structure of past situations; are not individual heredity and past experience relevant to the definition of today's situation? Surely, answers the situationist; all science follows the stream of time and regards the emergent present as an expression of continuing dynamic factors. (Murphy, 1947, p. 881)

Richard Lazarus (1961) considered Murphy to be fundamentally a field theorist like Lewin. For Murphy "the culture and the person cannot be independently defined. The personality is dependent upon the culture or the environment, and the culture cannot be conceived independently of the personalities of its members" (Lazarus, 1961, p. 133).

Dimensions, Networks, Domains, and Layers

Over time I have described field dynamics in various ways and so have my colleagues. Sylvia Crocker (1999) referred to "inseparable and interpenetrating dimensions," claiming that every human being "exists in numerous overlapping fields which influence his cognitions, feelings, and behavior" (pp. 17, 35). She later referred to the field as a "domain of interest" (2008, p. 129). People have used "sphere" in the same way as Crocker used "domain," saying, "the field is a sphere of influence in which experience occurs"

(Brownell, 2009a, p. 403). Joel Latner (2000) said, "The field perspective views all phenomena as inextricably linked, part of a vast network of interaction which is called the field" (p. 20). Kepner (2003) referred to an energetic field. More recently, Brian O'Neill (2008) referred to the "relativistic quantum field" and asserted that in that view people are the "instruments" of the field.

In 2001 portions of discussions on field theory held at Gstalt-L in 1998 were published in *Gestalt!* At that time Gerhard Stemberger made a helpful observation when he said:

> One has to distinguish strictly between the experienced, phenomenal world at the one hand, and the physical, transphenomenal world on the other hand. (1) My experienced, phenomenal world comprises not only my perceived environment (including my perceived body) but also my perceived bodily I (or, as LEWIN says: my life space comprises person and environment, meaning exclusively the phenomenal person and its phenomenal environment, not the physical organism and its physical environment). And this phenomenal world is not "neutral," but full of affordances, attractions, repulsions—it is a phenomenal FIELD in the strict sense of the EINSTEIN definition of a field. The physical bases of this phenomenal world are brain processes, but these cannot be perceived; they belong to the (2) transphenomenal world, which comprises my physical body and its physical environment (including the physical bodies of other persons). There is NO field relation of any known quality (electric, magnetic, gravitational) between my physical body and my physical environment (though there is a physical field in the physical brain). The attraction, repulsion etc. which links me to the persons or distances me from them are not the outcome of any field between our physical bodies, but in first instance of the field relations in my (and their respective) phenomenal worlds between the experienced I and the experienced others.
>
> [Viewed from this perspective, "organism," "environment" and so on are very ambiguous terms: one would have to clarify in each case, whether one is speaking of the physical body or the experienced body, of the physical environment or the experienced environment. Also the term "boundary" needs

> to be specified: is one talking about the boundary between the physical body and its physical environment—which would be the physical skin—or is one talking about the boundary between my perceived person and my perceived environment.] (Stemberger, 1998, np)

In 1998 I used "layers" to describe what I later called "spheres" and also have referred to as "dimensions of a unified field." Frank Staemmler (2006) distinguished among several conceptualizations of "field," emphasizing the difference between Lewin's concepts and those expressed by Perls, Hefferline, and Goodman. (He also echoed Stemberger's thoughts along the way.) Perhaps it helps to see the consistency between two gestalt theorists working independently almost a decade apart; the two perspectives can be compared in Table 6.1.

Consider the following integrative description of Lewin's and Goldstein's/Perls, Hefferline, and Goodman's conceptions:

> As Lewin has described them, there are the lifespace (one's field), what is in the physical and social world that doesn't affect the life space (what is not one's field), and the boundary of the life space, which constitutes parts of the physical or social world that do effect the life space but which may be out of awareness. These boundary entities, then, are actually part of the field, for everything having an effect is part of one's field, or as Goldstein called it, one's milieu. In his metaphor, the organism adapts to fulfill these boundary requirements of its environment. (Goldstein, 1995, p. 99)
>
> That the boundary itself is part of the life space was described at an early point in the development of Gestalt therapy. Bringing together both the functional and structural metaphors, Perls and Goodman stated, ". . . contacting occurs at the surface-boundary *in* the field of the organism/environment." (Perls, Hefferlein, & Goodman, 1951, p. 303)
>
> The boundary constitutes the substantive layer of the field, with which one forms a contact style, and from which one organizes the experiential layer of the field. Perls described this relationship by saying, ". . . we assume there is an objective world from which the individual creates his subjective

> world . . ." (Perls, 1969, p. 38). Elements of this objective world that have effect comprise Lewin's boundary, and he observed that the process of perception "is intimately linked with this boundary zone because what is perceived is partly determined by the physical 'stimuli', i.e., that part of the physical world which affects the sensory organs at that time" [Lewin, 1951, p. 57]. (Brownell 1998, np)

Contrary to the thinking of Stemberger, Staemmler (2006), O'Neill and Gaffney (2008), and I (1998) have affirmed a physical

Table 6.1

DIFFERENT EXPRESSIONS/SIMILAR MEANINGS

STAEMMLER 2006	BROWNELL 1998
Lewin: The phenomenal person and the phenomenal environment form a shared field, within which their respective forces influence each other in the lifespace	Experiential layer: Lewin's model, the lifespace, is a functional figure (what would now be called the phenomenal field)
Goldstein: The transphenomenal field of organism and surround	Substantive layer: Goldstein's field is a structural/biological figure (what would now be called the ontic field)
Perls, Hefferline, and Goodman: Organism and environment cannot be separated, as they are integral parts of the same unitary field	Experiential and Substantive layers of the unified field
A "boundary zone" of the life space: Certain parts of the physical or social world do affect the state of the life space at that time. The process of perception, for instance, is intimately linked with this boundary zone because what is perceived is partly determined by the physical stimuli; i.e., that part of the physical world that affects the sensory organs at that time (Lewin, 1951, p. 57)	Goldstein wrote of an organism with a membrane that acts as a buffer connecting it to its environment; Lewin spoke of a boundary that actually constitutes part of a person's lifespace. The substantive layer of the field is this buffer/boundary, carrying engrams of experience through contact with things as they are (in a critically realistic understanding).

Source: Adapted from Staemmler, 2006, and Brownell 1998.

aspect to the field in Perls, Hefferline, and Goodman's thinking, and recently I maintained that there is a physical correlate to the boundary—the executive system of the brain largely associated with the frontal and prefrontal cortex. Quoting Goldberg (2001), I wrote:

> The choices we make are not inherent in the situations at hand. They are a complex interplay between the properties of the situations and our own properties, our aspirations, our doubts, and our histories. It is only logical to expect that the prefrontal cortex is central to such decision making, since it is the only part of the brain where the inputs from within the organism converge with the inputs from the outside world. [Goldberg, 2001, p. 78]
>
> In saying this, Goldberg marked the anatomy of what gestalt therapists would recognize as the "boundary," making a case for the frontal lobes as the neurological center of the experience of self.... This is an important point. As will be seen, the neurological processes of the brain correlate directly with the resulting emergent self of the organism, and both are intrinsically related to the executive functions associated with self-regulation as the human organism negotiates contacting. (Brownell, 2009b, pp. 70–71)

THE HERMENEUTICS OF FIELD

Hermeneutics is a whole subject in itself. For the purposes of this discussion, what started as a means of understanding biblical texts was transformed by Schleiermacher, Dilthey, Heidegger, and Gadamer into a means of understanding the facticity of life. This method presupposes a field perspective:

> if we are to understand anything at all, we must already find ourselves "in" the world "along with" that which is to be understood. All understanding that is directed at the grasp of some particular subject matter is thus based in a prior "onto-logical" understanding—a prior hermeneutical situatedness. (Malpas, 2009, np)

In Heidegger–Gadamer, hermeneutics is not a set of rules by which one recreates the subjective experience and meaning of the author of some text of antiquity; it is the means of discerning the situated interest of the contemporary person seeking to understand, for it is that which is most related to the meaning of the text or the work of art or the experience at hand *for* the one seeking understanding (for whom it might be said that the situation is that person's field). Having said that, Gadamer was not so much opposed to the standard rules of interpretation as interested in a priority that he regarded as preceding them. He conceived of the process of interpretation as a dialogue, a conversation, between the familiar and the alien in which one's horizons (Klein, Blomberg, & Hubbard, 1993/2004; Malpas, 2003) presented an existing interest that drew one to the issues inherent in the situation but also posed a limit upon what one might discover. Thus, the dialogue was a means of challenging and enlarging a given horizon. In this regard, Gadamer's interpretation resembles Jean-Luc Marion's understanding of the saturated phenomenon that overwhelms one's horizon in the presentation of what could not be imagined or expected because it comes from a truly transcendental Other (Marion, 2004; Smith, 2002).

Meaning-making is the activity of interpretation, and it is so whether one is interpreting texts, dramatic enactments, or the drama of everyday life. Blending perhaps the most prominent "rule" of traditional interpretation with Heidegger–Gadamer, one comes to the importance of contextualizing. In writing of biblical hermeneutics, Klein, Blomberg, and Hubbard (1993/2004) capture the twin horizons involved:

> Contextualizing biblical truth requires interpretive bifocals. First, we need a lens to look back into the background of the biblical world to learn the intended meaning. Then, we need another lens to see the foreground to determine how to best express—contextualize—that sense for today's world. (p. 231)

Thus, a field-theoretical interpretive process will be concerned with the meaning-for-Other and the meaning-for-self (and there may be numerous "Others" involved in any given complex situation). These twin horizons then suggest dual contexts—the context of the self and the context of the Other (or the context of the therapist and the context of the client).

As we have seen already, there are various ways in which to view what a given context is, but I will reduce them to three categories relevant to any given situation: time, the process of figure forming (which is phenomenal), and the extratherapeutic factors brought to the meeting of client and therapist that constitute an ontological condition accounting for about 40% of outcomes in psychotherapy.

Time and Field

Lewin and other field theorists believed that any behavior or any other change in a psychological field "depends only upon the psychological field *at that time*" (Lewin, 1943, p. 294). Rather than looking at the history of a situation, one might gain more useful and relevant information by testing the present situation itself, and in order to do that one might consider the direction and velocity of change going on in the current moment.

The principle of contemporaneity (that one is concerned with the client in the *current moment*) calls for the consideration of a period of time. Think of it as a dot, and the size of that dot can be very small or rather large; if the situation is macroscopic, the dot will have a greater diameter, but if the situation is more microscopic, the dot may be quite small. Lewin (1943) drew a comparison between time–space quanta in physics and time–field in psychology, and he maintained that the current experience of the client in his or her situational unit (the dot) might contain awareness of more than simply the current activities:

> The individual sees not only his present situation; he has certain expectations, wishes, fears, daydreams for his future. His views about his own past and that of the rest of the physical and social world are often incorrect, but nevertheless constitute, in his life space, the "reality-level" of the past. In addition, a wish-level in regard to the past can frequently be observed. The discrepancy between the structure of the wish–or irreality-level of the psychological past and the

> reality-level plays an important role for the phenomenon of guilt. The structure of the psychological future is closely related, for instance, to hope and planning. . . . It is important to realize that the psychological past and the psychological future are simultaneous parts of the psychological field existing at a given time. (p. 303)

The Process of Figure Forming

Figure forming is a phenomenal process related to perception, cognition, and consciousness, but taken as a whole it forms an important context for the interpretation of experience and, thus, a field-theoretical hermeneutic.

We focus on figures of interest that loom large against a background by which they can be understood. For instance, if I give you the following statements, what words fit in each one (the context of the other words in a sentence suggests what fits in the blank)?

1 The ________ barked loudly as the stranger approached the house.
2 The deer were so numerous and so hungry that they __________ the fence between them and the garden and ___________ all our leafy vegetables.

The classic gestalt shift in figure-ground in which one can focus on the silhouettes or the vase, but not on both at the same time, has been seen over and over again. That is because the perception shifts according to which part of the graphic one attends. In order to understand the nature of the figure in the foreground, one must see it against the background to which it is related. There are various kinds of background possible.

Clinical History as Background

When a psychologist interviews a client in order to gain a history of the presenting problem, it is a phenomenal recollection, a recreation of the past, that is obtained. There are no recordings of raw footage in the client's life that can be consulted; it is the client's memory that supports such an interview. That is why it is helpful to ask "What was that like?" when gathering disjointed facts such as "In the sixth grade I crashed my bike and was in the hospital" or "When I was ten, my brother's friend messed with me." Observing the client while asking for such clarification allows one to register emotional surges, dead spots, and various split-off experiences as otherwise bare facts are being shared, and all that provides an understanding of some of the ground of a person's life.

One must conduct a thorough history in order to ascertain whether perhaps there are field factors active in the person's life that he or she is not aware of. Here, it is the implications of various phenomenal symptoms that may point beyond the phenomenal field to the ontic field (see below for discussion of these concepts), which is still relevant to the person's unified field. For example, Hux, Schneider, and Bennett (2009) screened 1,991 people for traumatic brain injury and found that 531 of them (26.56%) were positive to such a degree that it impacted their quality of life. These people struggled with memory challenges, headaches, depression, inability to concentrate, and anxiety. Although the gestalt therapist can certainly work with the phenomenal field of such people (what it is like to have memory challenges, headaches, depression, lack of concentration, and anxiety), the etiology of these symptoms for the 531 people in question was neurological and physical in origin, and so the approach to treatment would be rehabilitative and not psychodynamic. In other words, for such people headaches, seen against the background of traumatic brain injury, are not a reaction formation; they are a physical malady. The gestalt therapist can certainly work with a client who has a physical malady, but it helps to know what one is dealing with.[2]

Meaning as Ground for Subsequent Experience

Often the product of one hermeneutic process will serve as ground in another. Imagine a man who comes to a party but is not greeted by anyone upon entering the room. He interprets that to mean that he is not truly welcome, and then someone says to him, "Why'd *you* come to the party?"—at which point he feels ashamed, assumes people think he's an unwelcome intruder, and looks for the first chance to leave without calling even more uncomfortable attention to himself. This building and cascading effect is common in relationships where two people assume things about one another and then build on such assumptions with cascading consequences. The interpretation of experience provides meaning which serves as ground for subsequent experience.

Worldview as Background

A worldview is what Kant called a *Weltanschauung*, and it is a point of view on the world, or a way of looking at the whole order of existence from a particular perspective.

A worldview is a system of assumptions and frameworks about the nature of reality that people use to organize their lives (Hiebert, 2008). Phenomenologically, it can be thought of as the sum of a person's worlds and the integration of his or her attitudes (Luft, 1998).

The concept was used by Kierkegaard, Engels, and Dilthey to talk about Western culture (Hiebert, 2008). Worldviews are global images that explain elements of personal experience. They provide an orientation as a background anchor for dealing with life's various challenges. Any given worldview is

> a system of coordinates or a frame of reference in which everything presented to us by our diverse experiences can be placed. It is a symbolic system of representation that allows us to integrate everything we know about the world and ourselves into a global picture, one that illuminates reality as it is presented to us within a certain culture. (Aerts et al., 2007, p. 9)

Among those who study worldviews some believe individuals can construct them, but others believe that they are based on language, that they take years to form, and that only communities and societies form worldviews. This resembles the difference between those in gestalt therapy who emphasize the individual's phenomenology and those who emphasize the field that gives substance to the individual.

Discourse as Foreground

Discourse is not just what is said; it includes any given act of "speaking" and assumes there *is* speaking (an ontological consideration). This can be described by the formulation x performs the action of y by way of performing the action of z (Wolterstorff, 1995). For example, a client comes out of silence, finding that speaking out suddenly seems possible, and she expresses herself by way of throwing the box of tissues across the room. Thus, there are different ways in which discourse can occur.

What Is "Said" What is said is just that—*what* is said. It can be recorded, spoken, written, sung, and so on. It is, however, subject to the receiving capacities of others. In an exercise with couples, one person was asked simply to repeat what he heard his wife to be saying, exactly as he heard it said and without any commentary. He got it wrong. He added bits and pieces. He used other words for what he thought was the same concept. The concrete words themselves are in question here, and they are subject to the lexical and grammatical norms of customary speech.

How It Is "Said" This is the way in which the concrete words are communicated. This includes the medium one uses. One might use a handwritten note, an e-mail message, a voicemail message, a telephone conference call, and so on. Then there is the emotional tone that comes across in the presence of another person, his or her relative energy, the way he or she holds his or her body, and his or her facial expression. One of the standard tests in assessing a person's capacity to comprehend another person's inner world (called a theory of mind) is the ability to read the other person's facial expression, and that is based on the fact that we express our feelings through facial expressions, often before anything is actually said out loud.

The Foreground and Background of Discourse

As gestalt therapists know, in much of everyday life we do not have simple perceptual shifts such as the silhouette/vase figure of classic gestalt figure-formation fame to account for; our situations are more complex, and it is the background that provides the clue about the significance of the foreground. What matters is what a person attends to out of all the various things he or she *could* attend to. The same is true for the impact of what we say to other people. How we say what we say is important. Just as the general background is a stronger cue to meaning, because it contextualizes the figure in the foreground, our mannerisms as we speak are read as speaking more quickly than our concrete words, so both what is said and how it is said must be considered together. For instance, ponder the difference between someone saying "I promise I'll mow the grass before the weekend is over" while smirking and rolling his eyes and someone saying the same thing while looking you in the eyes, standing straight, and never hesitating, emphasizing the word "promise."

Thus, the words are foreground and the affect and physical presentation are background, but at another level the two together constitute a unified discourse. Discourse is not just audibly speaking out loud or the product of writing. Discourse is the whole person in coordinated expression. This is the basis for understanding gestalt's emphasis on observing the whole person and pointing to split-off behavior such as a bouncing foot, crossed arms, or sighing. The person is saying something by what he or she does, including speaking, and that whole discourse can be understood as foreground to the overall situation.

Extratherapeutic Factors

When the Other meets the therapist, he or she presents as an ontological reality, a truly Other—another person who is not merely an extension of the therapist's own imagination. This is the alterity mentioned in chapter 5. What that other person brings to the process of therapy is critical. Also, therapist and client meet in the flow of actual events with social and cultural factors. Often, the situation changes and moves the ground under each one's feet: a client gets a new and better job, an economic downturn affects both client and therapist, or the weather provides days of sunshine or weeks of dreary overcast.

Clients and therapists agree that the client contributes most to change in a therapeutic process (Thomas, 2006), and that can be laid at the feet of the client's field-relevant circumstances; it is, after all, the client's situation that is the subject matter of a therapeutic process (Hubble, Duncan, & Miller, 1999).

> It appears that client factors account for 40% of improvement in successful outcomes; the therapeutic relationship accounts for 30% of improvement in psychotherapy; placebo, hope, and expectancy accounts for 15% of the improvement; and specific techniques/models of treatment account for 15% of the improvement...the essence of "what works in therapy" are [*sic*] curative processes present in the client that become activated within a warm, empathic therapeutic relationship. The artistry of this process has much to do with the fostering of hope and expectancy and techniques that draw out the healing aspects in the client. (Mones & Schwarz, 2007, p. 315)

FIELD-RELATIVE PERSPECTIVES

There are many perspectives one could list here. Murray's sense of needs-and-press coincides with the gestalt therapy understanding of field being developed in this chapter and allows a succinct way of conceptualizing field dynamics.

> Murray maintained that the environment *as it is apprehended by the individual* determines behavior. This phenomenological emphasis can best be illustrated by reference to the concept of *press*. The environment or stimulus is phenomenal in nature; that is, it is based on a personal frame of reference. The stimulus is relevant to behavior because of its effect conceived by the individual; that is, the environment or a particular aspect of the environment is apprehended as relevant or irrelevant and as facilitating or obstructing important needs. The conceived harmful or beneficial effect of the stimulus is called "beta press." One may ask: "Does the object physically harm the subject, nourish him, excite him, exalt him, depreciate him, restrain, guide, aid, or inform him?" In essence, the

> aspect of the stimulus most correlated with behavior is the beta press. The objective situation, called "alpha press," is not the significant determinant of action, although the discrepancies between the objective environment and the perceived environment throw light on the reality-testing capacities of an individual and suggest areas of conflict. (Lazarus, 1961, pp. 109–110)

Beta press is the phenomenal field, and alpha press is the ontic field. To these I add the pneumenal field for those whose work makes that relevant and also to reflect the fact that some of the more interesting and contemporary thinking in phenomenology is being accomplished by French phenomenologists who have taken a "theological turn."[3]

Phenomenal Field

The phenomenal field can be thought of as the universe of experience open to a person at any given moment (Combs, 1952). This is what gestalt therapists work with directly. It is epistemic in nature, for it has to do with how a person experiences/knows whatever he or she is experiencing/knowing. Working from within this field, a therapist is not concerned with what "really" happened; rather, it is what the client reports about what happened, or is currently happening, that is of concern.

For example, one client came to therapy telling the story of being abused and belittled by her supervisor at work. She described one particularly shaming incident in which the supervisor had stood before her in an overbearing posture and yelled at her, saying, "You are *worthless*!" As she spoke about it, she trembled, her voice wavered, and her eyes grew moist. The tone of her voice was mildly complaining, as if to provide a subtext: "That is not fair." But she had to collect herself and move out of that moment to express the injustice of it more directly. Everything in her presentation was an expression of her phenomenal field—what it was/is like to be her in that situation. Whether the supervisor actually stood over her is not known. Whether he yelled is not known. Whether he said she was worthless is not known. Some would say these things are irrelevant, but that is not always the case. What is certain is that both the content of what she asserted (which is her version of reality on the subject) and the way she experienced herself in the telling of the story are aspects of her phenomenal field. The therapist is with the client inside the situational unit, because even though the incident happened in the past, the phenomenal field includes the current moment of retelling something that is clearly unfinished. The dyadic field of the therapist and client, then, becomes enveloped by the client's situation so that the therapist can actually sense what it is like to be the client at that time.

Ontic Field

The ontic field is about what actually is, what has being, and therefore is ontic. Ontological concerns focus on the study of Being, which undergirds each individual manifestation of Being in one being or another. Being as a whole comes to focus in the ontic (Parkes, 1992). Describing ontic fields, M. C. Dillon (1988/1997) wrote:

> Merleau-Ponty's ontology is predicated on the thesis of the ontological primacy of phenomena, and, as I have sought to show, he understands phenomena as both immanent and transcendent. Thus, the lived body, as a phenomenon, includes both the immanent agency of my conscious life and the transcendence of worldly objects. (p. 143)

This is consistent with the thinking of Levinas and others who view the Other as transcendent to the point of violence were one to thematize the Other in the effort to make a model of the Other from one's existing understanding rather than to accept the Other as given. It is the "as given" that connects one to an ontic field, and this occurs in gestalt therapy through contact.

Integrating the Phenomenal and Ontic Fields

Although there are many kinds of fields and many overlapping spheres of influence, ultimately they all fall into one of the two categories mentioned above. How these two kinds of fields are related to one another in a unified field theory has been described well by Donn Welton (2000):

> The world is understood in terms of the phenomenological notion of horizon. An *epistemic* characterization of the horizon attempts to clarify the constitution of significance or meaningfulness itself. An *ontic* characterization attempts to describe the constitution of regionally configured spheres or fields in which particular types of experience and discourse are situated. They are internally related in at least three ways:
>
> 1 The epistemic characterization accounts for the structure of significance on the basis of which we can have a world. The ontic characterization treats the world we do have in term of the transformations of significance that constitute it.
> 2 An epistemic account describes spheres of existing significance; an ontic analysis describes spheres having significant existence. The spheres of significance articulate spheres of existence; spheres of existence deploy spheres of significance.
> 3 The epistemic characterization accounts for the pregiven horizon of our embodied and discursive involvement with objects in the world. The ontic characterization gives us the pregiven horizon of the world's involvement with us. (p. 373)

Pneumenal Field

Exactly how many gestalt therapists believe in God or work comfortably and competently with those who believe in God is impossible to know. Suffice it to say that a concern for working with spirituality has been growing in clinical psychology generally, and in gestalt therapy as well. Here, I share a perspective on the unified field with which not many of my colleagues agree, but perhaps those who do not believe in God can appreciate it as an example of the application of field theory to a particular population (theistic oriented people from among the religions of Judaism, Christianity, and Islam). The approach might stand for applications to different populations and communities.

The pneumenal field is spiritual.[4] This field is all things having effect for a given person who is in contact with God in the ontic field. Building on Welton (2000), in the pneumenal field one finds existing significance having significant existence. The pneumenal field is the unified field viewed with a spiritual attitude, in which the spheres of significance articulate spheres of existence, and the spheres of existence deploy spheres of significance.

For any given person, the awareness of God's presence is a feature of the person's phenomenal experience. This includes the sense that God speaks, and it emerges from contact between that person and God in which faith provides the eyes to see and the ears to hear. Ontic contact and faith are the subvenient properties from which the awareness of God emerges and upon which the awareness of God, and thus one's conscious relationship with God, supervenes.

> Conversely, it is the awareness of God that exercises a downward causation deepening one's faith and contributing to one's sanctification. A person must believe that God exists. A person must develop the spiritual attitude that organizes his or her interests, perceptions, needs, experiences, and curiosities in such a way as to find God in the world where others, operating with a natural or unspiritual attitude, find no God at all. (Brownell, in press a, np)

Is this just a solipsism dressed up in metaphysical attire? There is a circularity to it, but it is one that is not in the form of a logical argument. Rather, it is the circularity one sees in feedback loops and relational dynamics, in which trust begets deeper levels of experience. In order to even begin in a relationship with a being one cannot perceive by the usual means, one must start with faith. Whoever hopes to come to God must believe that He exists and rewards those who seek Him (Hebrews 11:6); otherwise, one skips right past the presence of God without ever sensing that He is there. Faith opens up awareness.

The pneumenal field can also be understood as ground for the lives of individuals in Christian community. Figure 6.1 is a schematic conceptualization showing that the pneumenal field is relevant to

$$\frac{\left(\dfrac{((N-I)(Alt)(D))^{I+comm}}{\left(\dfrac{((FoS)(GoS))}{DoS}\right)\left(\dfrac{((N-I)(Alt)(D))^{I+div}}{DoS}\right)} \rightarrow (VoG \times VoM \times VoE)\right)}{PneuF} = ChComm$$

Figure 6.1 Relational factors in Christian community.

Note: Alt = alterity; ChComm = Christian community; D = dialogue; DoS = depth of sanctification; FoS = fruit of the spirit; GoS = gifts of the spirit; I + comm = relationships between an individual and others in community; I + div = relationship between an individual and God; N-I = non-independence; PneuF = pneumenal field; VoE = varieties of effects; VoG = varieties of gifts; VoM = varieties of ministries. (From Brownell [in press b, np]).

the situation of the community, as relationships between individuals and community are affected by nonindependence, alterity, and dialogue. It also shows that the relationship between an individual and God is affected by the same nonindependence, alterity, and dialogue, but attenuated by a person's depth or growth spiritually, a person's responsiveness to God—what is known as "sanctification." Rather than being isolated factors apart from the field, such things are parts of the whole. The field determines how many parts might be relevant to a situation, but in any given situation some parts are more proximate and salient than others, and those parts are such things as are listed in Figure 6.1. This kind of schematic can be drawn to represent field factors present in any given situation.

FIELD-THEORETICAL PSYCHOTHERAPEUTIC STRATEGIES

O'Neill and Gaffney (2008) listed seven strategic principles that serve the therapist working from a field-theoretical position. These are shown in Table 6.2.

To make things a little more concrete, let's start with the fact that ontic elements will have phenomenal antecedents. So, the therapist might want to attend to his or her office. Is it warm, rich, and nurturing, or is it bleak and sterile? Comfortable chairs or couches

Table 6.2

O'NEILL AND GAFFNEY'S SEVEN STRATEGIC PRINCIPLES

STRATEGIC PRINCIPLES	DESCRIPTION
Work from the whole to the parts	Pay attention to the environment, history, and culture. Consider phenomena from many perspectives, because nothing unconnected happens
Consider self to be process	A person is always of some field, fields are in flux, and personality can be seen as slow moving process[1]
Follow the organization of the field	The needs and interest of the person organize his or her field
Surrender to the paradoxical agency	Let things happen rather than try to make things happen
Attend to part-to-whole relationships	Converse to the first principle, there are times when the part weighs more heavily than the whole, even though the relationship between them remains intact
Watch for the field in action	Watch for unfolding patterns of homeostasis, polarization, and growth
Make way for emergent creation	Creativity is the generative nature of the field; get into step with and risk floating on the current which the field provides

[1]I acknowledge Gary Yontef for this concept.

Source: Adapted from O'Neill and Gaffney (2008).

arranged in configurations that support encounter without forcing premature intimacy would be in order. An easy-to-follow procedure for entering and maintaining attendance in therapy, including payment for services, would be helpful.

Second, expect phenomenal elements to lead to ontic adjustments. This is at the core of the paradoxical theory of change in gestalt therapy. If an exploration of the client's phenomenal world is effective and the client settles down in the current experience of being who he or she is at the moment, it will lead to adjustments being made by the client outside of therapy in the "real world" of the client's situation. The therapist would do well to expect such a thing and to work with an in-session/out-of-session mentality. When psychotherapy is working, the client will make changes in the ontic field apart from the physical presence of the therapist.

Third, watch with a wide-angle lens. Instead of focusing narrowly on the client, as is described in the process for diagnostic interviewing using the *DSM*, this kind of focus is an observation of the situation in motion, and it takes into consideration what is happening outside the therapy room as well as inside it; it considers what is happening for the therapist as well as the client, for the therapist is at some stage or another in joining the situation of the client.

Be willing to experiment with the complexity of the situation. This builds on O'Neill and Gaffney's point about creativity and it relates to the next chapter, on experimentation. The field will strive to maintain homeostasis, so if the therapist purposefully introduces something new, that will necessitate some kind of shift, and the results can be mined for understanding. Although this is not an intervention in the sense that a gestalt therapist can always know what the results will be, sometimes case management to broker new services for the client can be a very potent field-theoretical strategy (see chapter 10). Instead of continued psychotherapy for one elderly and depressed woman, I once recommended a home health nurse who would come in, not take no for an answer, and get the woman up, bathed, fed, dressed, and out of her apartment at least three or four times a week. That was not psychotherapy as we have traditionally thought of it, but it was a gestalt-consistent and field-theoretical strategic experiment.

Recognize that everything else that is true about gestalt therapy is present in the field; thus, a therapist who is working phenomenologically is working from a field perspective. The therapist who is involved in dialogue is working with a field. The therapist doing group work is in a field. All-things-having-effect is true for the phenomenal field Lewin called the "life space" and the ontic qualities of the organism and its surroundings incorporated into Perls, Hefferline, and Goodman.

CONCLUSION

Field theory has become the largest current consideration in the ongoing development of gestalt therapy praxis. It is being applied across the board to various kinds of clinical work by gestalt therapists, organizational consultants, and coaches. The term itself became so ubiquitous that it began to lose salience, but that trend has begun to turn around with the desire among gestalt therapists to be more refined in how they define the term.

The unified field is relative to any given person, and it is a unity of phenomenal and ontic characteristics. In addition, this unified field can be seen and experienced as any number of subsequent fields depending on the attitude with which one views it (which gives the appearance of there actually being many, many fields instead of a unified field for each person). An example of this was given in the form of the pneumenal field for those viewing the unified field with a spiritual attitude.

Finally, I agree with Lewin that field theory is a practical method. It has certainly become more of a theory that undergirds psychotherapy, group practice, and communal process than it was in Lewin's day, but mostly it is still a method. As such, it is a way of working with people rather than a means of drawing a map of what people do.

NOTES

1. Their work was preceded by many others in the wider context of psychology, including Lewin (1943), who defined field theory at an early period of its understanding; Hall and Lindzey (1957/1959) and Murphy (1947, 1949/1950), who explored the development of personality from a field perspective; and Hartmann (1942) and Lewin (1942), who explored learning from a field perspective.
2. Along with a history, one can also do neuropsychological assessment; psychological testing is a possible support for gestalt therapists (Brownell, 2002), not antithetical to the approach, and the therapist can benefit by using simple instruments such as a genogram with which to investigate the client's relational history or the performance-based assessments of cognitive function in tests such as the NEPSY or the D-KEFS.
3. Consult the work of Jean-Luc Marion, Michel Henry, and Jean-Louis Chrétien. Also see Dominique Janicaud's (2001) critique of this turn toward theology.

4. The Greek word for "wind in motion," later used for the concept of "spirit," is *pneuma*.

REFERENCES

Aerts, D., Apostel, L., De Moor, B., Hellemans, S., Maex, E., Van Belle, H., et al. (2007). World views: From fragmentation to integration, Internet edition, first published in 1994 by Vrije Universiteit Brussel Press: Brussels. Retrieved June 14, 2009, from http://www.vub.ac. be/CLEA/pub/books/worldviews

Brownell, P. (1998). Condensing the field: Internet communication and gestalt community. *Gestalt Review*, *2*(2), 143–153.

Brownell, P. (2002). Psychological testing, a place in gestalt therapy? *The British Gestalt Journal*, *11*(2), 99–107.

Brownell, P. (2009a). Gestalt therapy. In I. Marini & M. Stebnicki (Eds.), *The professional counselor's desk reference* (pp. 399–407). New York: Springer.

Brownell, P. (2009b). Executive functions: A neuropsychological understanding of self-regulation. *Gestalt Review*, *13*(1), 62–81.

Brownell, P. (in press a). Spirituality in the praxis of gestalt therapy. In J. H. Ellens (Ed.), *The healing power of spirituality, how religion helps humans thrive: Vol. 3. The psychodynamics of healing spirituality and religion* (np). Westport, CT: Praeger.

Brownell, P. (in press b). The healing potential in religious community. In J. H. Ellens (Ed.), *The healing power of spirituality, how religion helps humans thrive: Vol. 2. The healing power of religion* (np). Westport, CT: Praeger.

Combs, A. (1952). Intelligence from a perceptual point of view. *Journal of Abnormal and Social Psychology*, *47*(3), 662–673.

Crocker, S. (1999). *A well-lived life: Essays in gestalt therapy*. Cambridge, MA: Gestalt Institute of Cleveland Press.

Crocker, S. (2008). A unified theory. In P. Brownell (Ed.), *Handbook for theory, research, and practice in gestalt therapy* (pp. 124–150). Newcastle, UK: Cambridge Scholars Press.

Dillon, M. C. (1988/1997). *Merleau-Ponty's ontology* (2nd ed.). Evanston, IL: Northwestern University Press.

Goldberg, E. (2001). *The executive brain: Frontal lobes and the civilized mind*. Oxford: Oxford University Press.

Goldstein, K. (1995). *The organism*. New York: Urzone.

Hartmann, G. (1942). The field theory of learning and its educational consequences. In N. Henry (Ed.), *The forty-first yearbook of the national society for the study of education: Part II, the psychology of learning* (pp. 165–214). Chicago: University of Chicago Press.

Hiebert, P. (2008). *Transforming worldviews: An anthropological understanding of how people change*. Grand Rapids, MI: Baker Academic.

Hubble, M., Duncan, B., & Miller, S. (1999). *The heart and soul of change: What works in therapy*. Washington, DC: American Psychological Association.

Janicaud, D. (2001). *Phenomenology and the theological turn: The French debate. Perspectives in Continental Philosophy*. New York: Fordham University Press.

Kepner, J. (2003). The embodied field. *British Gestalt Journal, 12*(1), 6–14.

Kounin, J. (1963). Field theory in psychology: Kurt Lewin. In J. Wepman & R. Heine (Eds.), *Concepts of personality* (pp.142–161). Hawthorne, NY: Aldine.

Klein, W., Blomberg, C., & Hubbard, R., Jr. (1993/2004). *Introduction to biblical interpretation*. Nashville, TN: Thomas Nelson.

Latner, J. (2000). The theory of gestalt therapy. In E. Nevis (Ed.), *Gestalt therapy: Perspectives and applications* (pp. 13–56). Cambridge, MA: Gestalt Press.

Lazarus, R. (1961). Personality from a phenomenological point of view. *Adjustment and Personality* (pp. 104–136). McGraw-Hill series in psychology. New York: McGraw-Hill.

Lewin, K. (1942). Field theory and learning. In N. Henry (Ed.), *The forty-first yearbook of the national society for the study of education: Part II, the psychology of learning* (pp. 215–242). Chicago: University of Chicago Press.

Lewin, K. (1943). Defining the "field at a given time." *Psychological Review, 50*(3), 292–310.

Lewin, K. (1951). In D. Cartwright (Ed.), *Field theory in social science: Selected theoretical papers*. New York: Harper.

Luft, S. (1998). Husserl's phenomenological discovery of the natural attitude. *Continental Philosophy Review, 31*, 153–170.

MacKewn, J. (1997). *Developing gestalt counselling*. Thousand Oaks, CA: Sage.

Malpas, J. (2009). Hans-Georg Gadamer. In E. N. Zalta (Ed.), *The Stanford encyclopedia of philosophy* (np). Retrieved June 13, 2009, from http://plato.stanford.edu/entries/gadamer

Marion, J. L. (2004). *In excess: Studies in saturated phenomena*. New York: Fordham University Press.

Massarik, F. (2000). Field theory. In A. Kazdin (Ed.), *Encyclopedia of psychology: Vol. 3* (pp. 370–371). Washington, DC: American Psychological Association.

McConville, M., & Wheeler, G. (Eds.). (2001). *The heart of development: Gestalt approaches to working with children, adolescents and their worlds: Vol. 2. Adolescence*. Cambridge, MA: Gestalt Press.

Mones, A., & Schwartz, R. (2007). The functional hypothesis: A family systems contribution toward an understanding of the healing process of the common factors. *Journal of Psychotherapy Integration, 17*(4), 314–329.

Murphy, G. (1947). Field theory. *Personality: A biosocial approach to origins and structure* (pp. 880–902). New York: Harper.

Murphy, G. (1949/1950). The relationships of culture and personality. In S. S. Sargent & M. Smith (Eds.), *Culture and personality* (pp. 13–30). New York: Viking Fund.

O'Neill, B. (2008). Relativistic quantum field theory: Implications for gestalt therapy. *Gestalt Review, 12*(1), 7–23.

O'Neill, B., & Gaffney, S. (2008). Field theoretical strategy. In P. Brownell (Ed.), *Handbook for theory, research, and practice in gestalt therapy* (pp. 228–256). Newcastle, UK: Cambridge Scholars Press.

Parkes, G. (1992). *Heidegger and Asian thought*. Delhi, India: Motilal Banarsidas.

Parlett, M. (1991). Reflections on field theory. *British Gestalt Journal, 1*(2), 69–81.

Parlett, M. (1997). The unified field in practice. *Gestalt Review, 1*(1), 16–33.

Parlett, M., & Lee, R. (2005). Contemporary gestalt therapy: Field theory. In A. Woldt & S. Toman (Eds.), *Gestalt therapy history, theory, and practice* (pp. 41–63). Thousand Oaks, CA: Sage.

Perls, F. (1969). *Ego, hunger, and aggression*. New York: Random House.

Perls, F., Hefferline, R., & Goodman, P. (1951). *Gestalt therapy: Excitement and growth in the human personality*. New York: Julian.

Smith, J. K. A. (2002). *Speech and theology: Language and the logic of incarnation*. New York: Routledge.

Staemmler, F. (2006). A Babylonian confusion? On the uses and meanings of the term "field." *British Gestalt Journal, 15*(2), 64–83.

Thomas, M. (2006). The contributing factors of change in a therapeutic relationship. *Contemporary Family Therapy: An International Journal, 28*(2), 201–210.

Welton, D. (2000). *The other Husserl: The horizon of transcendental phenomenology*. Bloomington: Indiana University Press.

Wheeler, G. (1996). *Gestalt reconsidered: A new approach to contact and resistance*. Hillsdale, NJ: Analytic Press.

Wheeler, G. (2000). *Beyond individualism: Toward a new understanding of self, relationship, and experience*. Hillsdale, NJ: Analytic Press.

Wheeler, G., & McConville, M. (Eds.). (2002). *The heart of development: Gestalt approaches to working with children, adolescents and their worlds: Vol. 1. Childhood*. Cambridge, MA: Gestalt Press.

Wolterstorff, N. (1995). *Divine discourse: Philosophical reflections on the claim that God speaks*. Cambridge, UK: Cambridge University Press.

7 Move to Action

Gestalt therapy is experiential in nature. It was once described as phenomenological behaviorism. That is because, in gestalt therapy, people do not merely talk about something; they experience it directly in the moment through a variety of means gestalt therapists call "experiments." This chapter describes experiment and discusses how the move to the experiential can be strategic in support of awareness and change.

Gestalt therapy is perhaps best known for its experiential nature—what some have referred to as its "boom-boom" dramatic techniques. Because of that, unfortunately, many people think gestalt therapy is no more than an experiential method. They learn how to perform those techniques and think they are practicing gestalt therapy. See chapter 8 for the full description of why that is not so, but for now, know that gestalt therapy praxis is a unified approach, and one cannot extract its experiential experiments, turn them into techniques, and think that is all there is to "doing a little gestalt."

What follows is a general orientation to the "experiment" in gestalt therapy, more on action as a form of discourse, and then some descriptions of general categories of experiments with the understanding that a creative and spontaneous practice will modify and shape these categories to generate novel experiences.

BEHAVIOR, ENACTMENT, AND EXPERIENCE

Gestalt therapy has occasionally been referred to as phenomenological behaviorism, but it is not behaviorism at all. Behaviorism uses associative learning to train people in a predetermined path through stimulus and response, punishment or reward. John Watson viewed behaviorism as a scientific endeavor built on the idea that one attends only to what can be observed—what people do (with the idea that speech is something people do). Watson wrote,

> The rule, or measuring rod, which the behaviorist puts in front of him always is: Can I describe this bit of behavior I see in terms of "stimulus and response"? By stimulus we mean any object in the general environment or any change in the tissues themselves due to the physiological condition of the animal, such as the change we get when we keep an animal from sex activity, when we keep it from feeding, when we keep it from building a nest. By response we mean anything the animal does—such as turning towards or away from a light, jumping at a sound, and more highly organized activities such as building a skyscraper, drawing plans, having babies, writing books, and the like. (Watson, 1924/1997, pp. 6–7)

Just because something is observed does not make the act of observing into a form of behaviorism. It is true that through the phenomenal method the gestalt therapist observes the client and attempts to become very good at doing so. It is also true that experimentation takes place, introducing stimuli into people's lives. It is not true that this is done to train desired responses or behaviors or that gestalt therapy conceives of a line of cause-and-effect, as is implied in Watson's statement. There are causes and effects in gestalt therapy, but gestalt therapists understand the situation to necessitate multivaried, multidetermined, and complex contextual logic rather than linear causality.

Enactment is the process of acting something out. As such, it is not the same as spontaneously "acting out" and thereby expressing one's unconscious desires and conflicts. Often, children act out the frustrations and fears they cannot verbalize to themselves and others; just as play is a means for them to process life, so acting out is a means of accomplishing difficult emotional and psychological tasks. As necessary as acting out can be as the person makes creative adjustments to do his or her best with a difficult situation, it is not the same as the enactment of experiment in gestalt therapy.

Enactment puts into action something imagined, contingent, or potential. I once interviewed for a job as a road manager for a rock band, and the man who put these bands out on the road needed someone who could move to action when necessary. So, he asked me, "What would you do if you were walking down the sidewalk and you saw a house with smoke rolling out one of its windows?" I told him that I would go up and see if anyone was in the house, at which point he said, "Okay. Do it." I then attempted to simulate what I had previously described, and that was an enactment.

A special form, and more technical definition, of enactment is seen by Varela, Thompson, and Rosch (1991) and Thompson (2007) as perceptually guided action that includes cognitive structures and sensorimotor patterns. These authors integrate the study of consciousness with neuroscience and phenomenology. Accordingly, enactment is the action of the whole person, body and mind, in a situated plain of perception and contact.

Perception itself can be thought of as an enactive process, meaning that it includes sensorimotor activity and not just sensorireceptive activity (Gallagher & Zahavi, 2008). Such perception is often one part of an intersubjective dynamic in that perceiving involves the neural structures and functions that make intersubjectivity what it is. Through perception–action (motor activity associated with perceptive stimuli), a very young person (prenatal to neonatal) lays down "reference points," called mirror neurons, in his or her perceptual–motor pathways. Because these neurons sit right next to the motor neurons in the perceptual–motor pathways, the relationship between mirror neurons and motor neurons is important. People are able to understand the movement, or the verbal reference to the action of others' movement—and it "gets to" them at a visceral level—because observing others, hearing about others' actions, and so forth, stimulates a corresponding *simulation* in the perceptual–motor pathways of the observer. From a neuropsychological perspective, then, enactment can take place within the systems of the organism; it does not have to be a macro-level, outwardly visible form of behavior.

> Goal-directed motor acts are the nuclear building blocks around which action is produced, perceived, and understood. Taking advantage of the motor system's functional organization in terms of motor goals and motor intentions, the mirror neuron matching mechanism enables a direct comprehension of the actions of others. Such comprehension is prereflexively accomplished because the behavior of others consists of goal-directed motor acts and is recognized as such by virtue of the activation of the observer's brain of the neurons presiding over the motor accomplishment of that same act. (Gallese, Rocaht, Cossu, & Sinigaglia, 2009, p. 110)

To experience is to *go through* something. One must be situated, locked down to a time and a place. There must be an environmental and social context, for all of life is situated in some way, and the details of such a place help create what it is like to go through something there. It is one thing to meet with friends at an Irish pub, but it is another to meet with friends in judge's chambers.

To have experience is to learn, to come to know, because we also carry the residue of experience which forms the background of many figure/ground experiences. For instance, I have experienced a hurricane. I was in a particular time and place where a hurricane came through and I know, because I lived through it, what that is like. It produced experiential knowledge that I sometimes lean on when a big storm approaches.

The Greek verbs *ginōskō* and *geuōmai* refer to tasting, sensing, or perceiving something and, by extension, coming to know something through the senses—that is, to experience that something or to have experiential knowledge. The terms are used in this context from Aristotle forward (Schmitz, 1976). Thus, I can know about blueberries. I can know what a pie is. I can imagine what a blueberry pie might be like, but until I see one and taste a piece of blueberry pie, I do not really know what it is like. In the same way, I had taken classes on death and dying, I was a consultant to a hospice program, and as a minister I had been with many people who had lost loved ones, did grief counseling, and conducted funerals. However, I did not know what deep grief was like until my youngest brother was killed suddenly in an auto accident. That cut through me. It was then that knowing *about* grief became the experience *of* grieving. Theoretical knowledge is made more sure through experience. To know through personal intercourse is to have experience of something. Thus, this knowing is in the biblical sense of "to know," which actually refers to having sexual intercourse—to have intimate sexual knowledge of someone based on intimate experience.

"Experiment" in gestalt therapy is behavior, and it is enactment. Going through an experiment creates experience, and people learn. They come to know by means of doing; by means of experience. Still, this experience is not just receptive; it is also expressive. The result of an experiment is not just that a person might *hear from*, but also that a person might *speak to*.

ACTION AS DISCOURSE

Potentia is a potentiality—something available or even at hand but not fulfilled; *actus* is the fulfillment of potentia. To act is to realize or make real some kind of potentiality, and this is what Goldstein and later Maslow meant when they used the term *actualization* referring to making one's potential real—becoming self-actualized. A person comes more into being through action, through what he or she does.

In discussions of discourse, the idea of conventional generation alerts a person that he or she can accomplish one thing by doing another thing (Wolterstorff, 1995). For instance, a person can signal a turn by sticking an arm out of the window or by using the blinker. Standing at the airport and watching loved ones depart through the security lines, a person can say good-bye by waving a hand and smiling, or by crying with a hand on one's head, or by shouting loudly, "Good-bye!" All three will do, and one is not necessarily more right than the others; however, one form of saying good-bye may express a different kind of internal potential than another. These are all actions; they actualize the potential at hand

and express the agency of a person as creator of his or her experience. One person remains composed and simply waves; another person expresses utter dismay and actualizes emphatic grief by crying and putting a hand on top of her head.

Karol Wojtyla (1979) asserted that people reveal themselves by action. Someone might have an experience, in the sense that something happens to him or her, but when someone acts, he or she becomes the agent of experience. When I wave good-bye, I am the one expressing that sentiment through what I do. In action, both subjectivity and agency are united.

> Viewing subjectivity solely from the metaphysical standpoint, and stating that man as a type of being constitutes the true subject of existing and acting, autonomous individual being, we abstract, to a large extent from what is the source of our visualizations, the source of experience. It is far better, therefore, to try to coordinate and join together the two aspects, the aspect of being (man, person) with the aspect of consciousness; the aspect of acts (acting and action) with the aspect of experience. (Wojtyla, 1979, p. 57)

In other words, being/person is to consciousness as action/acting is to experience. Discourse depends on someone actually existing with whom conversation might be established, but once being is accepted, then the person is manifest in action. When a person acts, he or she self-actualizes and communicates a potential in some way, to some extent, to other beings, and that is discourse.

Thus, when a gestalt therapist moves from talk to action, it is not really a move from one category to another but from one aspect of a single category to another. Both talk and action are forms of discourse. The related action in experiment helps bring into clearer relief who the person is by what he or she does.

EXPERIMENT

Much is said these days about evidence-based practice, which people usually think of as the need to back up practice with facts based on research about the outcomes of psychotherapy. Experiment is so critical to research that a whole division of psychology is called "experimental psychology," referring to those who conduct research using experimental designs.

Experimental psychologists and gestalt therapists use the term *experiment* in different ways. Experimental design at one extreme consists of null hypothesis testing based on comparisons between a control group and a group in which some variable is being examined, with random assignment of subjects. For example, someone might compare a group of depressed clients receiving gestalt therapy with a group of depressed clients in some kind of waiting group (control group). The subjects would be randomly assigned and the therapy would be manualized to ensure that reasonably similar treatment was being applied across all patients by all therapists. Testing would be conducted at least pre- and posttreatment. This structured process would then be analyzed statistically to see if there were a significant difference, essentially, between doing nothing and doing gestalt therapy. This is not at all what a gestalt therapist means by "experiment."

A gestalt therapy experiment is a purposefully created experience in the support of increased awareness that facilitates change; it is unpredictable, and that is why experiments are also referred to as "safe emergencies." It is paradoxical in the sense that the therapist is not *aiming* to change the client (but to support the natural change that often occurs in the course of increased awareness); the therapist *is* aiming to help the client more fully experience himself or herself in some kind of behavior or enactment he or she would not otherwise likely have imagined or ventured into. For instance, in working with a young woman who had lost her first child during childbirth, I invited her to imagine the baby across from her in a cradle perched on the chair. I invited her to speak to the baby who had died, and then I asked her to imagine she was the baby talking back to herself. She did both, released herself from the guilt she felt because she had pushed during labor and the baby had strangled in its cord, and that facilitated her overall grieving.

> *Experimentation* is the act of trying something new in order to increase understanding. The experiment may result in

> enhanced emotions or in the realization of something that had been kept from awareness. Experimentation, trying something new, is an alternative to the purely verbal methods of psychoanalysis and the behavior control techniques of behavior therapy. (Yontef & Jacobs, 2007, p. 330)

So, through experiment people can unleash and experience emotions that serve as catalysts for catharsis, and that provides an affective rationale for doing experiments. However, that is not the whole story. Experiments also provide information.

For example, in a couple I was once working with, the woman was dying to connect emotionally with her husband, whose basic approach was to go "into his head" and think his way through a situation to find a solution by which he could fix it. She did not want to be "fixed" by his solutions; she wanted to sense him beside her, and to understand what she was feeling as they both traversed the situation together. As they were talking in one session I noticed that while he was sharing his ideas with her, the muscle that controlled his jaw was tightening, as if he were chewing on something. So, I asked him to touch that part of his face and then to speak from that place. He looked somewhat put out, but he did it, and as he was speaking his voice began to quiver and grow raspy as if his throat were going dry or tightening up. I said, "Do you hear that?" And he looked amazed. He said, "I feel that." Then I turned to his wife and asked, "Do you see that?" And she was jubilant. "Yes! He's feeling something." Out of this experiment, which was in the service and flow of dialogue, the couple learned that the man had the capacity for emotional experience, which opened up a whole new plane on which they might be able to walk together in the future.

As Melnick, Nevis, and Shub described it,

> Experiment is a teaching method that creates an experience in which clients can learn something that is part of their next growth step. Experiment is what transforms talking into doing, reminiscing and theorizing into presence and action. ...Every experiment has a strong behavioral component. (Melnick, Nevis, & Shub, 2005, p. 107)

Jungkyu Kim and Victor Daniels stated that experiment can guide a client toward discovery by participating in direct experience.

> She is invited to *act or to do something* rather than simply to talk about it. In the process of enactment, the "story" about the problem becomes a present event. Out of that event, unexpected dimensions of realization and discovery often emerge.... Experiment, as used in gestalt therapy... brings the client's words alive by drawing the client into the dimension of action, emotion, sensation, imagination, and verbal expression. (Kim & Daniels, 2008, p. 198)

While doing couples work, it is frequently the case that two people will open up and start talking. In fact, they frequently tell me that that is the only place where they *do* talk. I have also noticed that they often talk to me instead of to each other. I have found this diagnostic of the state in which they are with one another; if they engage each other directly, they are stronger than if they talk instead to me. So, one experiment I often suggest is to talk to each other (which means to face each other as well as address each other). This often changes the dynamic considerably, and it creates new experience that can be mined for understanding, especially if the therapist follows up by asking what it was like to talk directly *to* one another.

Sylvia Crocker described experiment as moving from talking to action, noting various benefits of experiments:

> Under the guidance of the therapist, the client actively experiments with elements of his experience, partly in the service of the client's greater self awareness, and partly as preparation for action. Through the use of the experiment in the safety of the therapeutic situation, the client can try out variations of current verbal and non-verbal behavior. In doing this he can practice different ways of interacting with significant others, and can get new perspectives on both current and important situations in the past. (Crocker, 1999, p. 29)

Creating an Experience That Supports Awareness

Our object-directed, intentional experience emerges out of the background of a precognitive intentionality that includes affective sensibility, motivation, and attention (Thompson, 2007). "The idea is that whatever comes into relief in experience must have already been affecting us and must have some kind of 'affective force' or 'affective allure' in relation to our attention and motivations" (Thompson, 2007, p. 30). It may be on the periphery of life, slightly out of focus. It might be an aspect of our ontic field that is having effect, but not yet part of our phenomenal field.

The most effective experiments are "in the room" before they are given structure and form. They arise out of the shared sense of the therapist and client. They feel like they belong to the process. It may be a polarity that emerges from dialogue or phenomenal exploration. It may be the client's split-off body behavior that grows on the therapist's attention. The most effective experiments are not "canned" and waiting on the shelf to be taken down and inserted; thus, an effective experiment is a response to and part of the ongoing experience.

If a therapist wants to create an experience that supports awareness, he or she therefore needs to step off of the experience that is already going on between the therapist and the client. One need not think up something totally new. The trick is not remembering 10 techniques that one can use and knowing which one is the right one to use at any particular moment.[1] The "trick" is to loosen up and brave the anxiety of an unpredictable situation, a ride the therapist suggests taking *with* the client. To suggest such a ride, the therapist can refer to various such "excursions" that gestalt therapists have taken with their clients in the past and modify one of them; but he or she can also think imaginatively of something unique, something that seems to suggest itself in the moment.

EXPERIMENTAL OPTIONS

There are many ways to organize possible experiments.[2] The following should be considered general categories that might lend themselves to the flow of any given therapeutic process. They should all be employed with ample support for both the client and the therapist.

Bilateral and Unilateral Experiments

A therapist can choose to negotiate with the client around a potential experiment or simply implement something on his or her own without warning. The first is a bilateral experiment, because it requires the consent of both parties, but the second requires only the decision of the therapist.

The first is negotiated, which means that the therapist introduces it with something like, "I am thinking of something we might try right now; would you be interested?" If the client signals tentative interest, then the therapist describes what he or she has in mind: "What would happen if you sat in this chair, and I sat on the couch?" The therapist puts out the crux of the experiment as a proposal or a question (what might happen, if…?), and the client has a chance to respond and to say, "Yes" or "No." Following the experiment there is a debriefing in which the therapist explores with the client what it was like to go through that experience. Often, no words will capture the impact, and all that is necessary is to say, "Wow."

A unilateral experiment is something the therapist has control over and can implement without any cooperation from the client. Thus, in couples therapy I may on occasion tell a client to say something directly to his or her partner, and then I may tell them to say it again but look into the other person's eyes. Since experiment also undergirds other ways of working in gestalt therapy, in the service of dialogue, and as a unilateral experiment, I may self-disclose what my experience is like while being with the client, and then ask what it was like to hear me say that. When using unilateral experiments it is important to gauge and understand the client's level of support, and provide support as needed so that the client might not become overwhelmed during experimental contact.

Augmenting

As stated previously, it is not necessary to create something completely new. One can simply augment, or heighten, what is already going on. For example a therapist might tell the client to notice what he or she is experiencing in the moment and describe that. When the client skips over something, the therapist might call the client back to it. The therapist might ask the client to say something again, and then to say it even again. Often saying something like "I never felt I belonged to anybody" can open up the client to areas long since submerged. The therapist can ask the client to emphasize one word above others ("I never felt I belonged to *anybody*" or "I never felt I *belonged* to anybody"). The therapist might ask the client to magnify some mannerism that the client is already doing. "I notice you waving your hand; can you wave it more? Keep waving it." Then, the therapist might ask the client to give that gesture some words. The therapist might ask the client to "go deeper" into a particular thought or "stay with" a specific feeling. The therapist might ask the client to make abstract statements concrete; if a person says it was a good day at work, the therapist might ask, "What made it a good day?" The therapist might discern that the client is speaking in minimizing language, either on purpose or out of awareness, and the therapist might ask the client to enlarge on something, and make it bigger, more serious, more troubling than it seems at that moment.

In a form of augmenting, the client can be invited to bring into the current meeting with the therapist matters about which he or she had been speaking as if they were abstract or distant. The therapist asks the client to speak about the issue, some event, or that other person as if these were right there in the same room. While the client is describing something that happened "out there," for example, the therapist asks, "What is it like to be telling me these things right now?" In other instances, the client might be encouraged to phrase things in the first person and to introduce them with, "I am thinking…" or "I am feeling…"

Since we are holistic beings, it makes sense that a person would have a physical side to any given psychological symptom or disorder. Therefore, one can direct the client's attention to his or her physical body, asking, "What sensations are you feeling in your body right now?" or "Where in your body do you feel that?"

Each of these examples takes a process or a manifestation already present, some presentation of the client, and works with it to enlarge it and call attention to its facets. In some cases, this augmentation triggers or jars loose something to which it is related, and then there is an emotional moment that can become quite important to positive outcomes (Greenberg, 2004). Greenberg, Auszra, and Herrmann (2007) discerned the following elements in good outcomes in psychotherapy, and I maintain that they are all relevant to the use of augmenting experiments in gestalt therapy: (1) the emotion in question is a primary emotion that is experienced in the present in a contactful and fully aware manner, (2) the experience involves the emotion being owned by the client, who experiences himself or herself as an agent instead of a victim of the feeling, (3) the emotion is not overwhelming, (4) the emotional process is fluid instead of blocked, and (5) the emotion is related to a therapeutically relevant issue.

Enacting

Enactment as a concept has already been described. Various forms of enactment lend themselves to gestalt experimentation.

Sometimes a person can be asked to put into embodied motion a thought previously expressed. A person who says she feels helpless might be asked to assume a posture that expresses her helpless feelings. Family sculpting is a form of enactment in which a person "paints" a picture of his family by putting people into a configuration, a "still life" of how he or she sees them.

In what is now a classic gestalt technique, the use of the "empty chair" allows a person to address polarized elements in his or her own mind, unfinished events, and interpersonal problems.

> An empty chair placed facing the client may carry out a projective dialogue, whether with another person or between parts of himself. This technique is often used to complete an unfinished situation from the past, in which case the person not available in the present is imagined to be sitting in the empty

> chair. Sometimes it is better to address issues in this manner than in a real encounter with the other person, because feelings can be expressed and acted out more safely in this situation. Once the cathartic expression of sadness, anger, jealousy, or other emotional behavior has been fully expressed toward the "person in" the empty chair, the client may more easily find a way to open up communication with the other. (Kim & Daniels, 2008, p. 214)

Sometime a client can be asked to "be the person" he or she is talking about. When I was in supervision with a gestalt therapist, he routinely asked me to "be" the client I was talking with him about, whereupon he would assume my role in that relationship, and we would play out the process. A variation on this is that sometimes a person can be asked to be the opposite of whatever is manifest. For instance, if a person is coming across as helpless and dependent, the therapist might ask him to "be" the strong and independent person.

Imagining

Imagination, the ability to imagine, involves forming mental images, including sensory approximations and cognitive concepts, when they are not perceived directly through sight or other perceptual operations. An early Muslim philosopher, Ibn Arabî (1165–1240), claimed that the heart has two eyes, reason and imagination. "The heart, which in itself is unitary consciousness, must become attuned to its own fluctuation, at one beat seeing God's incomparability with the eye of reason, at the next seeing his similarity with the eye of imagination" (Chittick, 2008, np). One can see that imagination's link to what a person thinks has been around for a long time. Imagination is not a free-floating fantasy, untethered from cognitive process—one's *reason*. To imagine is to imagine something, to be able to hold it in one's mind and turn it this way and that in order to consider it. That is imaginal.

A therapist might request that the client visualize certain scenarios. Someone fretting over receiving a poor review at work was asked, "What is the worst that could happen to you? Imagine that you are in that situation." A great deal of imaginal work can support working around phobias and various kinds of anxieties. The client is asked to imagine himself or herself near the feared object, and then to "hold" there and to relax the body. This is a form of desensitization, but it is not conducted as a behavioral intervention. It is done as a gestalt experiment in which no one really knows what will happen when *this* unique client attempts to do it. The results need to be monitored and processed within the in vivo context of the therapy session.

In classic gestalt dream work, the client imagines himself or herself as each aspect of the dream and describes or speaks from that position in the dream. "How does it feel to be that thing or that person?" "Is there someone in the dream you want to talk to?" "What do you want to say to that person?" "How safe do you feel?" "How hungry do you feel?"

One woman was dealing with the infidelity of her husband. She was having trouble letting go of the offense and fully reconciling, even though she consistently stated she was committed to the relationship. Her head told her she needed to move forward, but her heart told her to make sure she would not get hurt again. I asked her to imagine that it was 6 years down the line and she had given herself to the relationship, forgiven her husband, and moved on. I said, "One day a woman comes to your door and tearfully, regretfully confesses that she's been having an affair with your husband." Let that sink in. Each person will take such an experience in a unique direction. She could have realized it was not worth the chance of such pain ever again. She could have realized that she would hurt but that she could live through it. The point is that such an imaginal experience, an experiment, changes the inner arrangement in one's perception of the situation, and it is impossible to simply remain in exactly the same place one inhabited before the experiment. Thus, experiment also leads to paradoxical change.

Diminishing

Sometimes a suppressive technique works nicely, particularly with a practice that is counterproductive. In a group setting, for instance, telling theories about why members do what they do is not as helpful as direct contact and experience between members; consequently, some groups create a "no aboutism" rule to suppress the tendency to figure out "why" and allow people to move on to more productive ground (Kim & Daniels, 2008). In a similar vein, "shouldisms," which rule how a person ought to be or act, what a person should believe and value, are sometimes better simply confronted rather than set aside. When an introject (something accepted uncritically that rules in some manner) appears, it can be directly challenged. "What happens if you say to yourself, 'That is not true'?" Or if a client lacks sufficient self support but is suffering under the load of some rule-bound existence, the therapist can simply offer a new introject (on the way to a better solution), by saying, "That doesn't fit with the facts." Again, these are done as experiments and need to be tracked for the ongoing process.

Giving Homework

Often, giving a client something to try in the world outside of therapy can lead to discovery, for example, keeping diaries; making schedules; use of relaxation techniques. Making suggestions as to what a person might do in the midst of his or her troubled situation is homework. A client may not attempt these suggestions, or may throw himself or herself into them wholeheartedly. They may "work" or not, but that is not the main point. There is no success or failure with an experiment, only more experience that one can sift through to build understanding.

One couple came to me complaining of not being able to communicate. I suggested that they take a walk together on the beach and explicitly not talk about anything. Just walk together down the beach. They agreed to do it. The next time we met, the man declared, "Well it didn't work." I wondered what happened, and he said, "We didn't do it." Brushing aside the assertion that something had not "worked," I asked, "*How* did you not do it? What happened?" In the process of reviewing what each had done, we discovered that their practice was to defer to the other and then respond to someone else's initiative. So, the work then focused more on that pattern.

CONCLUSION

Experiment, broadly understood, is the action step of gestalt therapy theory. Experiment is moving to action, but when one considers that anything a person does is action, and any action says something about who that person is, then we see experiment is intrinsically linked to individual experience, relational dialogue, and field theoretical strategies. Without experiment, nothing would be accomplished. The modified phenomenological method is experimental. Dialogue is experimental. Field theory is experimental.

Experiments are the tools by which a gestalt therapist explores the client's phenomenal field and encounters the client in a therapeutic relationship. Experiments arise out of the natural ground of the situation and are not canned techniques a therapist takes down from the clinical shelf to prescribe like medication to reduce symptoms. Experiments are the behavioral and experiential component of gestalt therapy, but gestalt therapists employ them and understand them differently, differentiating gestalt therapy from behaviorism and experiential therapy even while finding some consilience in these approaches.

NOTES

1. Incidentally, that is one reason gestalt therapy does not easily lend itself to a practice of empirically supported treatments—gestalt therapists do not prescribe treatments like medications to reduce symptoms; they work with the whole person, moving from in situ to in vivo and back again, and they flex with a novel and living experience.
2. For this section, I am largely in debt to Kim and Daniels's (2008) chapter on experiment.

REFERENCES

Chittick, W. (2008). Ibn Arabi. In E. N. Zalta (Ed.), *The Stanford encyclopedia of philosophy*. Downloaded June 19, 2009, from http://plato.stanford.edu/entries/ibn-arabi.

Crocker, S. (1999). *A well-lived life: Essays in gestalt therapy*. Cambridge, MA: Gestalt Institute of Cleveland Press.

Gallagher, S., & Zahavi, D. (2008). *The phenomenological mind: An introduction to philosophy of mind and cognitive science*. New York: Routledge.

Gallese, V., Rochat, M., Cossu, G., & Sinigaglia, C. (2009). Motor cognition and its role in the phylogeny and ontogeny of action understanding. *Developmental Psychology, 45*(1), 103–113.

Greenberg, L. (2004). Emotion-focused therapy. *Clinical Psychology & Psychotherapy, 11*(1), 3–16.

Greenberg, L., Auszra, L., & Herrmann, I. (2007). The relationship among emotional productivity, emotional arousal and outcome in experiential therapy of depression. *Psychotherapy Research, 17*(6), 482–493.

Kim, J., & Daniels, V. (2008). Experimental freedom. In P. Brownell (Ed.), *Handbook for theory, research, and practice in gestalt therapy* (pp. 198–227). Newcastle, England: Cambridge Scholars.

Melnick, J., Nevis, S. M., & Shub, N. (2005). Gestalt therapy methodology. In A. Wold & S. Toman (Eds.), *Gestalt therapy, history, theory, and practice* (pp. 101–115). Thousand Oaks, CA: Sage.

Schmitz, E. D. (1976). Gin sk . In C. Brown (Ed.), *Dictionary of new testament theology* (Vol. 2, pp. 392–406). Grand Rapids, MI: Zondervan.

Thompson, E. (2007). *Mind in life: Biology, phenomenology, and the sciences of mind.* Cambridge, MA: The Belknap Press of Harvard University Press.

Varela, F., Thompson, E., & Rosch, E. (1991). *The embodied mind: Cognitive science and human experience.* Boston: MIT Press.

Watson, J. B. (1924/1997). *Behaviorism*. Piscataway, NJ: Transaction.

Wojtyla, K. (1979). *The acting person: Analecta Husserliana, the yearbook of phenomenological research* (Vol. X). Dordrecht, Netherlands: D. Reidel.

Wolterstorff, N. (1995). *Divine discourse: Philosophical reflections on the claim that God speaks.* Cambridge, England: Cambridge University Press.

Yontef, G., & Jacobs, L. (2007). Gestalt therapy. In R. Corsini & D. Wedding (Eds.), *Current psychotherapies* (8th ed., pp. 328–367). Florence, KY: Cengage.

8 Practice a Unified Approach

Gestalt therapy is not simply multimodal. That is, at any given time all the elements of its theory are at play in the therapeutic process. The unity of practice is discussed in terms of the holism inherent in gestalt therapy, and therapists are shown how to make space for all the elements even though they might, at any given time, emphasize one over another as a way of working in the moment.

Gestalt therapy has a mix of influences. As Sylvia Crocker and Peter Philippson (2005) described them, many threads make up the tapestry of gestalt therapy's theory and method. Among the most important of such threads are the following:

1. The psychoanalysis of Freud, Horney, Rank, and Reich
2. The holism of Goldstein and the gestalt psychologists
3. Kurt Lewin's development of field theory for the social sciences
4. The experimental and problem-solving approaches of pragmatists like Dewey and James
5. The philosophy of Aristotle and Kant
6. The phenomenology of Brentano, Husserl, Merleau-Ponty, and Levinas

7 The existentialism of Hiedegger, Kierkegaard, Tillich, and Buber
8 Several ideas from Taoism and Buddhism

From this, one might think that gestalt therapy is not really a coherent system. Certainly, all its various contributions were not aligned; each has been a movement or system in itself. Gestalt therapy might seem simply like a number of rocks one finds along a hiking trail; they were all found on the same journey, but each came to be on the trail through very different processes. Yet, what started out as separate influences has continued to develop, as if all the rocks were taken to a foundry and melted down into one, new gem.

Charlie Bowman described how that "melting down" process, toward an integrated praxis, developed over the years:

> The broadest overview of Gestalt therapy identifies a changing weltanschauung as responsible for Gestalt therapy's development. *Weltanschauung* connotes more than the dictionary definition, "a shared worldview." It is how we apprehend the world—how we are involved in it, perceive it, and bring our personal history to bear on it. This collective perspective creates momentum and becomes an engine for change. In Gestalt therapy, the result has been movement (a) from deconstructive views of the world toward holistic models of existence; (b) from linear causality toward field theoretical paradigms; and (c) from individualistic psychology toward a dialogical or relational perspective. (Bowman, 2005, pp. 4–5)

One might be tempted to consider gestalt therapy to be merely multimodal—not one gem but several newly formed stones all lined up together. Instead of having a coherent system, gestalt therapy would then be seen as additive—incorporating phenomenology plus existentialism, plus intersubjectivity and relational philosophies, plus holism and field theory, plus behavioral and experiential experimentation. This view would allow one to factor out various parts for study without doing damage to any of the other parts, or seriously affecting the overall approach. It is tempting to do this in research, for instance, if one simply wants to study the dialogue of gestalt therapy as it relates to dyadic assessment; one could then pretend that dialogue had nothing to do with individual experience or the complex and unified field. However, things do not work that way, and in practice gestalt therapy does not work that way; so, one would need a practice-based approach (Brownell, 2008) to doing research on gestalt therapy and that would require maintaining the integrity of gestalt therapy's theoretical core. Gestalt therapy is a holistic approach that is also a unified system of praxis.

Praxis is a word that denotes theory and practice combined. Thus, in the same book Sylvia Crocker (2008) identified components of gestalt therapy's unified theory, and Gary Yontef and Peter Philippson (2008) identified elements of gestalt therapy's unified practice. Just how theory and practice are related to one another in gestalt therapy stands behind the *claim* of a unified praxis (see below).

THE UNITY OF PRAXIS

Theories explain or predict experience and guide practice (Crocker, 2008). That is the basic relationship between theory and practice that forms the nature of one's praxis. How well does one's theory inform and guide one's practice? Can gestalt therapists actually track the use of theory through the course of therapy? Yes. That can, and is done both in training and in private practice.

Holism

Holism asserts that the whole is larger than the sum of its parts. Methodological holism asserts that an understanding of a complex system requires examination of principles governing the whole system as opposed to those governing individual parts. Metaphysical holism breaks down into three categories: ontological holism, property holism, and nomological holism. *Ontological holism* asserts that some objects are not wholly composed of parts. *Property holism* asserts that some objects have properties that are not determined by the physical properties of their basic physical parts, and *nomological holism* asserts that some objects obey laws not determined by fundamental physical laws governing the structure and behavior of their parts (Healey, 2008).

In terms of a whole family, then, it is the communal nature of a family that organizes the being and action of its individual members. In terms of a community of professional therapists, such as the Association for the Advancement of Gestalt Therapy (AAGT) or the European Association for Gestalt Therapy (EAGT), it is the nature of the association that gives meaning and outlines the parameters of behavior of its members. The AAGT is concerned with the advancement of gestalt therapy as a discipline and a practice, but the EAGT is concerned with the advancement of gestalt therapists as disciplined practitioners. The AAGT is nonregulatory, grants no certificates, and exercises no ethical authority over its members, while the EAGT is regulatory, grants certificates, and exercises ethical authority over its members. The nature of the whole determines the function and experience of the parts.

Gestalt therapy theory applies holism at several levels of its structure, and gestalt therapy practice views that practice as one whole process. The theory of gestalt therapy is both a property and a nomological holism; that is, its characteristics can only be understood in the context of the whole approach, and its principles work together. The practice of gestalt therapy is a methodological holism, given that the laws of each part of gestalt therapy are shaped by all the laws of all the parts working together rather than by any set of laws alone.

As a gestalt therapist, I cannot ignore all other elements of gestalt therapy to simply use one particular tenet in its theory. I might focus on that one thing, but what I find is that, because of my experiential training and the overall system being what it is, all the various tenets come along. Frankly, this is what allows me to enjoy the practice of gestalt therapy, because I can settle into a natural way of being with people, confident that other elements of the approach are not being neglected.

The characteristics of gestalt therapy theory are not simply additive; rather, personal experience influences gestalt's dialogical way of being with another person, and dialogue is the forming of a two-person field, all of which is worked out in the lives of people through action—what people do in therapy. What people do is in contexts and speaks about who they are at any given moment. These are theoretical commitments in gestalt therapy theory. They point to the properties and "laws" that inform about what gestalt therapy theory is and how it operates. The theoretical tenets of gestalt therapy may once have been separate "parts" of diverse wholes, but they have come together—they have been forged into a new whole in which no part is separate from other parts, and each part is in play whenever one part is focused on.

The principles governing the system of gestalt therapy practice do not constitute isolated interventions that can be employed or studied on their own outside the whole system of gestalt therapy methodology. At any given moment in therapeutic practice, one or another way of working as a gestalt therapist may be in the foreground while others are in the background. In addition, during "choice points" in that process a therapist may choose to work experimentally, phenomenologically, dialogically, or with the field, but when moving to one of these methods, a therapist is not abandoning all the other options. Some simply recede to the background as others move into the foreground of the therapist's figure–ground dynamic. This process itself is a current flowing between the therapist and the client in which each has effect on the other, but the therapist takes responsibility to facilitate or navigate that flow, and all elements of theory are always present in his or her practice.

A Tracking Matrix for Gestalt Therapeutic Process

It is possible to track the way any given therapist "navigates" the flow in the therapist–client field by (1) watching the therapist's figures of interest, on the one hand, and (2) the ways in which the therapist chooses to work, on the other (keeping in mind that how one works in gestalt therapy is a matter of emphasis). These things can be cast in a matrix (Brownell, 2000, 2005), which could then be used by students in training groups and by researchers checking to see how much a truly gestalt practice was being used. (See Figure 8.1.)

Ways of Working →

Focuses of Work ↓

	Modified Phenomeno-logical Method	Dialogic Relationship	Field Theoretical Strategy	Experimental Freedom
Therapist and/or Client Figure # 1				
Therapist and/or Client Figure # 2				
Therapist and/or Client Figure # 3, etc.				

Figure 8.1 A gestalt therapy matrix for training, practice, and research. (Adapted from Brownell [2000, 2005])

THE CONCEPT OF A UNIFIED APPROACH

People have long thought that everything is connected. Religious convictions over centuries prior to the Enlightenment found that connection in the mind and work of God. When people began questioning and wanting to know more about *how* God did what had been done, they started investigating the principles by which the universe worked, and putting together theories about its various parts. The first to develop a unified theory of everything was Roger Boscovich, a Dalmatian Jesuit, poet, and architectural advisor to popes, who extended Newton's thinking to propose a grand, unified force law that eventually influenced Faraday, Maxwell, and Kelvin. He introduced ideas new for his time that "still form the intuition of scientists" today (Barrow, 2007).

> He emphasized the atomistic notion that Nature was composed of identical elementary particles and then aimed to show that the existence in Nature of larger objects with finite

> sizes was a consequence of the way their elementary constituents interact with one another. The resulting structures were equilibrium states between opposing forces of attraction and repulsion.... Boscovich proposed a grand unified force law which included all known physical effects ... he was the first to envisage, seek, and propose a unified mathematical theory of all the forces of Nature. (Barrow, 2007, pp. 20–21)

In thinking holistically, and using mathematics to explain forces in a unified theory of everything, Boscovich is the ultimate predecessor of Goldstein's holism and Kurt Lewin's approach to field theory. Grand unifying theories have come and gone since Boscovich. For instance, string theories have recently been supplanted by M-theory. Those working on psychotherapy integration are also seeking a version of a grand theory of everything. The Society for the Exploration of Psychotherapy Integration's official journal, *Psychotherapy Integration*, is published by the American Psychological Association and carries articles reflecting the desire to enhance the interface, or rapprochement, and bring about the convergence among these various clinical approaches.

I contend that gestalt therapy could function as a grand unifying theory of psychotherapy—a heuristic of convergence—and I understand that that is an audacious claim. Three factors support this assertion: the construct of consilience (and the consilience that exists between gestalt theoretical tenets and those of other approaches), the observation of common factors in psychotherapy outcomes research (that embody basic gestalt therapy commitments), and the emerging convergence of various schools of psychotherapy along the lines of existing gestalt therapy theory (whether they recognize that as such or not).

Consilience

Consilience as a construct points to the unity of knowledge. It is an idea developed by William Whewell when he wrote of the construct of induction as it pertained to his philosophy of science. Whewell said that the evidence in favor of an induction was more potent when it enabled a person to explain *different kinds* of cases from those contemplated in forming the hypothesis. Whewell called this kind of evidence a "jumping together" or "consilience" of inductions. "An induction, which results from the colligation of one class of facts, is found also to colligate successfully facts belonging to another class" (Kockelmans, 1999, p. 74; Snyder, 2006, np).

Consilience, as I am using that term, is related to abduction in science. Abduction is the inference to the best explanation from several possible theories contemplated at the same time. "Abduction, by its very nature, forces people into estimates of consilience, or how well a theory fits with theories from other domains" (Brownell, Meara, & Polák, 2008, p. 9). If one can contemplate several theories for consideration of the best explanation of a phenomenon within one domain of study, then one can contemplate several domains as well, considering aspects of each to find any matches. If matches occur, then *where* they are indicates a "point" of consilience—something that explains how things work in divergent domains.

When gestalt therapy is compared in this way to other domains, one can find many matches, or points of consilience. Probably the clearest case of consilience is between gestalt therapy's field perspective and the various organismic and field theories that proliferated in neuroscience, medicine, and physics in the early and mid-20th century. Within social science there is a consilience between gestalt field theory and systems or ecological psychotherapy; between the concept of dialogical relationship and object relations, attachment theory, client-centered therapy, and the transference-oriented approaches; between the existential, phenomenological, and hermeneutical aspects of gestalt therapy and the constructivist aspects of cognitive therapy; and between gestalt therapy's commitment to awareness and the natural processes of healing and the mindfulness, acceptance, and Buddhist techniques adopted by cognitive behavioral therapy.

COMMON FACTORS

Psychotherapy research has identified various "common factors" resident in all major forms of psychotherapy that also contribute to positive outcomes. Many research studies have identified an overlapping array of factors (Asay & Lambert, 1999; Beitman, 2005; Bickman, 2005; Drisko, 2004; Duncan, 2002; Gallo, Ceroni, Neri, & Scardovi, 2005; Meione & Chenail, 1999), and Table 8.1 shows how some of the most common are consistent with gestalt therapy theory.

Table 8.1

COMMON FACTORS RESIDENT IN GESTALT THERAPY

COMMON FACTOR	GESTALT THERAPY MANIFESTATIONS
Client and extratherapeutic factors	This is the field—all things having effect/the lifespace of the client. This is what the client brings to the therapeutic process; it includes the client's cognitive-intellectual capacities, elements of culture, history, finance, and any legal issues related to the client
Therapist qualities	This relates to the authentic presence of the therapist, the capacity of the therapist for contact, and his or her training and experience. It includes the lifespace of the therapist
Relationship	This concerns the relational and dialogical skills of the therapist in the working alliance: presence, inclusion, commitment to dialogue, and the creating of conditions supportive of dialogue
Specific method	This relates to the gestalt therapist's reliance on a modified phenomenological method, dialogue, strategic use of the field, and experiment (among other things)
Expectancy	This relates to faith in the paradoxical theory of change; it is a faith position more generally as well because gestalt therapists trust in the desire for growth in the client and that the field will supply what is needed

Adapted from Brownell (2008).

People who advocate a common factors approach to understanding psychotherapy effectiveness use the outcomes data to argue against the need for an empirically supported treatments' approach, but the point here is that there *are* common factors. What is effective in one approach is effective in all major approaches, or so the theory of common factors goes. The idea of common factors levels the ground between diverse clinical perspectives. It takes the idea of consilience and provides research data delineating just *how* divergent systems of psychotherapy like cognitive behavioral therapy (CBT), psychoanalysis, and gestalt therapy are consilient.

Convergence

If there is a general consilience that is made more specific in common factors, then what makes gestalt therapy so special? Could we not just as easily say that everything is converging around one of the other approaches? No. Not really. I say that, because these other two main approaches (CBT and psychoanalysis) are adopting long-held main tenets of gestalt therapy instead of the other way around.

Occasionally, but it seems consistently, I will read of someone doing some kind of psychotherapy, and when I read the details—the description of the work in question—I say to myself, "That's gestalt therapy." I am not the only one to notice this (Gold & Zahm, 2008). I do not believe these psychotherapists are ruthless thieves who knowingly steal gestalt therapy's thunder and lack the ethical standards to at least acknowledge where they got it from; I think they are discovering things, given the march of thought, that were known in gestalt therapy all along.

Probably the most direct convergence to date can be seen in a form of psychotherapy called existential–phenomenological psychotherapy (Langdridge, 2004) with a close second in dialogical–existential therapy (Portnoy, 2008). Exponents focus on the continental philosophy that was the foundation of gestalt therapy, and, like gestalt therapists, they continue to track the contemporary developments in writers from both existentialism and phenomenology. For instance, the staff at Seattle University has developed a graduate program emphasizing the existential–phenomenological approach (Halling, McNabb, & Rowe, 2006) and a brochure available at the Web site for that program describes it without mentioning gestalt therapy at all:

> This approach to psychology is inspired by the philosophical tradition developed by thinkers such as Buber, Kierkegaard, Nietzsche, Husserl, Heidegger, Gadamer, Sartre, Marcel, Merleau-Ponty, and Emmanuel Levinas. Existential-phenomenology seeks to develop an in-depth understanding of human existence. It challenges traditions that study the person in a reductionistic manner or promote dualistic modes of thinking (e.g., mind vs. body or freedom vs. determinism).... Existential–Phenomenological Psychology is humanistic in that it challenges the modern tendency to interpret the human condition through narrow technological lenses. It also appreciates the wisdom accumulated by the long tradition of the humanities. The existential dimension deepens our understanding of persons living in their everyday circumstances through in-depth reflection on the psychological meanings expressed in both experience and action. The phenomenological dimension encourages openness toward psychological reality by identifying and putting aside theoretical and ideological prejudgments. As a whole this approach is therapeutic in that it focuses on the psychosocial conditions that help people deal with the difficulties of life. (Seattle University, 2009, p. 2)

For some time now, relational psychoanalysis has been flirting with the intersubjective nature of the working alliance. Lynne Jacobs described some of the aspects of this converging toward gestalt therapy's perspective when she wrote that the schools of intersubjectivity theory and American relational psychoanalysis

> seem to me to have a closer affinity to gestalt therapy than they have to early, "classical" psychoanalysis. The intersubjectivity theorists have even been campaigning to develop a phenomenological psychoanalysis, one that they in fact describe as "a phenomenological field theory or dynamic systems theory" (pg 6)! That is a campaign that might warm the heart of Perls,

> Hefferline and Goodman, who championed phenomenological field theory in their 1951 opus, Gestalt Therapy. Notice how closely the following paragraph aligns with statements in PHG:
>
> "It is our view that the persisting dichotomies between the intrapsychic and the interpersonal, between one- and two-person psychologies, are obsolete, reified, absolutized relics of the Cartesian bifurcation. The very phrase two-person psychology continues to embody an atomistic, isolated-mind philosophy in that two separated mental entities, two thinking things, are seen to bump into each other. We should speak instead of a contextual psychology in which experiential worlds and intersubjective fields are seen to mutually constitute one another. Unlike Cartesian isolated minds, experiential worlds—as they form and evolve within a nexus of living, relational systems—are recognized as being exquisitely context-sensitive and context-dependent. In this conception, the Cartesian subject-object split is mended, and inner and outer are seen to interweave seamlessly. We inhabit our experiential worlds even as they inhabit us. *Mind is pictured here as an emergent property of the person–environment system, not as a Cartesian entity localized inside the cranium.*" (p. 9) (Italics added) (Jacobs, 2002, np)

In addition to these psychoanalytic and psychodynamic trends, Gold and Zahm (2008) take note of converging trends from other directions:

> Another example is the importance many approaches now place on acceptance of what is, awareness, and the present moment—as if these are novel concepts for psychotherapy when they are, in fact, cornerstones of gestalt therapy theory and method.... Steven Hayes, developer of acceptance and commitment therapy, or ACT (Hayes, 2007) writes that in the last ten years, a number of approaches to therapy have entered the mainstream based on the core idea that the more we struggle to change or get away from what our experience is, the more stuck we can become. He lists mindfulness based cognitive therapy (MBCT), dialectical behavior therapy (DBT) and ACT, as all agreeing that a first step toward fundamental

> change is to embrace the present moment, even if the experience is difficult or painful. (Gold & Zahm, pp. 30–31)

Living in the current moment, the "here and now," is basic to gestalt therapy, so gestalt therapists have had an interest in opening dialogue with Daniel Stern (Jacobs, Philippson, & Wheeler, 2007) when he began theorizing about the power of exactly that—the current moment. Stern wrote of the importance of contact ("moments of meeting") in what he called "now moments" (Stern, 2007). However, Stern's work also emphasizes (1) the shift to a two-person psychology—intersubjective and interpersonal processes rather than on intrapsychic dynamics—and (2) the impact of home visits, where in-home facilitators come face to face with the family as a system, or a defined element in the infant's overall field (Stern, 2008). Because of Stern's work, his psychoanalytic colleagues have wondered if he has not actually become more gestalt than psychoanalytic, but at least one concluded that his work is revolutionary and relevant for the field of psychoanalysis (Wilkinson, 2003).

The affective-focused body psychotherapy (ABP) approach is similar to gestalt's commitment to tracking a holistic process through the modified phenomenological method and has elements of dialogue and experiment:

> The ABP therapist attempts to facilitate the patient's awareness of his or her experience by directing the patient's attention to various aspects of his or her in-the-moment experiencing, both while working hands-on or by instructing the patient to perform a movement and while simply being in the room together. (Levy Berg, Sandell, & Sandahl, 2009)

Remaining with the body for a moment, the impact of Antonio Damasio's (2005) studies in neuroscience ignited the interest of gestalt therapists with his rejection of Descartes' dualism (*Descartes' Error: Emotion, Reason, and the Human Brain*) and his exploration of consciousness in daily experience (*The Feeling of What Happens: Body and Emotion in the Making of Consciousness*). Damasio, while writing firmly from within the domain of neuroscience/neuropsychology, shares many interests with gestalt therapists.

The neurological antecedents for conscious experience also lead gestalt therapists back to their roots in Goldstein and neuropsychology (Brownell, 1998).

Addressing the issue of a unifying core for the integration of psychotherapy, Anchin suggested that some kind of mix between what he called systems theory and a biopsychosocial model provided enough scaffolding on which to hang meta-theories and interventions. He claimed that

> foundational to systems theory is an all-inclusive, holistic conception of the human being that at one and the same time embraces the multilevel structural complexity of human personality and yet the inherently unified manner in which this structure functions within the contextual circumstances at hand. The biopsychosocial model of health and illness comprehensively defines the composition of this integrated complexity. It encompasses and delineates the multiple and intricately constituted subsystems, from microlevels to macrolevels, that in thoroughly interdependent fashion comprise the individual qua living system: in the biological domain, genetic, anatomical, physiological, and biochemical subsystems; in the psychological domain, cognitive, affective, and motivational subsystems, each of whose constitutive processes occur along a continuum of awareness ranging from acute consciousness to thoroughgoing unconsciousness; and in the social domain, the verbal/linguistic subsystem of speech and the overt behavioral subsystem, which is itself composed of multiple nonverbal channels. Further, the social domain of the biopsychosocial model underscores that events occurring within and among all of the aforementioned subsystems continuously spin out in relation to and are reciprocally interpenetrated by an individual's social surround, a multiplex environment that is itself a domain of systems-within-systems (e.g., dyadic, familial, community, cultural groups, society). (Anchin, 2008, p. 325)

And once again there is convergence, because what Anchin states could stand as a reasonable description of gestalt therapy's holistic field theory, wedded to gestalt's relational and phenomenological tenets. A rose by such another name does smell just as sweet.

Finally, Scott Henggeler and his colleagues (2009) indicated another convergence in the multisystemic approach he champions in the treatment of antisocial adolescents. He pointed to the mediators of change in the use of multisystemic therapy to treat juvenile sex offenders, but multisystemic therapy is a field-theoretical concept; it is a social-ecological theory of development and behavior (Saldana & Henggeler, 2006).

CONCLUSION

Magnavita (2008, p. 275) maintained that, to be a unified theory, a theory of psychotherapy would have to include the following characteristics:

- Unified theory emphasizes the essential function, structure, and processes common to all human systems.
- Unified theory attempts to establish the interconnectedness of all the domains of human functioning.
- Unified theory attempts to shift to a meta-theoretical model or total paradigmatic matrix.
- Unified theory attempts to offer a theory of the functioning of the entire ecological system of human functioning, including all pertinent areas of psychology, especially psychopathology/maladaptation, personality theory, developmental processes, as well as psychotherapeutic processes.
- Unified theory attempts to recognize all the major domain systems of the human biosphere.
- The personality system is seen as the central organizing system of human adaptation, function, and dysfunction.
- Unified theory relies on multiple paradigms for knowing, believing that each one offers some aspect that deepens understanding.

In order for a psychotherapy theory to be both unified and *unifying*, a clinical perspective must accomplish Magnavita's tasks but also the theory must find consilience with significant features of other approaches, obviously manifest the common factors that make for good outcomes across the board of all major approaches to psychotherapy, and constitute a point of convergence as other approaches either borrow directly from its theory and practice or discover anew the features in its praxis.

This is the picture of gestalt therapy. This book has not made much of the extensive development of gestalt therapy's theory of self, because exploring every facet of the gestalt therapy approach would take too much space for one volume; however, gestalt therapy's theory of self is fully developed in Perls, Hefferline, and Goodman's (1951) original text and also in such recent volumes as Peter Philippson's *Self in Relation* and *The Emergent Self: An Existential-Gestalt Approach* (2009), and in Ansel Woldt and Sarah Toman's book, *Gestalt Therapy History, Theory, and Practice* (2005). In addition, Mark McConville and Gordon Wheeler (2001, 2002) offered a two-volume set with a developmental model built around gestalt therapy's phenomenological field theory. With the addition of the theory of self, then, gestalt therapy satisfies all of Magnavita's requirements for a unified theory of psychotherapy; it finds many points of consilience with other approaches, manifests the most salient common factors, and provides a very suitable focal point for convergence.

REFERENCES

Anchin, J. (2008). Pursuing a unifying paradigm for psychotherapy: Tasks, dialectical considerations, and biopsychosocial systems metatheory. *Journal of Psychotherapy Integration, 18*(3), 310–349.

Asay, T., & Lambert, M. (1999). The empirical case for the common factors in therapy: Quantitative findings. In M. Hubble, B. Duncan, & S. Miller (Eds.), *The heart and soul of change* (pp. 33–56). Washington, DC: American Psychological Association.

Barrow, J. (2007). *New theories of everything*. Oxford, England: Oxford University Press.

Beitman, B. (2005). To the editor: Defining the core processes of psychotherapy. *American Journal of Psychiatry, 168*(2), 1549–1550.

Bickman, L. (2005). Common factors approach to improving mental health services. *Mental Health Services Research, 7*(1), 1–4.

Bowman, C. (2005). The history and development of gestalt therapy. In A. Woldt & S. Toman (Eds.), *Gestalt therapy history, theory, and practice* (pp. 3–20). Thousand Oaks, CA: Sage.

Brownell, P. (1998). Renewing our roots in neuropsychology: A gestalt perspective on the work of Joseph LeDoux. *Gestalt!* 2(1), np. Downloaded June 23, 2009, from http://www.g-gej.org/2-1/ledouxreview.html.

Brownell, P. (2000). A gestalt theoretical matrix for training and practice. *The Australian Gestalt Journal, 4*(1), 51–61.

Brownell, P. (2005). Contemporary gestalt therapy theory: Organizing perspective for juvenile sex offender treatment. *Gestalt Review,* 9(2), 175–190.

Brownell, P. (2008). Practice-based evidence. In P. Brownell (Ed.), *Handbook for theory, research, and practice in gestalt therapy* (pp. 90–103). Newcastle, England: Cambridge Scholars Publishing.

Brownell, P., Meara, A., & Polák, A. (2008). Introduction and purpose of the handbook. In P. Brownell (Ed.), *Handbook for theory, research, and practice in gestalt therapy* (pp. 2–26). Newcastle, England: Cambridge Scholars.

Crocker, S. (2008). A unified theory. In P. Brownell (Ed.), *Handbook for theory, research, and practice in gestalt therapy* (pp.124–150). Newcastle, England: Cambridge Scholars.

Crocker, S., & Philippson, P. (2005). Phenomenology, existentialism and eastern thought in gestalt therapy. In A. Woldt & S. Toman (Eds.), *Gestalt therapy history, theory, and practice* (pp. 65–80). Thousand Oaks, CA: Sage.

Damasio, A. (2000). *The feeling of what happens: Body and emotion in the making of consciousness.* New York: Vintage Books.

Damasio, A. (2005). *Descartes' error: Emotion, reason, and the human brain*. New York: Penguin Classics.

Drisko, J. (2004). Common factors in psychotherapy outcome: Meta-analytic findings and their implications for practice and research. *Families in Society, 85*(1), 81–90.

Duncan, B. (2002). The founder of common factors: A conversation with Saul Rosenzweig. *Journal of Psychotherapy Integration*, 12(1), 10–31.

Gallo, E., Ceroni, G., Neri, C., & Scardovi, A. (2005). Specific common therapeutic factors in psychotherapies and in other treatments. *Rivista di Psichiatria, 40*(2), 63–81.

Gold, E. & Zahm, S. (2008). The need for gestalt therapy research, in P. Brownell (Ed.) *Handbook for theory, research, and practice in gestalt therapy*, pp. 27–36. Newcastle, England: Cambridge Scholars Publishing.

Halling, S., McNabb, M., & Rowe, J. (2006). Existential–phenomenological psychotherapy in the trenches: A collaborative approach to serving the underserved. *Journal of Phenomenological Psychology, 37*(2), 171–196.

Healey, R. (2008). Holism and nonseparability in physics. In E. N. Zalta (Ed.), *The Stanford encyclopedia of philosophy*. Downloaded June 20, 2009, from http://plato.stanford.edu/entries/physics-holism.

Henggeler, S, Letourneau, E., Chapman, J., Borduin, C., Schewa, P., & McCart, M. (2009). Mediators of change for multisystemic therapy with juvenile sexual offenders. *Journal of Consulting and Clinical Psychology, 77*(3), 451–462.

Jacobs, L. (2002). It's not easy to be a field theorist: Commentary on "Cartesian and post-Cartesian trends in relational psychoanalysis." *Gestalt!* 6(2), np. Downloaded June 21, 2009, from http://www.g-gej.org/6-2/jacobsreview.html.

Jacobs, L., Philippson, P., & Wheeler, G. (2007). Self, subject, and intersubjectivity: Gestalt therapists reply to questions from the editors and from Daniel Stern and Michael Mahoney. *Studies in Gestalt Therapy: Dialogical Bridges, 1*(1), 13–38.

Kockelmans, J. (1999). *Philosophy of science: The historical background.* Piscataway, NJ: Transaction.

Langdridge, D. (2004). The hermeneutic phenomenology of Paul Ricoeur: Problems and possibilities for existential–phenomenological psychotherapy. *Existential Analysis, 15*(2), 243–255.

Levy Berg, A., Sandell, R., & Sandahl, C. (2009). Affect-focused body psychotherapy in patients with generalized anxiety disorder: Evaluation of an integrative method. *Journal of Psychotherapy Integration, 19*(1), 67–85.

Magnavita, J. (2008). Toward unification of clinical science: The next wave in the evolution of psychotherapy? *Journal of Psychotherapy Integration, 18*(3), 264–291.

McConville, M., & Wheeler, G. (Eds.). (2001). *The heart of development: Gestalt approaches to working with children, adolescents and their worlds, Vol. II: Adolescence.* Cambridge, MA: Gestalt Press.

Meione, P., & Chenail, R. (1999). Qualitative inquiry in psychotherapy: Research on the common factors. In M. Hubble, B. Duncan, & S. Miller (Eds.), *The heart and soul of change* (pp. 57–88). Washington, DC: American Psychological Association.

Perls, F., Hefferline, R., & Goodman, P. (1951). *Gestalt therapy: Excitement and growth in the human personality.* New York: Julian.

Philippson, P. (2002). *Self in relation.* Highland, NJ: Gestalt Journal Press.

Philippson, P. (2009). *The emergent self: An existential-gestalt approach.* London: Karnac Books.

Portnoy, D. (2008). Relatedness: Where existential and psychoanalytic approaches converge. In Kirk Schneider (Ed.), *Existential-integrative psychotherapy: Guideposts to the core of practice* (pp. 268–281). New York: Routledge/Taylor & Francis Group.

Saldana, L., & Henggeler, S. (2006). Multisystemic therapy in the treatment of adolescent conduct disorder. In M. Nelson III, A. Finch, Jr., & K. Hart (Eds.), *Conduct disorders: A practitioner's guide to comparative treatments* (pp. 217–258). New York: Springer.

Seattle University. (2009). Master's degree in Psychology Brochure. Downloaded June 22, 2009, from http://www2.seattleu.edu/artsci/psychology/Default.aspx?id=3506.

Snyder, L. (2006). William Whewell. In E. N. Zalta (Ed.), *The Stanford encyclopedia of philosophy.* Downloaded June 21, 2009, from http://plato.stanford.edu/entries/whewell.

Stern, D. (2007). Applying developmental and neuroscience findings on other-centered participation to the process of change in psychotherapy. In S. Braten (Ed.), *On being moved: From mirror neurons to empathy. Advances in consciousness research* (pp. 35–47). Amsterdam: John Benjamins.

Stern, D. (2008). The clinical relevance of infancy: A progress report. *Infant Mental Health Journal, 29*(3), 177–188.

Wheeler, G., & McConville, M. (Eds.). (2002). *The heart of development: Gestalt approaches to working with children, adolescents and their worlds, vol. I: Childhood.* Cambridge, MA: Gestalt Press.

Wilkinson, H. (2003). Review article: The shadow of Freud: Is Daniel Stern still a psychoanalyst? The creative tension between the present moment and the past in psychoanalytic and existential psychotherapies, in Daniel Stern's The Present Moment, and his humanistic-existential partners in dialogue. *International Journal of Psychotherapy, 8*(3), 235–254.

Yontef, G., & Philippson, P. (2008). A unified practice. In P. Brownell (Ed.), *Handbook for theory, research, and practice in gestalt therapy* (pp. 257–276). Newcastle, England: Cambridge Scholars.

PART III

Specific Clinical Issues

9 Assessment in Gestalt Therapy

In this chapter assessment and diagnosis are defined. Elements of dimensional scaling, currently being debated and assimilated into the thinking on the *Diagnostic and Statistical Manual of Mental Disorders,* 5th edition (*DSM-V*), are discussed as more consilient to gestalt therapy. The features of a gestalt system of diagnosis are compared and contrasted to the *DSM* so that therapists can work within both and accomplish the tasks required by the profession.

At various times, gestalt therapists have either shunned assessment or yearned for a distinctively gestalt therapy *version* of it. Related to that, many gestalt therapists have also turned away from psychological testing (not trusting anything that resembles a positivist philosophy of science) as a means of understanding people. Gestalt therapists also live in the real world, however, and they have a pragmatic need to operate professionally and responsibly in that world. Whether one uses the *DSM* or the *International Classification of Diseases* (ICD), he or she will need some kind of rationale for assessing and diagnosing clients—if for no other reason than to be able to bill correctly and stand shoulder to shoulder with professional colleagues from other modalities. A much better reason, in my opinion, is that case conceptualization guides a therapist in his or her work. Therefore, it behooves one to think through the implications of the concepts in this chapter and to work out one's own integration of the divergent conceptions of assessment and its place in a clinical practice of gestalt therapy.

This chapter discusses diagnosis, psychological testing, and a within-process form of analysis, and concludes with a suggested method for gestalt therapists to use in assessment and diagnosis.

PRELIMINARY CONSIDERATIONS

Before getting into the pragmatic issues, a basic question of phenomenological ethics pleads for attention. What of Emmanuel Levinas's quarrel with thematizing? Is not assessment thematizing magnified? Is there not a tendency to evaluate someone and then speak as if that assessment is what the person is? In this way, the process of evaluation leads to an end—a complete understanding. The person *is* a borderline, the person *is* an anxiety disorder, or in the watered-down version, we refer to the person by name but think of his or her disorder instead of regarding the person with a fresh perspective each time we meet.

Emmanuel Levinas and Jean-Luc Marion would call this "violence" because it steals transcendent personhood from the client. How do we speak *about* the client without doing damage *to* the client?

James K. A. Smith (2002) found a way through the apparent impasse that Levinas poses in his concept of alterity. To simplify somewhat opaque philosophical reasoning, the problem resolution goes something like this:

1. We cannot think or speak *about* another (intentionality) without objectifying, conceptualizing, or *thematizing* that Other.
2. If we do think or speak about another, we destroy the person's transcendent status as Other by limiting him or her to our own horizon, our own world, our own thinking and frames of reference, making the person not other at all, but the same—an extension of ourselves.

3. However, not all thought about another, not all predicating of various factors to another, makes the Other an object that is an end in itself.
4. Building on the thought of St. Augustine, there are idols that are ends in themselves, and there are icons that point beyond themselves to something greater.
5. Thoughts and words about another can be idols or icons; when thoughts and words about another are icons, they are held loosely as pointers to a transcendent entity that is ultimately mysterious and wondrous and that can be experienced but never grasped completely.
6. Iconic intentionality does no violence to the Other.

The therapist faces two questions when assessing a person in a situation using iconic intentionality: (1) to think in terms of nouns and categories or in terms of verbs and processes; and (2) to conceptualize in regard to structures or dimensions.

Nouns and Categories, Verbs and Dimensions

Nouns lend themselves to categories, because we tend to put things into boxes. From childhood we are taught to clean up our stuff and put it away. This *thing* goes with *that* thing.

In one of the subtests of the Wechsler Intelligence Scale for Children, 4th edition (WISC-IV), a block of several boxes is arranged in a matrix, with a figure in all but one box, which is empty. Below the matrix are a number of figures that could possibly fit in the empty block. What the test pulls for is that part of our intelligence that can see patterns and recognize what *goes with* and what falls outside (or does *not* go with) the pattern presented in the overall gestalt of the matrix.

At one level of assessment, the evaluation process is like taking this matrix reasoning subtest. The therapist is attempting to find which gestalt in the DSM or ICD the person's symptoms go with, and he or she uses a categorical system to do this, identifying an array of symptoms and adding them up until a threshold is reached in which the client either qualifies/matches the overall gestalt of a certain disorder or does not. One person may "go with" posttraumatic stress disorder while another fits with generalized anxiety disorder.

Often, a client actually displays symptoms from many different disorders, and the therapist first has to identify a general category: mood disorder, anxiety disorder, substance disorder, thought disorder, and so on. Sometimes it is not a clear call, because a client will have points that match several categories or not enough matching points to "qualify" as any one disorder. In such instances, when the general category (family) can be identified but the client's presentation and history do not provide enough evidence to refine the diagnosis to a specific disorder (genus), let alone its severity and longevity (species), catch-all categories of "not otherwise specified" are useful. Thus, the categorical system of assessment encourages people to deal in symptoms (nouns) and clusters of systems (categories), and these form taxonomic structures such as found in the DSM and the ICD.

When verbs are used to structure assessments, therapists are looking at what people have done or are doing, and this leads to a focus on process. A verb is not a thing; it is an action or a state of being, and in gestalt therapy verbs point to functional processes in self experience (Crocker, 1999; van Baalen, 1999). Something is happening; something is going on. *What* is happening, and *how* is it going on? These are the classic questions of gestalt therapy: "What?" and "How?" To be more precise, the phrasing goes like this: "Here and now; what and how?" One question identifies a process and sets it apart for study, and the other investigates the means, relational components, dynamic factors, and dimensions of time and place in which the flow of experience has been or is going on. Kurt Lewin called this the *situational unit* (see chapter 6), and it relates to the speed and direction of behavior (Corsini, 1999).

When people reduce a complex situation into manageable parts, they often sort the gray into black and white. Something is either this or that. Gestalt therapists are familiar with the concept of polarities, but they often view them as pathological, because typically a person will identify with one end of a polarity and reject or deny the other. However, that is not a necessary condition of forming a polarity; a person can hold both ends at once and gradually work toward the middle.

A polarity is simply one of the first organizations of meaning when dealing with complexity; it serves as a useful concept here, because it relates to the issue of dimensional scaling in assessment. Instead of locating a person in this or that box, as being a *this* or a *that*, dimensional assessment locates the current functioning of the client within a range, or along a continuum. Dimensional systems also have the advantage that they can use interval-type data instead of nominative data, so they lend themselves more to research. One example of this is the NEO-PI-R, a test built on the Big Five personality theory; it provides a read on the client's position along five dimensions of functioning: neuroticism, extraversion, openness to experience, agreeableness, and conscientiousness (Piedmont, 1998).

- Neuroticism assesses affective adjustment versus emotional instability. People who score at the high end of this dimension experience psychological distress, unrealistic thinking, excessive cravings, and maladaptive coping.
- Extraversion measures the quality and intensity of interpersonal interaction, the need for stimulation, and the capacity for joy. People at the two ends of this dimension are sociable, active, person-oriented at one end and reserved, sober, retiring, and quiet at the other.
- Openness to Experience is the proactive seeking and appreciation of experience for its own sake and tolerating the exploration of the unfamiliar. The contrast in this dimension is between curious, original, untraditional, and creative functioning and conventional, unartistic, an nonanalytical.
- Agreeableness examines an individual's attitudes toward other people. These attitudes can be "pro-person, compassionate, trusting, forgiving, and soft-hearted on one end to very antagonistic, cynical, manipulative, vengeful, and ruthless on the other."
- Conscientiousness assesses a person's degree of organization, persistence, and motivated, goal-directed behavior.

> "This dimension contrasts dependable, fastidious people with those who are lackadaisical and sloppy" (Piedmont, 1998, pp. 84–90).

Consistent with such dimensional scaling, Daan Van Baalen (1999) developed a dimensional approach to gestalt diagnosis involving several scales or polarities and described their implications for assessment. He formulated seven steps in making an assessment, and developed dimensional scaling for the first three. Table 9.1 extends the dimensional scaling of his system to all seven steps. Psychological and relational disorder and dysfunction can be correlated to the characteristics and dynamics of each step. For instance, van Baalen sees psychotic process associated with dysfunction of the first step; this remains to be researched, but the heuristic in the table provides a dimensional scaling system that lends itself to such an effort.

Structures and Processes

Gary Yontef and Talia Levine Bar Yoseph refer to personality structure as "slow moving process" (Yontef & Bar Yoseph, 2008, p. 184), but is there really an enduring personality that might be conceived of as a structure—not a process but a fixed *thing*? That is a subject that goes way beyond the scope of this book. However, it is important to point out that gestalt therapists do not hold to a person within a body—the homunculus. Rather, the "self" is viewed as constantly forming at the boundary of contact in the environment. Thus, there may be many different experiences of self—many "selves," all related to the various contexts in which one is situated at any given time. The self, though, when it emerges, is composed of id, ego, and personality functions.

A function is an activity natural to a person. Thus, the person has self-experience and engages in activities that involve the three major ways in which a person might manifest himself or herself in gestalt therapy: id function, ego function, and personality function.

> The id function is defined as the organism's capacity to make contact with the environment by means of (a) the sensory-motor background of assimilated contacts; (b) physiological needs; and (c) bodily experiences and sensations that are perceived "as if inside the skin" (including past unfinished situations).... Ego function expresses a different capacity of the self in contact: the capacity to identify oneself with or alienate oneself from parts of the field (this *is* me, this *is not* me), the power to want and to decide that characterizes the uniqueness of individual choices.... In Gestalt therapy, personality function expresses one's capacity to make contact with the environment on the basis of one's given definition of self. (Lobb & Lichtenberg, 2005, pp. 28–30)

Thus, when I have sensations and my body does its physiological thing as I bump my way through the ontic field, my body registers that experience and my brain gives rise to my mind, and this first elemental level is the id function of my emergent self. When, I begin to make choices, and especially when I distinguish between what is syntonic and what is dystonic, then my mind starts to exert downward causation, guiding my brain–body, and I operate using the ego function of my self. When I look back over time, or when I realize the dissonance that comes from doing something "not like me," then my mind is engaged in comparing the current circumstances with the residue of my past experiences, and I use the personality function of my self—I tell myself a story about who I am in order to make sense of my life. That story has a structure; so, at least in part and in some way, the personality is not just a slow moving process:

> Gestalt therapists have traditionally maintained that self forms at the boundary and is a constantly reforming sense of one's experience. As such, the self has been characterized as "the figure/background process in contact situations" (Perls, Hefferline, & Goodman [hereafter PHG], 1951, p. 374). Still, self as process is not the only way to think about it, for self as concept is also important and present in every contact episode. As such, it is through meeting what is *not me* that one

Table 9.1

A DIMENSIONAL ASSESSMENT APPROACH FOR GESTALT THERAPY

STEP	DIMENSIONAL SCALING
1. Is contact boundary formed, or does the field organize? Does a situation of fore contact lead to contacting?	0----1----2----3----4----5----6----7----8----9----10 <— Field does not organize; no contact boundary possible —> Field organizes; contact boundary possible
2. Contact boundary forms. The field organizes yet collapses easily with little dynamic and/or organizes in a fixed, stereotypical figure/ground formation.	0----1----2----3----4----5----6----7----8----9----10 <— Field organization or contact boundary collapses easily —> Field organization/contact boundary does not collapse
3. Which figures form and how flexible is the process of figure formation and resolution?	0----1----2----3----4----5----6----7----8----9----10 <— Not flexible; no development —> Flexible, showing fluid development
4. How does the appearance and disappearance of figure formation proceed; how does the contact cycle develop?	<— Fore contact supports the forming of a figure —> 0----1----2----3----4----5----6----7----8----9----10 <— Contacting results in identification with a figure —> 0----1----2----3----4----5----6----7----8----9----10 <— Final contact that prepares for transition—> 0----1----2----3----4----5----6----7----8----9----10 <— Post contact that moves back to spontaneity —> 0----1----2----3----4----5----6----7----8----9----10

5. What is the field that fits a certain figure? What is the next wider gestalt in which the figure/ground formation organizes?	0----1----2----3----4----5----6----7----8----9----10 <—— ——> No sense of context and wider developmental field — Sense of context emerges with awareness of position in field
6. How are awareness of the capacities of the field formed by the diagnostician and the one being diagnosed?	0----1----2----3----4----5----6----7----8----9----10 <—— ——> Diagnostician as subject to client as object — Diagnostician as subject to client as subject
7. How is the self-organizing taking place? Id function = "I need/I want," personality function = "I am," ego function = "I choose"	<——Id function evident and clear——> 0----1----2----3----4----5----6----7----8----9----10 <——Ego function evident and moderating——> 0----1----2----3----4----5----6----7----8----9----10 <——Personality function evident and orienting——> 0----1----2----3----4----5----6----7----8----9----10

Adapted from Van Baalen (1999).

> sketches the outlines of what *is me* (Polster & Polster, 1973; Yontef, 1993). Over time these distinctives take on continuity, and the story one tells oneself regarding one's identity persists, but is it the story that sets up the contacting or the contacting that results in the story? What one believes about oneself contributes to the support one organises for contacting (Korb, Gorrell, & Van De Riet, 1989). (Brownell, 2002, p. 100)

ASSESSMENT AS DIAGNOSIS

In a gestalt-informed diagnostic process, the client, through dialogue, informs the therapist, and the two construct an intersubjective awareness regarding the nature of the situation. This is accomplished by the quality of contacting within the relationship they enjoy (Francesetti & Gecele, 2009; Schmid, 2004). This is true of all dialogic processes, some of which are found in client-centered therapy as well.

In the broader field of mental health, axis I disorders (in the DSM system) are id- and ego-function based while axis II disorders are personality- and ego-function based. This is an important distinction even though it is impossible to completely compartmentalize these things, because an axis I disorder is found in a person with personality function and a person with an axis II disorder still has id and ego function to account for. When a person has major depression, for instance, that is a DSM categorical way of speaking about it, but in each case it is true that the unique person sitting in front of a therapist is doing major depression his or her own way. That person is experiencing bodily sensations and choosing and making meaning out of the experience he or she is going through. It is a phenomenal field that the therapist encounters, and that field is a combination of id functional processes and ego functional processes (the person feels lethargic and decides to be isolated and lay around on the couch all day). Similar things could be said about an axis II disorder such as narcissistic personality disorder. The therapist encounters a phenomenal field, which is a combination of personality functional processes and ego functional processes (the person tells himself that he is smarter, better, and more competent than those around him and decides those others are not worth his attention).

In arriving at a full DSM diagnosis, the clinician uses five axes. The first is for disorders relatively amenable to change with adequate treatment (arrived at through a categorical identification of key symptoms). The second is for relatively fixed, or slow-moving disorders of the personality that can change but only over a longer period of time (again through categorical identification of symptoms). The third axis is for physical conditions relevant to the situation (this is what a gestalt therapist might call a field factor that the client has some kind of id-ego experience around). The fourth axis is for psychosocial stressors, or what Murray would have called "press," and this too is a field dynamic for the client. Axis V is a dimensional scale called the Global Assessment of Function (GAF); the scale ranges from 1 to 100 (1 represents low functioning and 100 is high functioning). The GAF scale is composed of what I call a pain scale and a performance scale. Pain refers to discomfort that motivates one to change the situation because of the degree of unacceptable suffering. Performance means the ability to get things done and remain organized in accomplishing goals in the various contexts of life. As pain goes up, performance goes down and the composite of these two subdimensions results in the GAF score, usually a short range, such as GAF = 55–60 (current).

In the latest version of the DSM, a relational dimension has been added—the Global Assessment of Relational Functioning (GARF) scale. The GARF scale is designed to be used in relationship system functioning rather than individual functioning; therefore, it is appropriate for use in working with family systems, but it can be adapted to work with any relational system, such as in organizations, or any subsystem within a family structure (Yingling, 1998).

ASSESSMENT AS PSYCHOLOGICAL TESTING

In some ways, psychological testing is a catch-all term. There are many psychological tests, because some people make a living at generating and selling them. Like software, best sellers are constantly being upgraded and improved and new ones being created. Beyond that, psychological tests fall into different categories according to their use. Some are for assessing axis I psychological disorders and others are primarily for working with axis II personality disorders. Some tests evaluate the cognitive and intellectual capacities of a person, while others address neuropsychological functioning, and still others are designed for various kinds of perceptual-motor or achievement-oriented evaluations.

For gestalt therapists, it does not matter how many tests there are, because the real question in their minds is how valid they are and how relevant to the actual person who meets with them in a novel, intersubjective encounter in which both therapist and client contribute to the experience in a moment-by-moment process.

> Validity is an overall evaluative judgment of the degree to which empirical evidence and theoretical rationales support the adequacy and appropriateness of interpretations and actions on the basis of test scores or other modes of assessment.... Validity is not a property of the test or assessment as such, but rather of the meaning of the test scores. These scores are a function not only of the items or stimulus conditions, but also of the persons responding as well as the context of the assessment. (Messick, 1998, p. 241)

Psychological testing can be understood in gestalt therapy terms as experiment (Brownell, 2002). The giving/taking of any given psychological test is a unique experience using a fixed form that has been carried out under rigorous conditions so that the test-taker's responses can be assessed statistically compared to a norm group. However, the basic question of a gestalt experiment holds for psychological testing: "I wonder what might happen if..."; "I wonder how the client will respond to the test taking challenge."

The Minnesota Multiphasic Personality Inventory (MMPI-2) has validity scales that indicate whether or not a person is responding in a haphazard fashion, trying to look good, or trying to look bad. What response pattern is the client adopting? This goes to the results of the test in terms of content, but process results can also be included. Many peripheral observations can be made of the client as he or she enters the testing environment, and a gestalt therapist can learn something about how the client responds to a performance demand in the testing process. This information is not related just to the client's history; the test-taking situation creates a mini-crisis in which the person understands he or she is going to be evaluated in some way. As a clinical psychologist *and* a gestalt therapist, I have learned to make abundant use of the testing process in order to *be with* my clients at those times so as to learn more of what it is like to be that person. These are things that can be followed up on between the therapist and the client. Test results are something a therapist can go back over in the debriefing that accompanies psychological testing, to more fully understand the world of the client. Thus, the experiment of psychological testing includes the reason for such an undertaking, the approach to test taking, the manner in which the person takes the test, and the debriefing afterwards. All of this is a kind of safe emergency that arrives with a set scaffold.

In one instance, a young man came for evaluation at the request of his mother, because he had declined in most spheres after attempting college. The man agreed to have his mother attend the debriefing session; he sat on one couch, while she sat on the other. Each reacted to the findings of the brief assessment in a different way. She looked thoughtful and considered each point seriously, while he smiled inappropriately, let his eyes wander, rolled his head on his shoulders, and spoke in hushed whispers as if telling himself inside jokes that nobody else was included in. The results suggested an emerging schizophrenia that was consistent with his inappropriate affect and loose associations. However, there were other possibilities, and as I interacted with the two people, I laid out these possibilities and suggested a course of action for each. All of this was done in a dialogical fashion, checking with the two people and at times pointing the mother to her son's bizarre behavior. Indeed, it was no surprise to her, as that was part of the reason she had asked him to come in the first place; it constituted a significant part of the situation.

Every occasion for assessment and diagnosis is embedded within the stream of life of the client, in which various things have been going on. Seen that way, the assessment is merely one part in an unfolding process, and it offers just as many clinical opportunities as anything else traditionally associated with gestalt therapy. Although every occasion for psychological testing can be seen as an experiment in which some kind of action is taking place (i.e., taking a psychological test), the tests themselves can largely be sorted into self-report questionnaires and performance-based tasks.

Self-Report Assessment Procedures

A self-report assessment instrument asks a number of questions to which the test taker responds, usually indicating something as being true or false about him or her. Sometimes the possible responses are cast in Likert scales offering a range of possible answers from extremely in one direction to extremely in the opposite direction, and the subject selects his or her degree of agreement along a continuum. Such self-report instruments have been used to predict major affective disorders in adolescents (Aebi, Mezke, & Steinhausen, 2009), to evaluate executive functioning (Janssen, De May, & Egger, 2009; Walker & D'Amato, 2006), to assess one's ability to attend to one's own psychological states and processes and to reflect on them, resulting in insight (Nyklíček & Denollet, 2009), and to evaluate the outcomes of psychotherapy (Lambert, Okiishi, Finch, & Johnson, 2003).

One of the values of self-report scales and questionnaires is that often they provide information that no one else knows (Baldwin, 2000). In such cases, concise definitions and clear questions are important. Often the juxtaposition between self-report and performance-based measures, when multiple methods are used in assessment (Eid & Diener, 2006), provides depth and human interest to the process of evaluation. However, self-report is suspect, given people's tendency to discern the intent of such scales when face validity is high. For instance, one sorting test used in the managed care of employee assistance clients asked such questions as when was the last time you lied or conned others, when was the last time you shoved or hit someone, made and sold drugs, or took something from the store without paying for it? Obviously, a person can figure out that if they have done these things and answer truthfully, they might get into trouble or suffer loss. To account for this, some self-report instruments like the MMPI-2 have built-in validity scales sensitive to self-serving response sets.

Performance-Based Assessment Procedures

Performance-based assessment is just what it sounds like. Someone does something—chooses from among several options to complete a gestalt in matrix reasoning; sorts eight cards with pictures of animals, in various colors and borders, into two groups of four cards each; or responds to the projective pull in an inkblot—and the result is compared to how a norm group performed on the same exercise. This is done in the presence of the test giver, who monitors the way the test taker handles the demands made on him or her. Does the person make side comments, go off task, fidget, or just glide right through as if he or she is not bothered in the least? All such things are part of the phenomenal field, and so not outside the concern of a gestalt therapy–oriented psychologist.

In education, performance-based assessments have been used to help teachers target specific academic goals for students and promote productive and practical learning experiences (Gallavan, 2009). Students provide evidence of what they can actually do, and that is related to what the teacher has been attempting to teach them. In the same way, the feedback available to a gestalt therapist through dialogical encounter gives evidence to the change taking place in the client.

Performance-based measures allow clinical psychologists to avoid the variety of ways in which people defend against recognition of true mental distress (Fowler & Groat, 2008). In clinical psychology, performance-based assessment is accomplished with projective tests such as the Rorschach and the Thematic Apperception Test.

ASSESSMENT AS GESTALT THERAPY "ANALYSIS"

Many gestalt therapists approach the analysis of a situation in a different way. Instead of a top-down judgment, in which a deduction is made and put upon the situation or person, gestalt analysis, as described by Perls, Hefferline, and Goodman (1951), is a bottom-up presentation of the situation in an experience-near fashion—as if one is attempting to recreate the experience for the purpose of observation.

Perls, Hefferling, and Goodman referred to such a method of assessment, when they said (in typically demanding construction) that

> the only useful method of argument is to bring into the picture the total context of the problem, including the conditions of experiencing it, the social milieu and the personal "defences" of the observer. That is, to subject the opinion and his holding of it to a gestalt-analysis. A basic error is not refuted—indeed, a strong error, as St. Thomas said, is better than a weak truth—it can be altered only by changing the conditions of raw experience. Then, our method is as follows: we show that in the observer's conditions of experience he *must* hold the opinion, and then, by the play of awareness on the limiting conditions, we allow for the emergence of a better judgement (in him and in ourselves). (Perls, Hefferline, & Goodman, 1951, p. 243)

Thus, a gestalt assessment might not present the conclusion but the process by which a conclusion might emerge. This would be frustrating to many people who just want that code number to input into the third-party payer system. They want the conclusion. However, gestalt assessment is more interested in processes that develop out of what people do over time and how they navigate contact in the unified field.

ASSESSMENT AS THERAPEUTIC PROCESS

What people do over time in therapy results in a felt sense of the other for each one. That is informative, and it can be diagnostic. Recently, for instance, in a meeting with a couple, the woman complained that she was always having to remind the man and follow up after him. I listened and began to wonder if the man had an attention deficit that had never been assessed in childhood. I offered dialogically my curiosity and then painted a word picture of a person with adult ADD; the woman's eyes brightened and she said, "That's him!" While understanding a dynamic as an executive dysfunction instead of a lack of caring did not remove the annoying behavior, it did put a different set of clothes on it.

Whenever I get a referral of a child from a parent who comes with voluminous documentation of what is going on with the child, I always insist on meeting with the child him or herself before interacting with the data from schools and other clinicians; this is so I can get a "feel" for that child myself. Each person is different, and I want to see what it is like to be with that person. The contact provides first-person experience that contextualizes any observations made by others.

Sometimes the need for formal assessment procedures emerges from the therapeutic context, because a clinician realizes something is going on about which he or she would like to find out more. In the course of a dialogical approach, this interest in what the results of psychological testing might show can be shared with the client. Conversely, when the process begins with the need for assessment, the results of testing can become quite important therapeutically. For instance, when I do assessments that are formal psychological evaluations to begin with (i.e., referrals from another clinician, an agency, or a department of community mental health that expressly request a certain kind of psychological evaluation), I always meet with the subject afterwards to go over the results, not just to satisfy ethical propriety but actually to get a sense of the person's reaction. That reaction becomes part of the assessment because hearing those results affects the client and must be monitored for its significance. A counseling piece accompanies the process of giving feedback on the testing. In that sense, all assessment is, to me, part of an advancing therapeutic relationship.

> Two different horizons exist in which to situate diagnosis in therapy: the first is the naturalistic model, the second the hermeneutic model. The naturalistic model implies an objectifying relationship that is not oriented towards intersubjective contact. It is the medical model whereby the clinic maps symptoms and then uses this map for treatment, without

> concerning itself with the subjectivity of the patient. In the hermeneutic model, on the other hand, the diagnostic process is co-constructed, pooling together the knowledge (and foreknowledge) of the therapist and patient. (Francesetti & Gecele, 2009, np)

Assessment in a therapeutic situation is, by nature, a constantly evolving process.

> The therapist and client are always noting, evaluating, responding, or reacting to the transactions of therapy, each person using his own internal process to interpret and comprehend what has transpired. It is difficult, therefore, to comprehend any form of assessment as truly static or objective. Assessment is multisided. Three basic observational positions are recognized in formal, structured assessment. *Outsider* evaluation is described as the use of a clinical rating scale by an observer/therapist/team or researcher. *Insider* methods use client self-report about his or her experience of system functioning. *Insider-outsider* methods use a more collaborative process whereby the client and therapist develop criteria delineating desired change in a well-defined manner. (Yingling, 1998, p. 36)

A SUGGESTED METHOD OF ASSESSMENT AND DIAGNOSIS

We now come to how assessment and diagnosis might be handled by a gestalt therapist, especially by a gestalt therapist working within a mental health system dominated by the DSM (or the ICD).

First, one must attend to the pragmatic demands of the system. That means attending to the categorical sorting that results in a DSM code/diagnosis, and if one is preparing an official report, it also means preparing the five-axes diagnosis. These are not merely busy work, for as stated previously, elements in those five axes tap field factors and processes of suffering and performance that are represented in a dimensional scale. These can be conceptualized from a gestalt perspective without losing ground.

Beyond this level of assessment, however, the gestalt therapist is interested in the manner in which the client navigates contact in the two-person field comprising the therapeutic relationship (or beyond that to the more extended field outside of the therapy room). Does the client show sustained ability to maintain contact and to show presence, or does he or she interrupt the contact in some fashion by externalizing and projecting on others, going up "into the head," being overly intellectualized and analytic about everything, or does he become deflective and divert attention to peripheral issues and objects and away from the meeting that is possible? There are many ways in which a person can break contact. Further, it is possible to develop a contact style in which one characteristically interacts with others. When that style becomes fixed and rigid, and also interpersonally problematic, people begin to suspect an axis II disorder.

The gestalt therapist is also interested in how the client makes meaning out of his or her experience. First, the therapist is interested in how the client senses and navigates the ontic field, which cannot be seen or understood except through the byproducts of such navigation; with a modified phenomenological method, however, it is possible to slow down a client's process as if to take one frame at a time and examine what is happening in the whole person at that time.

Now all this is done, as implied, in the midst of the two-person field, the working alliance. And further, the therapist works out the assessment by using that relationship and presenting to the client his or her observations and self-disclosures of what it is like to *be with* the client. As the client responds, the therapist and client together come to an understanding about the nature of what is going on with the client. This does not mean that the client knows just as much about it as the therapist, but the client knows more about his or her own experience than the therapist. As that experience is made more available to the therapist (through exploration of the client's phenomenal field and the dialogic encounter between them), the therapist is able to come to a more informed understanding and diagnosis. Yet, this is something they work out together rather than something the therapist alone performs on or for the client.

Some gestalt therapists have made much of assessing the client's figure formation and resolution skills, using the cycle of experience (Melnick & March Nevis, 2000), but I am not going down that road. The cycle of experience is regarded as a useful teaching heuristic but not a diagnostic instrument that assumes the existence of such a thing in itself.

Each gestalt therapist will get the feel of the client in his or her own way. This assessment emerges out of the whole process of therapy; however, this is how I do it in my own practice:

1. In the first meeting, I note if there is an openness in the client that engages with me, or if we avoid one another in some way. Does he or she tell a coherent story or throw out one-liners that do not go anywhere? I may have my first glimpse of a contact style, and I notice in myself if I am working harder than usual, fearful that I will not make something happen, and so on. I regard this, if I see it, to be a product of the meeting between myself and this particular client.
2. I want to get a sense of the need and press, the field dynamic, all things having effect, and so I might ask the client to tell me parts of his or her history that do not have an apparently direct relationship to the situation at hand.
3. In assessment, I am evaluating the situation, not the individual person detached from the situation. And when the client comes to me, I suddenly have become part of that situation. So, the work with the client becomes similar to a piece of action research, which is a form of hermeneutics.

   Hermeneutics, from which are derived appreciative inquiry, cooperative inquiry and action research, seeks to derive a rich understanding of the context and focuses on the formation of meaning. In its pursuit of knowledge, it opens a recursive dialogue between subjects and the object of inquiry to mine deeper into an understanding of what exactly happens to generate a more complete interpretation of events. This approach investigates the researcher as much as the topic, and involves the researcher in the explanatory process (Barber & Brownell, 2008, p. 44).

4. I hold all theories loosely and continually check them out with the client; I watch for the reaction to answer the experimental question: What happens when I share this with the client?
5. I ask myself if the client's primary problem is (a) one of individual experiencing (i.e., an inability to sense herself in her body, form good figures, make good contact with nonpersonal aspects of her ontic field and process percepts, etc.), (b) one of interrupting or not even establishing contact with personal Others—people—and thus of relating, or (c) a matter of disabling field effects or unfinished business from past relationships and/or events.
6. I am constantly weaving my awareness of the DSM into the ongoing process so that my growing understanding of the client informs my professional responsibility, shaping my understanding of the process elements and dimensional scaling possible that complements the categorical system in the DSM. Should the DSM-V include more obvious dimensional considerations in differential diagnosis, then gestalt therapy would be poised to use it more explicitly, referring to verbal processes instead of nominative categories.

CONCLUSION

Diagnosis is a critical need in mental health practice, and the field is already dominated by the DSM and the necessity of inputting DSM-based code numbers into various databases. Rather than argue for a totally new system, gestalt therapists need to become proficient in using categorical assessment systems such as the DSM and the ICD in order to fulfill their professional requirements. To be sure, gestalt therapists working in government-funded and nonprofit-based community mental health do this. So do those working in practices largely funded by third-party payers that are highly managed. Further than that, though, it would be helpful if more gestalt therapists worked at integrating the established method, with its emphasis on nouns, categories, and structures and a system of assessment built on verbs, dimensions, and processes that is more in keeping with gestalt therapy theory and practice. As in many related clinical issues, the gestalt therapy perspective provides a coherent alternative and check against potentially harmful objectifying of clients and simplifying of the processes of assessment and diagnosis.

REFERENCES

Aebi, M., Meszke, C., & Steinhousen, H.-C. (2009). Prediction of major affective disorders in adolescents by self-report measures. *Journal of Affective Disorders, 115*(1–2), 140–149.

Baldwin, W. (2000). Information no one else knows: The value of self-report. In A. Stone, J. Turkkan, C. Bachrach, J. Jobe, H. Kurzman, & V. Cain (Eds.), *The science of self-report: Implications for research and practice*. Mahwah, NJ.: Lawrence Erlbaum Associates.

Barber, P., & Brownell, P. (2008). Qualitative research. In *Handbook for theory, research, and practice in gestalt therapy*. Newcastle, England: Cambridge Scholars.

Brownell, P. (2002). Psychological testing—a place in gestalt therapy? *British Gestalt Journal, 11*(2), 99–107.

Corsini, R. (1999). *The dictionary of psychology*. Philadelphia: Brunner/Mazel.

Crocker, S. (1999). *A well-lived life: Essay in gestalt therapy*. Cambridge, MA: Gestalt Institute of Cleveland Press.

Eid, M., & Diener, E. (2006). *Handbook of multimethod measurement in psychology*. Washington, DC: American Psychological Association.

Fowler, J. C., & Groat, M. D. (2008). Personality assessment using implicit (projective) methods. In M. Hersen & A. Gross (Eds.), *Handbook of clinical psychology, vol 1: Adults* (pp. 475–494). Hoboken, NJ: John Wiley & Sons.

Francesetti, G.& Gecele, M. (2009) A gestalt therapy perspective on psychopathology and diagnosis. *British gestalt journal*, 18(2), 5–20.

Gallavan, N. (2009). *Developing performance-based assessments, Grades 6–12*. Thousand Oaks, CA: Corwin Press.

Janssen, G. T. L., De May, H. R. A., & Egger, J. I. M. (2009). Executive functioning in college students: Evaluation of the Dutch executive function index (EFI-NL). *International Journal of Neuroscience, 119*(6), 792–805.

Korb, M., Gorrell, J., & Van De Riet, V. (1989). *Gestalt therapy, practice and theory*. New York: Pergamon Press.

Lambert, M., Okiishi, J., Finch, A., & Johnson, L. (2003). Outcome assessment: From conceptualization to implementation. In Alan Kazdin (Ed.), *Methodological issues & strategies in clinical research* (3rd ed., pp. 619–633). Washington, DC: American Psychological Association.

Lobb, M. S., & Lichtenberg, P. (2005). Classical gestalt therapy theory. In A. Woldt & S. Toman (Eds.), *Gestalt therapy history, theory, and practice* (pp. 21–39). Thousand Oaks, CA: Sage.

Melnick, J., & March Nevis, S. (2000). Diagnosis: The struggle for a meaningful paradigm. In E. Nevis (Ed.), *Gestalt therapy: Perspectives and applications* (pp. 57–78). Cambridge, MA: Gestalt Press.

Messick, S. (1998). Validity of psychological assessment: Validation of inferences from person's responses and performances as scientific inquiry into score meaning. In A. Kazdin (Ed.), *Methodological issues & strategies in clinical research* (2nd ed., pp. 241–260. Washington, DC: American Psychological Association.

Nyklíček, I., & Denollet, J. (2009). Development and evaluation of the balanced index of psychological mindedness (BIPM). *Psychological Assessment, 21*(1), 32–44.

Perls, F., Hefferline, R., & Goodman, P. (1951). *Gestalt therapy: Excitement and growth in the human personality.* New York: Julian Press.

Piedmont, R. (1998). *The revised NEO personality inventory: Clinical and research applications.* New York and London: Plenum Press.

Polster, E., & Polster, M. (1973). *Gestalt therapy: Contours of theory and practice.* New York: Vintage Books.

Schmid, P. (2004). Back to the client: A phenomenological approach to the process of understanding and diagnosis. *Person-Centered and Experiential Psychotherapies,* 3(1), 36–51.

Smith, J. A. K. (2002). *Speech and theology: Language and the logic of incarnation.* London and New York: Routledge.

Van Baalen, D. (1999). *Gestalt diagnosis.* Norsk Gestaltinstitutt, AC; Senter for Psykoterapi. Oslo, Norway.

Walker, J. M., & D'Amato, R. C. (2006). Review of behavior rating inventory of executive functioning—self report version. *Journal of Psychoeducational Assessment,* 24(4), 394–398.

Yingling, Y. (1998). *GARF assessment sourcebook.* New York: Routledge.

Yontef, G. (1993). *Awareness, dialogue, and process: Essays on gestalt therapy.* Highland, NY: Gestalt Journal Press.

Yontef, G., & Bar Yoseph, T. L. (2008). Dialogical relationship. In P.Brownell (Ed.) *Handbook for theory, research, and practice in gestalt therapy,* pp. 184–197. Newcastle, England: Cambridge Scholars.

10 Treatment Planning and Case Management in Gestalt Therapy

This chapter discusses case conceptualization, treatment planning, and case management as relevant to gestalt therapy. Approaches to treatment planning are offered, with hypothetical examples from a gestalt perspective, and a field theoretical consideration of case management that assimilates it as a strategy available to gestalt therapists.

Treatment planning is often driven by a problem–solution approach that has proven counterintuitive to solution-focused and strengths-based therapies. While gestalt therapy is not essentially solution focused, it is very much strengths based. Therefore, this chapter offers a gestalt-friendly approach to treatment planning that works around what gestalt therapists know as the "figures of interest" for the client. In addition, case management is often a related task required of clinicians; therefore, this chapter provides a gestalt therapy orientation to case management as a decidedly field-theoretical strategy.

TREATMENT PLANNING

It is now common practice to construct a treatment plan and to do so in conjunction with the client. This is a practice in keeping with gestalt therapy; specifically, it includes a dialogical negotiation between the therapist and client with respect to the amount of time and money that will be spent on any given therapeutic process. Gestalt therapists do not conceptualize cases, nor conduct their practices, in straight lines between cause and effect, between problem and solution, or between interventions and results. They are trained to think more contextually, relationally, and with a view to unfolding process. Consequently, gestalt therapists do conceptualize cases and do organize themselves to meet the perceived figures of interest emerging from the meetings between themselves and their clients. This presents some interesting alternatives to people unfamiliar with gestalt therapy, even as it necessitates that gestalt therapists operate with a parallel process to forge treatment plans commensurate with professional standards in mental health, on the one hand, as well as those that make more sense theoretically to gestalt therapists, on the other.

Treatment planning is a standard subject taught in most accredited graduate programs in psychotherapy. We do not need to start from scratch on the subject. As most people know, it is a problem–solution kind of process that is commonly worked out in conjunction with the client so that the client actually "signs off" on it at the end. When I worked in community mental health in North Carolina (before the state went out of the business of providing direct services), it was standard practice to meet with the client, do a diagnostic interview, and then, using the screen-driven computer system, create a treatment plan identifying at least two "problems," and each with several options for meeting the client's needs expressed in that problem. Thus, to me, and probably to all my clients, this was a fairly task-driven process that offered little time to build rapport or for the client to really tell his or her story. We had only an hour, after all, to accomplish it all!

That said, treatment planning is directly related to case conceptualization (Hersen & Porzelius, 2002), which is related to assessment and diagnosis (see previous chapter). Case conceptualization

> organizes assessment data into a meaningful outline, applying research and theory to make sense of a client's current

> presentation. Although the diagnosis summarizes a client's symptoms, it is not enough. Therapists must know more about their clients than symptoms and diagnosis. Therapists must go beyond diagnosis, developing hypotheses to explain how the clients came to have a particular set of psychological and interpersonal problems. Therapists review all potential contributors to the problem, examining distal and proximal factors; causal, maintaining, and precipitating factors; and internal and environmental factors. Therapists then identify the most central contributors, develop explicit hypotheses about clients' problems, develop treatment plans based on the hypotheses, and intentionally test the hypotheses during treatment. (Hersen & Porzelius, 2002, p. 4)

That is a great deal of objectifying of the client; so, how might a gestalt therapist approach responsible case conceptualization, leading to effective treatment planning? For that matter, how might a gestalt therapist translate such a linear process into a more contextual logic? There are philosophical and ethical considerations as well as evidence-based, professional considerations. This book is not the place for a complete development of these two subjects, but a brief overview will alert the reader to what is involved.

Philosophical and Ethical Considerations

Philosophically, of course, gestalt therapy is built on continental philosophy, more specifically on phenomenology, and it incorporates Heidegger's sense of being in the world among others. However, in terms of assessment there are also hermeneutical considerations to keep in mind; by what principles does one interpret one's experience of the client, and what happens when one reduces such a human being to a set of symptoms and then evaluates that set against the criteria in various clinical categories? These questions concern the ethical thinking of Emmanuel Levinas and the hermeneutics of Hans-Georg Gadamer (Bruns, 2004).

To the point, Levinas (as stated previously) abhorred objectifying other people, calling it an ethical violence. Rather, he viewed the Other (in this case, the client) as a stranger who calls to him (the therapist), and calls him out of his usual ways of knowing. The therapist does not exist *for* herself, but for the Other. This alters the syntax of relationship—the case in which a therapist operates—setting her in the accusative, so that she becomes a *me* instead of an *I*. Thus, the process goes like this: the client affects *me* rather than *I* figure out the client. The client transcends my usual ways of knowing, and the client must be allowed to do so free from the therapist's conceptualizing. This ethical principle presents a practical problem for the therapist, who must figure out what is going on with the client in order to organize his or her approach to the work they do together.

That leads to the subject of hermeneutics. Instead of a system that provides for the interpretation of texts, this kind of hermeneutics provides an orientation for the interpretation of experience. The therapist operates with at least a tacit guideline that informs how he or she will make sense of meeting the client and coming to know the client experientially.

Related to this, Gadamer offered a way of knowing that avoids extreme objectifying:

> Gadamer, for example, thinks of understanding on the model of Aristotle's concept of φϱόνησις, or practical wisdom, which is a ground-level or dialectical mode of thinking different both from theoretical consciousness (έπιστήμη), or knowing what things are, and from technical know-how (tecnhv), or knowing how things are made or how they work. φϱόνησις involves responsiveness to what particular situations call for in the way of action, where knowing how to act cannot be determined in advance by an appeal to rules, principles, or general theories (WM304–5/TM321–22). Knowledge here cannot be conceptualized or codified in general terms because it has to do with singular and unprecedented states of affairs, particularly as these involve us with other people. (Bruns, 2004, p. 34)

This fits well with a gestalt approach because both Gadamer's hermeneutic and gestalt therapy are concerned with a situation and not just with an isolated individual who bears the markings of various symptoms and can be classified accordingly. This harkens back to Francesetti and Gecele's (2009) point in the previous chapter about the diagnosis of action at the boundary between self and other.

Case conceptualization, like therapeutic process itself in gestalt therapy, is the interpretation of situational and relational elements contributing to the client's clinical presentation. Just as the client and the therapist are a two-person field in therapy, the client is part of a larger field including therapy, and the therapist's task is to be with the client, to perceive the client as an *icon* pointing to the situation of which the client is a part. This is true for the process of case management as well as it is for psychotherapy.

An icon can be contrasted with an idol. An idol is an object of adoration, and one's attention and interest are focused on it as an end in itself. Much of diagnosis, case conceptualization, and treatment planning in the past has been focused on the individual and his or her symptoms as if the client were the sole factor involved. An icon, by contrast, is not an end in itself. It is a symbol and a pointer to something beyond itself, usually conceived of as a greater reality and a more salient consideration (Smith, 2002).

Thinking of the client as iconic, a therapist can avoid the ethical violence of shattering alterity by objectifying and thematizing the client; a gestalt therapist sees the client as an icon pointing beyond the individual to the transcendent reality of the individual in situ. This is how a gestalt therapist conceptualizes any given case, paying attention to the ways in which the client affects contact at the boundary of self and other in a complex field.

It is also a process consideration, that is, the configuration of contact for any given current moment (field is a current consideration), so it can change in the next moment, and then again in the next. Thus, case conceptualization leaves one open and watchful, realizing that the client in situ is not static.

Evidence-Based and Professional Considerations

As in medicine, social science has adopted an evidence-based approach to mental health services. Evidence-based practice can be defined as the purposeful and explicit use of the best available scientific evidence in decision making; "it is the use of treatments for which there is sufficient persuasive evidence to support their effectiveness in attaining desired outcomes" (Roberts, Yeager, & Regehr, 2006, p. 6). To help refine the definition of evidence-based practice, the American Psychological Association commissioned work to define both the means and the results of achieving "evidence" in the construct of evidence-based practice:

> The American Psychological Association adopted a working definition of evidence-based practice, and they asserted that *evidence-based practice in psychology* (EBPP) is the integration of the best available research with clinical expertise in the context of patient characteristics, culture, and preferences (APA, 2006). They went on to make a critical distinction between empirically supported treatments and evidence-based practice and to open up multiple and relative streams of support as "evidence:" … The APA task force pointed to a range of research designs that all contribute to the body of knowledge relevant to evidence-based practice. They include clinical observation, qualitative research, systematic case study, single-case experimental designs to examine causal factors in outcome with regard to a single patient, process-outcome studies to examine mechanisms of change, effectiveness studies in natural settings, Random Controlled Treatments and efficacy studies for drawing causal inferences in groups, and meta-analysis for observing patterns across multiple studies and for understanding effect sizes. With regard to any particular treatment intervention, the task force identified two considerations: does the treatment work—a question of its efficacy, which is most related to internal validity, and does it generalize or transport to the local setting where it is to be used—a question of its effectiveness, which is most related to external validity. (Brownell, 2008, pp. 94–95)

Questions that arise from practice, that are practice-based (Brownell, 2008), and questions that focus on benefits to the client—the type of client, the proposed course of action, and the pertinent findings in research literature (Yeager & Roberts, 2006)—are most conducive to evidence-based case management. Here, it is not necessary to find an exact match for population, disorder, and treatment in the research literature. The best fit is what carries the day, and in regard to that, it is helpful to pay attention to the consilience that might exist between one construct in a piece of research and another construct used in a parallel approach to therapy.

For instance, much is made these days of mindfulness and acceptance therapy, especially as practiced in cognitive behavioral therapy (CBT), but gestalt therapy has been practicing mindfulness and acceptance from its very inception, and gestalt therapists locate these ideas nested in the constructs of awareness and paradoxical growth. Therefore, it is reasonable that research directly supporting mindfulness and acceptance therapy would be applicable to gestalt therapy's use of awareness and paradoxical change by virtue of consilience. Indeed, the assimilation of mindfulness and acceptance techniques and strategies run along the lines of awareness work relying on gestalt therapy's paradoxical theory of change. This goodness-of-fit in accordance with consilience is also similar to what happens when studies conducted on one population are attributed as relevant to a different, but similar (in many ways), population somewhere else.

According to Vourlekis, Ell, and Padgett (2005), a comprehensive, evidence-based practice in social services and case management includes four sets of activities: (1) It uses evidence-based strategies to identify people for social work services within certain settings; (2) it demonstrates the accuracy and validity of assessment processes that lead to clinically relevant decisions; (3) it uses interventions or treatments with established effectiveness and guidelines based on systematic inquiry; (4) it examines practice processes and outcomes for quality and goal achievement.

With regard to the assessment and case conceptualization foundational to treatment planning,

> cognitive strategies that have demonstrated potential for improving judgment outcomes include (a) needing to simultaneously consider several alternative diagnoses, explanations, and treatment plans; (b) addressing environmental as well as internal factors influencing client behaviors; (c) decreasing reliance on memory alone in decision-making tasks; and

(d) using formal decision aids such as diagnostic criteria, norms, and base rates to improve accuracy. (Falvey, Bray, & Hebert, 2005, p. 348)

Two Metaphors for Treatment Planning

A treatment plan can be like a budget, and it can also be like a road trip. When a treatment plan is like a budget, the therapist essentially knows that he or she has only so many sessions that managed care will likely fund, after which the client will have to pick up the rest or simply stop. So, the therapist makes a plan to cover x, y, and z in the amount of time available. In identifying several problems, for instance, the therapist might sort them and negotiate with the client to choose the *one* thing they will work on together. That would leave other issues either to be addressed at a later point or for the client to attend to with other people or by his or her own means. Further, the therapist writes goals, like commodities to be purchased with the time available, in terms of client accomplishments. Thus, a typical treatment plan, from a gestalt therapist working in community mental health or managed care, might look like what is depicted in Figure 10.1.

Notice that it is not good enough to "prescribe" a whole form of therapy as an intervention (such as, "cognitive behavioral therapy

Client/Customer: Joe Smith

Problem #1: Mood darkens and energy dissipates
- Experiment #1-1: Client will engage in cardiovascular exercise for at least 30 minutes daily
- Intervention #1-1: Client will debrief and explore experiment #1 dialogically

Problem #2: Defeatist introjects ruling awareness and destroying hope
- Intervention #2-1: Client will engage therapist in exploration of the client's phenomenal field, keeping watch for (a) negative cognitive processes; (b) defeating introjects; (c) lagging hope
- Experiment #2-1: Client agrees to challenge an introject in vivo with two-chair work and therapist support

Figure 10.1 Example of a budget-model gestalt therapy treatment plan.

for depression"). Rather, the descriptions of the problems are experience-based and phenomenal, and the interventions and experiments are process-oriented. These are the kinds of things a gestalt therapist would include in his or her "budget" for spending the resources of time and third-party funding that support therapy. In addition, in order to be evidence-based, the gestalt therapist needs to refer to research evidence supporting gestalt therapy and/or demonstrate points of consilience with established research in other modalities.

In other ways, a treatment plan is like a road trip. A road trip is an adventure in which the charm is the purposeful encounter of the unexpected. A person planning a road trip will establish some general parameters but leave open and undefined most of what will take place, because the person wants to be flexible enough to adjust and take advantage of the opportunities that arise along the way. Using that model, a gestalt-oriented treatment plan might resemble Figure 10.2.

Notice that in the road trip metaphor the treatment plan is written in terms of therapist-driven procedures, and that is because it is the therapist who is driving. He or she takes responsibility to fill that tank, kick the tires, and keep the car on the road; but beyond that, the driver must remain aware of the scenery, the opportunities that present themselves as the car goes down the road, and the experience of the passenger who wanted to go on the road trip to begin with. Neither passenger nor driver

Client/Customer: Joe Smith

Problem #1: Mood darkens and energy dissipates
- Experiment #1-1: Establish presence and wait on Mr. Smith to enter into dialogue; stay present in the dialogue
- Intervention #1-2: Track the phenomenal experience of the client with a modified phenomenological method.

Problem #2: Defeatist introjects ruling awareness and destroying hope
- Intervention #2-1: Turning to the client's field, explore where he got those rules, how old he feels with them, who taught them to him, etc.
- Intervention #2-2: Stay attentive to the client's figures and possible open doors to in vivo experiments

Figure 10.2 Example of a road-trip model gestalt therapy treatment plan.

can know what he or she will encounter (the client's issues and responses; the therapist's countertransference), but the therapist/driver can be reasonably sure of some of the first turns he intends to make on the process.

Two Criteria for Planning Therapy

Both outcome research and clinical reasoning need to be used by the therapist in constructing and monitoring responsible treatment plans.

> If the major theoretical orientations all have a respectable standing nomothetically, then idiographic questions become especially salient, particularly the old, venerable question of what works best for whom. To clinicians, comparing the group effects of alternative treatments might be less important than assessing the etiology of disturbance in a given client. Treatment planning based on individual case formulation has the potential to link the nomothetic and idiographic levels of psychotherapy. (Shapiro, 2009, p. 51)

Since, as has already been discussed, gestalt therapy would be expected to enjoy roughly the same outcomes as CBT, and since the research that has compared the two shows favorable comparisons, Shapiro's point that clinical reasoning is important looms large. When writing a treatment plan, the gestalt therapist will want to pay close attention to the individual needs and interests of the specific client in question.

CASE MANAGEMENT

When I was program coordinator and clinical supervisor at a community resource center for children and families in mid-Multnomah County, Portland, Oregon, one of my jobs was to help therapists adapt to the growing demand that they also shoulder the role and responsibilities of case managers. They did not train for that. They did not sign up for that. They viewed themselves as therapists, and that is what they wanted to remain. Unfortunately, that was not the direction in which the profession had been running. Consequently, it was satisfying to realize that case management is an exquisite way in which to conduct therapy according to a gestalt therapy understanding of field dynamics.

Case management is just what it sounds like: case *management*. Instead of providing services, the case manager identifies client needs and matches them to provider resources in the community. The case manager is a service broker, not a service provider (if case management is not seen as a service in itself). The case manager monitors the provision of services, and that involves interface with the service provider and the client. The case manager keeps responsibility for the case, even as various service providers assume responsibility for certain aspects of the client's case. The case manager *organizes* and *superintends* all that. Case management is not simply referring the client to someone else and then letting go, because an active role of involvement, monitoring, and continuity of care with regard to the client remains for the case manager, and this takes place within a complex of various community and social elements.

Case management has been shown to play important roles in the complex situations facing patients in medical care and clients in mental health care (Olbort et al., 2009; Walsh & Holton, 2008). It is most apparent in the demands for highly effective coordination and organization inherent to multisystemic therapy (Leonard, 2009 Tolman, Mueller, Daleiden, Stumpf, & Pestle, 2008), which is consilient with field theoretical strategies in gestalt therapy.

If the field is all things having effect (a phenomenal consideration) and also all actual effects (an ontic consideration), then changing anything in a person's ontic field may well result in changes in his or her phenomenal field. Let me explore that a bit more.

Lewin's life world (all things having effect) is a phenomenal construct; that is, it is all things the subject is aware of affecting him or her. The effects in the phenomenal field are actual (existent), but not all things existent are phenomenal effects (the currents of liquid gas on one of the outer planets, a traveler hiking in Nepal, etc.). However, some things that are effects (for any given person) are not phenomenal (a matter of a person's aware experience); some things affect a person unawares. There is a part-to-whole relationship here; the phenomenal field is part of the ontic field. All phenomenal effects are therefore actual, but not all actual effects are phenomenal. Do ontic effects result in phenomenal effects, and if so, how and how much?

It seems that the phenomenal field emerges from the ontic field and supervenes on it. It could emerge without supervening, but if the phenomenal field does supervene on the ontic, then no change in the phenomenal field can take place without a concomitant change in the ontic field (gestalt therapists must hold to this if they hold to an emergent and supervenient self/mind). I do not believe we can say that any change in the person's ontic field results in a change in the person's phenomenal field (and this is one difference between field theory and systems theory), not immediately anyhow. Someone can develop cancer unawares. On the other hand, the slowdown in metabolism as a person ages definitely results in phenomenal experience. We are all in process, so that some elements of the ontic field affect the phenomenal field when they attain a certain threshold of awareness.

Thus, case management can be seen as active intervention at the level of the field, because the case manager is actively introducing new effects into the client's field, and each time the case manager brokers services and the client meets with a new service provider, an experiment is underway (to say nothing of the effect of the relationship between the client and the case manger him or herself!). How will these two get along? Will the client get what he or she needs? What happens when I, as a gestalt therapist, case manage in this way?

In one study, homeless people who were offered housing and case management experienced less need for hospitalization (Sadowski, Kee, VanderWeele, & Buchanan, 2009). A study of the seriously and chronically mentally ill who received case management in Hong Kong indicated that case management reduced the number of hospitalizations and shortened durations of inpatient treatment when they were hospitalized (Wong, Yeung, & Ching, 2009). In a good example of how such case management works,

Wohl et al. (2009) found that 72% of goals established at baseline were achieved and 74% of referrals were completed in a case management approach for HIV-positive patients in a public care setting. The most common goals were adherence in taking medications and cooperating with case management interventions, housing, and nutrition.

Because the patient is sent out into the community to gain these supports and services, this approach constitutes a huge experiment at the level of the client's field. What happens when the client has to navigate the dentist? the rapid transit system? the local parent-teachers' association? applying for a job? How far will the therapist go in following up with service providers involved with his or her client? A thoroughly field theoretical strategy that opens up to the potential in case management changes the concept of gestalt therapy from a one-to-one individual therapy to a complex, situational, socially active approach.

For gestalt therapists in private practice and perhaps working with a higher functioning or less stressed population, a case-management experiment might be quite appropriate. On one occasion, the daughter of an elderly, severely depressed woman came to help in processing her anxiety and concern. After meeting with her, and after meeting with her mother, I suggested that the daughter employ a home health nurse to visit her mother's apartment, not take "no" for an answer, and get the woman up, showered, and dressed for a walk in town at least three times a week. We could have sat for a long time discussing the concepts involved with time of life, depression, reversed generational roles, and so forth, but the provision of the home health nurse changed something in the field and made all the difference.

CONCLUSION

Treatment planning and case management are linked because the treatment plan will often require some case management. Treatment planning can be goal oriented and written in terms of client benchmarks, considering the expenditure of resources from a budgetary viewpoint, or it can be open-ended and exploratory, following a few principles that allow the process to direct the outcome and written in terms of therapist facilitation, considering the unpredictability of psychotherapy as a road trip. Ultimately, case management is a field-level intervention that relies on the paradoxical theory of change and contextual logic for positive outcomes.

REFERENCES

American Psychological Association (APA). (2006). Presidential task force on evidence-based practice. Evidence-based practice in psychology. *American Psychologist, 61*(4), 271–285.

Brownell, P. (2008). Practice-based evidence. In P. Brownell (Ed.), *Handbook for theory, research, and practice in gestalt therapy* (pp. 90–103). Newcastle, England: Cambridge Scholars.

Bruns, G. (2004). On the coherence of hermeneutics and ethics: An essay on Gadamer and Levinas. In B. Kajewski (Ed.), *Gadamer's repercussions: Reconsidering philosophical hermeneutics* (pp. 30–54). Berkeley: University of California Press.

Falvey, J., Bray, T., & Hebert, D. (2005). Case conceptualization and treatment planning: investigation of problem-solving and clinical judgment. *Journal of Mental Health Counseling, 27*(4), 348–372.

Francesetti, G., & Gecele, M. (2009) A gestalt therapy perspective on psychopathology and diagnosis. *British Gestalt Journal*, 18(2), 5–20.

Hersen, M., & Porzelius, L. (2002), *Diagnosis, conceptualization, and treatment planning for adults: A step-by-step guide*. Mahwah, NJ: Lawrence Erlbaum Associates.

Leonard, C. (2009). Runaway youth and multisystemic therapy (MST): A program model. *Dissertation Abstracts International: Section B: The Sciences and Engineering, 69*(9), 5771.

Olbort, R., Mahler, C., Campbell, S., Reuschenbach, B., Müller-Tasch, T., Szecsenyi, J., et al. (2009). Doctors' assistants' views case management to improve chronic heart failure care in general practice: A qualitative study. *Journal of Advanced Nursing, 65*(4), 799–808.

Roberts, A., Yeager, R., & Regehr, C. (2006). Bridging evidence-based health care and social work. In A. Roberts & K. Yeager (Eds.), *Foundations of evidence-based social work practice* (pp. 3–20). New York: Oxford University Press.

Sadowski, L., Kee, R., VanderWeele, T., & Buchanan, D. (2009). Effect of a housing and case management program on emergency department visits and hospitalizations among chronically homeless adults: A randomized trial. *JAMA: Journal of the American Medical Association, 301*(17), 1771–1778.

Shapiro, J. (2009). Integrating outcome research and clinical reasoning in psychotherapy planning. *Professional Psychology: Research and Practice, 40*(1), 46–53.

Smith, J. K. A. (2002). *Speech and theology: Language and the logic of incarnation.* London and New York: Routledge.

Tolman, R., Meuller, C., Daleiden, E., Stumpf, R., & Pestle, S. (2008). Outcomes from multisystemic therapy in a statewide system of care. *Journal of Child and Family Studies, 17*(6), 894–908.

Vourlekis, B., Ell, K., & Padgett, D. (2005). Evidence-based assessment in case management to improve abnormal cancer screen follow-up. *Health and Social Work, 30*(2), 98–106.

Walsh, J., & Holton, V. (2008). Case management. In W. Rowe, L. Rapp-Paglicci, K. Sower, & C. Dulmus (Eds.), *Comprehensive handbook of social work and social welfare, volume 3: Social work practice* (pp. 139–160). Hoboken, NJ: John Wiley.

Wohl, A., Garland, W., Witt, M., Valencia, R., Boger, A., Squires, K., et al. (2009). An adherence-focused case management intervention for HIV-positive patients in a public care setting. *Journal of HIV/AIDS & Social Services, 8*(1), 80–94.

Wong, D. F. K., Yeung, M. P. M., & Ching, C. K. (2009). Evaluating a case management model for people with severe mental illness in Hong Kong: A preliminary study. *Hong Kong Journal of Psychiatry, 19*(1), 11–17.

Yeager, K., & Roberts, A. (2006). A practical approach to formulating evidence-based questions in social work. In A. Roberts & K. Yeager (Eds.), *Foundations of evidence-based social work practice* (pp. 47–58). New York: Oxford University Press.

PART IV

Training and Certification

11 Training, Certification, and Professional Development in Gestalt Therapy

This chapter describes the means by which people become trained and certified as gestalt therapists. It includes means for attending continuing education. It describes the historical development of postgraduate-level gestalt therapy training institutes worldwide, and provides identifying and contact information for a number of them. This chapter also helps the reader understand the experiential nature of gestalt therapy training. In addition, as certification conveys different connotations, depending on where one practices, these are discussed, describing options for credentialing that coordinate with interests and professional needs. Finally, gestalt therapists have affiliated with one another in various regional and even international associations. These are described so that the reader can fully understand their similarities and differences.

Training and certification often go hand in hand, but not always. Some forms of training do not lead to certification, because the professional landscape does not require it.

Beyond the issue of certification, though, is the issue of what it takes to train a competent gestalt therapist.

TRAINING

There are all kinds of training models that one might encounter in the field of mental health. Formal academic requirements prevail in most jurisdictions, but they are not uniform. Thus, in most places in the United States, the term *psychologist* is restricted to those with an earned doctorate, while *psychological associate* is reserved for those with an earned master's degree. In the United Kingdom, someone with less than a doctorate can become chartered and attain to the title of psychologist. In Europe a psychotherapy certificate is like licensing in the United States. Many gestalt training institutes in Europe are accredited to grant such a certificate, and so their training programs reflect the more stringent requirements of a regulated field.

As can be seen in chapter 3, the gestalt therapy training institutes spread rapidly as those trained began sharing their newly developed expertise with others, and the spread was in all directions: Europe, South America, Australia, and beyond. Joe Melnick described that growth as follows:

> The gestalt approach developed not in higher institutions of learning but in evolving communities, in the gestalt institutes. The growth of these institutes was influenced by a number of varying factors that impacted the various institutes in different ways. As a result, each institute, even today, is both different and similar to other gestalt institutes. For example, they differ in terms of training (short term vs. long term, beginner vs. advanced students) scope of application (individual psychotherapy vs. organizational development), internal organization (hierarchy vs. collective), theoretical approach (orthodox vs. expansionistic), etc. However, they are similar in terms of a large number of basic values, such as an emphasis on self-awareness and personal experience, living in the here-and-now, the co-creation of the moment, and a phenomenological approach to experience. (Brownell & Melnick, 2008, p. 281)

Usually, the standard training program in gestalt therapy is 3 or 4 years. The 4-year program at the Gestalt Training Institute of West Australia (Perth) starts with 100% experiential learning in the first year. In the second year, trainees begin to augment experiential training with supervision and reading, and by the third and fourth years, the mix of experiential and supervision and reading is 50%–50%. The Gestalt Institute of Cleveland, however, has no multiyear program as such; they offer a cafeteria-style, elective system of workshops and classes, some being prerequisites for others. It is up to the trainee to take those workshops that directly benefit and advance specific goals in personal and professional growth. The Gestalt Training Institute of Malta is built on the model created by the European Association for Gestalt Therapy (EAGT). It provides what it calls a basic course in gestalt therapy during the first and second years, and an advanced course in the third and fourth. The Gestalt Centre of London breaks up a Master's in Gestalt Therapy Theory Studies into 3 years, with a fourth post-master's year for those who want a Psychotherapy Practitioner Diploma. This reflects the growing trend toward accreditation of gestalt therapy training programs in Australia, New Zealand, the United Kingdom, and Europe more generally.

What people actually learn in these various years and systems varies. In the regulated programs under the guidance of the EAGT, subjects are made explicit, but when they are taken over the 4 years required to complete the programs varies. Table 11.1 shows the breakdown of EAGT course requirements.

I trained in the United States, where there is no regulated need for certification. I was simultaneously completing a doctorate in clinical psychology, so I knew that the demands of the profession of clinical psychology would be met by completing my formal course of study at the university—that, and the licensing process, which is regulated at the state level.

In my training group were massage therapists and body workers, one shamanistic counselor, a psychiatrist, several social workers, a nurse, several licensed professional counselors, a college professor, some students like myself, and one conductor of a national symphony orchestra. In gestalt training groups, trainees commonly do actual pieces of personal work, for when the trainees practice—the experiential learning referred to above—they do not play a

Table 11.1

EUROPEAN ASSOCIATION FOR GESTALT THERAPY CURRICULUM REQUIREMENTS

Topic 1	*History and Roots of Gestalt Therapy:* philosophy; anthropology; psychoanalysis; existentialism; phenomenology; gestalt theory; Eastern philosophies
Topic 2	*Theory of Gestalt Therapy:* organism/environment field; figure/ground resolution; creative adjustment; model of change; authenticity; contact-withdrawal experience; theory of self; awareness/consciousness; polarities; resistances; therapeutic process, and so on
Topic 3	*Human Organism and Environment:* theory of personality; health and sickness; child development; person in society
Topic 4	*Techniques of Gestalt Therapy:* experiment; amplification; dream work, and so on
Topic 5	*Diagnosis:* differential diagnosis; *DSM-IV*; psychodynamic diagnosis; gestalt diagnosis
Topic 6	*Different Clinical Approaches:* neurosis; psychosis; borderline; psychosomatic; addictions
Topic 7	*Fields and Strategies of Application:* individual; couple; families; groups; addictions; therapeutic communities; organizations, and so on
Topic 8	*The Gestalt Therapist in the Therapeutic Relationship:* transference; countertransference; dialogue; contacting
Topic 9	*Principles and Applications of Ethics*

Adapted from EAGT (2008).

role and assume an "as if" posture. No one says, "Now I'll be a depressed person and you can practice working with a depressed person." Rather, one trainee works as client and the other as therapist for about a 20-to-30–minute piece of work, and it is around the real figures of interest, the real issues in the life of the trainee who is assuming the place of the client. When the piece of in situ work is done, the other trainees typically offer the impact that had on them, so those working feel supported, and then the training group considers and discusses that piece of work so they might all learn from it. The purpose of such an experience is to allow people to learn what gestalt therapy feels like. Just as learning a foreign language is often enhanced by immersion in an environment where the language is spoken, these experiential pieces of gestalt work, and the theoretical and supervisory debriefing that follows, provide for a kind of immersion in the world of gestalt therapy.

Because gestalt therapy is what it is, this kind of experiential learning is a must. It is not enough to read about gestalt therapy or even to discuss it with colleagues. One must gain a "feel" for it. Here, I am reminded of Schleiermacher's construct of *feeling* in reference to religious experience. He was against the hyper-rational approach that created dry dogma detached from daily living, and suggested instead that people needed to experience God and complement any cognizing about God with feeling. In gestalt therapy, one must know in one's gut where to turn in the lively encounter with the client. It is not enough to just *think* one's way through it. One must combine feeling with any cognizing about gestalt therapy, and that comes through the experience of working as therapist, working as client, conducting experiential exercises, and then debriefing the process.

There are core concepts that need to be learned, as seen in Table 11.1. Every institute has a sense, either explicit in a tangible curriculum or more implicit in the flow of working together, of what a competent gestalt therapist knows and can do. Thus, in some cases, an institute will also adopt a set of competencies that their trainees must demonstrate before being certified. For example, the Illawarra Gestalt Institute sees a relationship between core areas of philosophy and core abilities in practice (Bar-Yoseph, Philippson, O'Neill, & Brownell, 2008):

> The practice competencies are to be acquired via theoretical understanding, demonstration and experimentation supported by on-going [*sic*] supervision. There is a need for an ongoing honing of the student's skills through feedback and reference to theory. These skills are taught through each unit, and are particularly focused on in the supervision meetings. (Bar-Yoseph et al., 2008, p. 115)

What cannot be stressed enough is that gestalt therapy is not a bag of tricks. It is not a set of techniques that can be patched into an existing eclectic practice in the sense some people might say, "I do a little gestalt." Either one does gestalt therapy or one does not. Either one practices a unified approach that uses, in a practical therapeutic flow, all the major tenets of gestalt theory, or one rips up the theoretical core of gestalt therapy and practices a counterfeit hybrid that is essentially technique driven, but cannot be called "gestalt therapy." When gestalt therapists assimilate aspects of other approaches, they identify consilient points of commonality in theory and practice, and they digest those aspects so that what emerges is a thoroughly consistent practice of gestalt therapy. It takes several years of training to get to that point. Thus, to be trained to function as a gestalt therapist, say for a research project in which therapists followed a manual and provided gestalt therapy, requires that the therapists in question stick close to the central theoretical core of gestalt therapy outlined in this book and others (Brownell, 2008; Houston, 2003; MacKewn, 1997; Woldt & Toman, 2005).

CERTIFICATION

Certification in the United States amounts to little more than a given institute providing a piece of paper showing that so and so completed one of their programs. That is because the regulation of psychotherapy is handled by state governments, and it has more to do with completion of a formal course of study at the university than with completion of an ancillary training course.

As mentioned previously, however, certification in Europe and Australia is part of the regulatory process, and gestalt therapy there is well-situated to provide certification that satisfies regulatory rigorousness. Gestalt training institutes often struggle with the administrative demands necessary to satisfy government regulation, but the benefit is that people practicing as gestalt therapist, having completed such a program, have a bit of "heft" to go with their training.

CONTINUING EDUCATION

Continuing education is usually available through various training institutes. Therapists can also attend the national and international conferences of various associations of gestalt therapists. Novices or those outside the gestalt community (just looking to pick up some needed continuing education credits), can contact the closest gestalt training institute to see what might be available or check out the Web site of a major association of gestalt therapists and attend their next major conference. The Association for the Advancement of Gestalt Therapy (AAGT) conducts an international conference every 2 years, and information about upcoming conferences is available at www.aagt.org. Conferences not only offer numerous workshops, but also introduce attendees to the people who practice gestalt therapy. In addition to the biennial conferences, regional conferences are also held in the southwest, southeast, and northeast United States, and a growing regional network promises increased development of regional conferencing in other countries as well.

GESTALT TRAINING ORGANIZATIONS

The programs of training organizations themselves vary in scope, cost, duration, and requirements. The reader would be best served to use the world wide web to examine some of the institutes listed in Table 11.2.

The information in Table 11.2 is not exhaustive; rather, it lists select organizations based on criteria such as number of years as a training organization, presence of significant faculty, contribution to the field, and availability for inspection on the Internet. In addition, the reader can find European national gestalt organizations with links to local training centers and institutes in most countries in Europe, the Middle East, and Russia at http://www.eagt.org/national_organizations_list.html.

Table 11.2

EXAMPLES OF GESTALT TRAINING ORGANIZATIONS

NAME (LOCATION)	FACULTY	PROGRAMS	CONTACT INFORMATION
Gestalt Associates Training Los Angeles (Los Angeles, California, USA)	Bob Resnick, Rita Resnick, and Todd Burley	Gestalt therapy training for work with individuals and couples	www.gatla.org
Pacific Gestalt Institute (Los Angeles, California, USA)	Gary Yontef, Lynne Jacobs, Lillian Norton, Jan Ruckert, Friedemann Schulz	Training in relational gestalt therapy	www.gestalttherapy.org
Portland Gestalt Therapy Training Institute (Portland, Oregon, USA)	Carol Swanson, Jeffrey Sher	Training in gestalt therapy	www.pgti.org
Gestalt Therapy Training Center-Northwest (Portland, Oregon, USA)	Steve Zahm, Eva Gold, and Jon Frew	Training in gestalt therapy; beginning and advanced groups	www.gttcnw.org
Gestalt Institute of Cleveland (Cleveland, Ohio, USA)	Numerous faculty including Marlene Blumenthal, Michael Clemmens, and Isabel Fredericson	Training in gestalt therapy, organizational development, and coaching	www.gestaltcleveland.org
Gestalt Therapy Institute of Philadelphia, Pennsylvania, USA	Mary Lou Schack, Philip Lichtenberg, David Henrich	Training in gestalt therapy and coaching	www.gestaltphila.org

New York Institute for Gestalt Therapy (New York, New York, USA)	Some members include Bud Feder, Dan Bloom, and Susan Gregory	Seminar approach to ongoing self-learning	www.newyorkgestalt.org
Gestalt Associates for Psychotherapy	Many faculty, among whom are Alan Cohen, Ruella Frank, and Arleen Maiorano	Four-year training program in gestalt therapy	www.gestaltassociates.org
Gestalt International Training Center	Edwin Nevis, Sonia March Nevis, Penny Backman, Joe Melnick, and others	The Cape Cod Model of Individual and Couples Therapy; Organizational Development	www.gisc.org
Gestalt Institute of Toronto, Canada	JoAnne Greenham, Jay Tropianskala, and others	Training in gestalt therapy	www.gestalt.on.ca
Gestalt Training Institute of Bermuda	Philip Brownell, Sue Congram, Talia Levin Bar-Yoseph, Dan Bloom	Training in gestalt therapy, organizational development, and coaching	www.gtib.org
Manchester Gestalt Centre, Manchester, England	Peter Philippson, Joy Appleby, Danny Porter, others	Training and supervision in individual and group gestalt therapy	www.mgc.org.uk
The Metanoia Institute, London, England	Lynda Osborne, with many others	Training, Supervision, credentialed course in gestalt therapy and other approaches	www.metanoia.ac.uk
The Gestalt Centre of London, England	Michael Ellis, Toni Gilligan, and several others	Training in gestalt therapy and organizational work	www.gestaltcentre.co.uk

(Continued)

EXAMPLES OF GESTALT TRAINING ORGANIZATIONS *(Continued)*

NAME (LOCATION)	FACULTY	PROGRAMS	CONTACT INFORMATION
The Istituto di Gestalt, H.C.C., Italy	Margherita Spagnuolo Lobb, Giovanni Salonia, and others	Training and supervision in gestalt therapy; publishing of gestalt literature	www.gestalt.it
Institut Francais de Gestalt-théraie, France	Jean-Marie Robine, Brigitte Lapeyronnie-Robine, and others	Gestalt therapy training and supervision; publishing of gestalt literature	www.gestalt-ifgt.com
MultidiMens, Antwerp, Belgium and The Netherlands		Training in gestalt therapy and organizational work	www.multidimens.be
Gestalt Institut Köln, Germany	Erhard Doubrawa	Training in gestalt therapy and publishing	www.gestalt.de
Instytut Terapii Gestalt, Kraków, Poland	Katarzyna Weglorz-Makuch, Tomasz Rebeta, and others	Training and supervision in gestalt therapy leading to a European certificate; publishing the *Gestalt Magazine*	www.gestalt.pl
Norsk Gestaltinstitutt, Oslo, Norway	Daan van Baalen, Gro Skottun, Svein Johansen, and others	Training in gestalt therapy and organizational development	www.gestalt.no
Moscow Institute of Gestalt Therapy and Counseling, Russia[1]	Oleg Nemirinsky, Olga Silnova, and others	Training in gestalt therapy and organizational work	www.gestalt-therapy.ru

Riga Gestalt Institute, Riga, Latvia	Artur Dombrovsky, Nikolay Shcherbakov, Daiga Auzina, and Baiba Pumpina	Training in applications of gestalt therapy to individual, couples and families	www.gestalt.lv
Centro de Estudos de Gestalt Terapia de Brasilia	Elaine Magaldi Daemon, Fádua Helou, and others	Training in gestalt therapy	www.cegest.org.br
Centro de Estudos e Atividades Gestálticas, Brasilia	Angelo Carlos Mineri, Christiane Silveira Becker Correa, and Mria Goretti Bunn Zomer	Training and supervision in gestalt therapy and organizational development	www.gestalt.com.br
Instituto Humanista de Psicoterapia Gestalt, A.C.	Myriam Munoz Polit and others	Extensive training program related to gestalt psychotherapy	www.gestalthumanista.com
Sidney Gestalt Institute	Philip Oldfield, Rhonda Gibson-Long, and others	Training in gestalt therapy in accord with GANZ guidelines	www.gestaltsydney.com
The Illawarra Gestalt Centre	Brian and Jenny O'Neill, Seán Gaffney, and others	Training in gestalt therapy and couples work	www.illawarragestalt.com
Gestalt Institute of New Zealand	Brenda Levien, Stephen Parkinson, and others	Training in gestalt therapy in keeping with national and GANZ standards	www.gestalt.org.nz

PROFESSIONAL AFFILIATIONS AND GESTALT COMMUNITIES

Gestalt therapy is alive and evolving through the communal efforts of gestalt therapists all over the world. What started in New York in the mid-20th century has spread, and at this writing gestalt therapy is more popular and prevalent in Europe and South America than it is in the United States, its birthplace. National associations have formed to support the individual gestalt therapists in those areas. For instance, in Argentina the Asociación Gestáltica de Beunos Aires serves as a national association of gestalt therapists and it frequently sponsors national conferences. In England the Gestalt Psychotherapy & Training Institute (GPTI) is actually a member organization attending to training standards across the board in the United Kingdom. It is a member of the United Kingdom Council for Psychotherapy (UKCP) and can list its qualified members on the Register for Psychotherapists. GPTI supports an e-mail discussion list for the networking of its members and the discussion of current and relevant topics in the field.

Beyond national groups like those mentioned above, however, three multinational or international associations of gestalt therapists stand out.

Gestalt Australia and New Zealand (GANZ) is an association of gestalt therapists in these two nations. It holds conferences, publishes a journal, and attends to the regulatory needs of gestalt therapists who want to practice in those two countries. Because of its need to advocate in the midst of an increasingly regulated environment, GANZ also attends to training standards for its member training organizations.

The European Association for Gestalt Therapy (EAGT) is much the same kind of organization as GANZ, only it involves many more nations in the European fold. It holds conferences but does not publish a journal. It sees to training standards consistent with the requirements in Europe and offers a certificate that qualifies as a European authorization to practice psychotherapy.

Unlike either GANZ or EAGT, the Association for the Advancement of Gestalt Therapy (AAGT), an international community, has no regulatory function. It does not grant any certificates.

It is a member organization whose stated purpose is to advance gestalt therapy through the associating of its members. The focus is not on permission to practice gestalt therapy but rather on the subject of gestalt therapy itself and the enjoyment of fellowship and camaraderie with other gestalt practitioners. The AAGT is not geographically limited. It has a regional system with regional contact people all over the world, and many of these regions hold mini-conferences of their own. Biennial conferences are held in various locations, where more intensive training and therapeutic experiences are available in preconference format, and about 50 peer-reviewed conference presentations are routinely offered within the conference itself.

Many gestalt therapists are members of two or three such associations: GANZ or EAGT and AAGT, and a regional subgroup of the AAGT. They provide a well-developed network of support for both individual members and organizational members.

As gestalt therapy continues to spread and to evolve, these two kinds of associations—those largely focused on the advancement of gestalt therapists and those focused on the advancement of gestalt therapy—will continue to be needed. They represent two facets of the same concern, for where gestalt therapists are shut out by regulatory and public policy decisions, the discipline of gestalt therapy must be sublimated to some other approach.

CONCLUSION

More could be said about the diverse training approaches. Training is sometimes done in an apprentice model, sometimes in a mentor model, and sometimes in an academic model. Brownell, Levin, and O'Neill (1997) offered several metaphors reflecting on such models and training practices. The various competencies many gestalt training institutes expect their trainees to demonstrate for certification, and how they ascertain such competencies, could have been described in more detail, but these requirements vary and it is best to consult the particular institute of interest for more information. The original gestalt institute in New York, for instance, does not regard itself as a training organization at all; rather, it is a collegial, membership organization that meets regularly for the presentation and discussion of papers presented by its members.

Being a gestalt therapy trainer is a career in itself, because it is an absorbing pursuit. Many people continue the trend set by the early gestalt trainers, who traveled often great distances to offer the gestalt approach to people who had never heard of it. Today, most people have heard of it, but they often have a poor base in theory and practice, having simply sampled gestalt techniques during a graduate program. Today's gestalt therapy trainers are also often writers who are extending and evolving gestalt therapy theory (see chapter 3).

NOTES

1. As in many places, there is an extensive development of gestalt training organizations and online resources in Russia. The following list of places and Web sites illustrates that fact:
   - The Byelorussian Gestalt Institute (http://gestalt-by.org);
   - Workshop of the Gestalt of Elena Petrovoj (http://www.gestalt.sp.ru);
   - The Moscow Institute the Gestalt and Psiphodrem (http://www.migip.ru);
   - SPb Institute of the Gestalt (http://www.gestalt.spb.ru);
   - Moscow the Gestalt of Institute (http://www.gestalt.ru);
   - The East Europe Gestalt Institute—EEGI (http://www.vegi.ru);
   - One more site EEGI (http://www.vegizerkalo.narod.ru);
   - Moscow Institute Geshtaltterapii and Consultations (http://www.gestalt-therapy.ru);
   - The Kiev representation, Moscow the Gestalt of Institute (http://gestalt.kiev.ua/our_partners)
   - NIKA—a Gestalt the center in Kiev (http://www.nika.net.ua/);
   - Gestalt the Line—club of professional psychologists (http://gestaltline.com);
   - The Byelorussian Gestalt center (http://www.gestalt.by);
   - Mihail Papush center (http://www.psychotechnica.ru);
   - Articles on the Gestalt of therapy (http://www.kulichki.com/inkwell/special/psyho/gestalt.htm);
   - Novosibirsk Gestalt the Center (http://gestaltnsk1.narod.ru);
   - Gestalt therapist, Polina Gaverdovskaja. Moscow (http://www.gaverdovskaya.ru);
   - Gestalt therapist, Jarosh Natalia (http://gestalt.in.ua/);
   - Nina Rubshtejn's Educacional Center (http://rubstein.ru/);
   - Gestalt therapist, Shelepova Olga (http://www.psy.by/);
   - Gestalt therapist, Konstantin Loginov (http://www.psyforum.ru).

REFERENCES

Bar-Yoseph, T. L., Philippson, P., O'Neill, B., & Brownell, P. (2008). Training of therapists. In P. Brownell (Ed.), *Handbook for theory, research, and practice in gestalt therapy* (pp. 104–121). Newcastle, England: Cambridge Scholars.

Brownell, P. (2008). *Handbook for theory, research, and practice in gestalt therapy*. Newcastle, England: Cambridge Scholars.

Brownell, P., Levin, J., & O'Neill, B. (1997). Ethics and training practices. *Gestalt!*, *1*(2), np. Downloaded June 26, 2009, from http://www.g-gej.org/1-2/issues-n-ethics.html.

Brownell, P., & Melnick, J. (2008). Gestalt therapy research communities. In *Handbook for theory, research, and practice in gestalt therapy*. Newcastle, England: Cambridge Scholars.

European Association for Gestalt Therapy (EAGT). (2005). The accreditation of gestalt institutes, NOG's and organizations. Downloaded March 14, 2008, from http://www.eagt.org.

Houston, G. (2003). *Brief gestalt therapy*. London: Sage.

MacKewn, J. (1997). *Developing gestalt counselling*. London: Sage.

Woldt, A., & Toman, S. (2005). *Gestalt therapy history, theory, and practice*. Thousand Oaks, CA: Sage.

Epilogue

This book has outlined the core of gestalt therapy theory and practice. It has not tackled everything. Many people have written thought-provoking essays on a multitude of facets in gestalt praxis, and many more are exploring the still growing edges in gestalt therapy. This has not, hopefully, been a watered-down version of gestalt therapy, for I realize I have raised some difficult issues and taken slants on them that not everyone would agree with. However, this is a limited view, not necessarily a safe view.

The discussion has been limited to the core of gestalt therapy—phenomenology, dialogue, field theory, and experiment—for the purpose of making it more explicit. My interest here is in contributing to the establishment of a heuristic, an easily understood definition of what gestalt therapy is and how it is practiced. My critics will say, "Well, you left out this," and "You left out that." Correct. But I included those major tenets that make gestalt therapy what it is, that hang together in a clearly unified approach, and that comprise a core that can also be researched.

One of my concerns is that gestalt therapy will generate its own research tradition. In a dialogue in *American Psychologist*, Alan Kazdin (2008, 2009) engaged his colleagues in an encouraging discussion about the need for research to "bridge" to practice. He suggested "evaluating the mechanisms of change in psychotherapy so we know what is critical to include in practice, evaluating who responds to treatment in ways that can be integrated into practice, and increasing the use of qualitative research" (Kazdin, 2009, p. 276). His colleagues were energized and contributed several thoughts of their own. Looking at this, I sense that gestalt therapy is poised on a ledge and about to leap off. Gestalt therapists have just begun to wake up to the possibilities in research, and I believe we can contribute successfully to all of Kazdin's forward-thinking suggestions.

In 2009, the AAGT sanctioned the creation of a Gestalt Research Task Force, and that task force is considering implementing various initiatives in support of research, including research into the mechanisms of change and the use of qualitative methods. *The Handbook for Theory, Research, and Practice in Gestalt Therapy* is currently being translated into French, Spanish, Czech, Chinese, Russian, and Korean. There is a growing way forward in the expansion of gestalt therapy, including its active dialogue with other modalities and its legitimate contribution to the fields of psychotherapy, organizational consulting, coaching, and research.

I'm looking forward to seeing how it comes together.

REFERENCES

Kazdin, A. (2008). Evidence-based treatment and practice: New opportunities to bridge clinical research and practice, enhance the knowledge base, and improve patient care. *American Psychologist, 63*, 146–159.

Kazdin, A. (2009). Bridging science and practice to improve patient care. *American Psychologist, 64*(4), 276–278.

Index

Note: Page numbers in italics indicate tables

38535233R00158

Made in the USA
Lexington, KY
13 January 2015